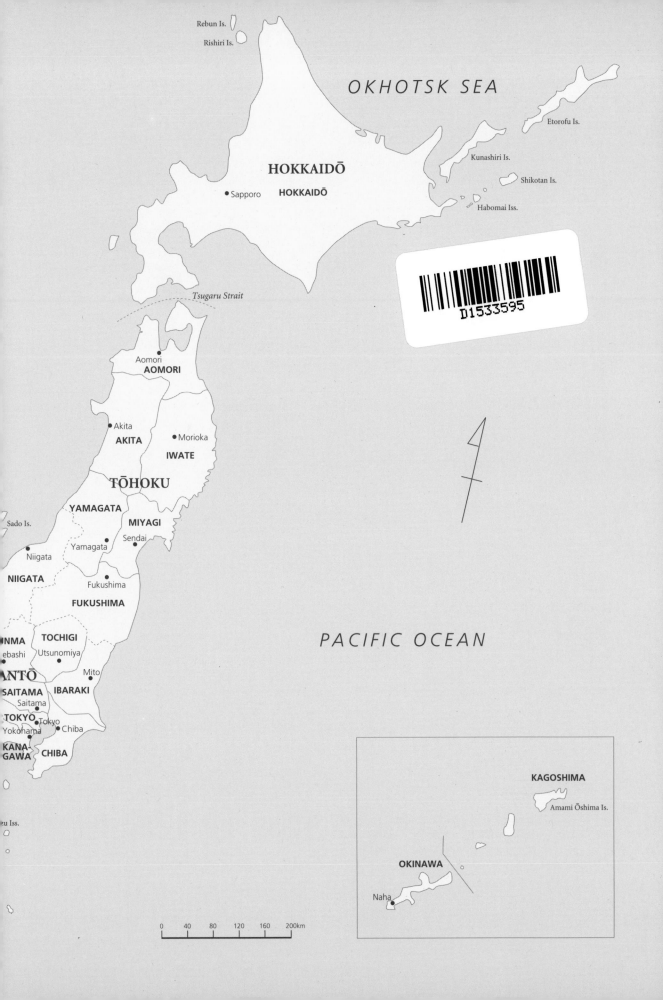

REBUN IS.
RISHIRI IS.

OKHOTSK SEA

HOKKAIDŌ

HOKKAIDŌ

• Sapporo

Etorofu Is.

Kunashiri Is.

Shikotan Is.

Habomai Iss.

Tsugaru Strait

Aomori
AOMORI

• Akita

AKITA

• Morioka

IWATE

TŌHOKU

YAMAGATA

Sado Is.

MIYAGI

Yamagata • • Sendai

• Niigata

NIIGATA

Fukushima •

FUKUSHIMA

NMA

TOCHIGI

ebashi Utsunomiya

ANTŌ

• Mito

SAITAMA **IBARAKI**

Saitama

TOKYO • Tokyo

Yokohama • Chiba

KANA-
GAWA **CHIBA**

zu Iss.

PACIFIC OCEAN

KAGOSHIMA

Amami Ōshima Is.

OKINAWA

Naha •

0   40   80   120   160   200km

JAPANESE FOR BUSY PEOPLE **I**

JAPANESE FOR BUSY PEOPLE

Revised 3rd Edition

I

Kana Version

Association for Japanese-Language Teaching
AJALT

KODANSHA INTERNATIONAL
Tokyo • New York • London

The Association for Japanese-Language Teaching (AJALT) was recognized as a nonprofit organization by the Ministry of Education in 1977. It was established to meet the practical needs of people who are not necessarily specialists on Japan but who wish to communicate effectively in Japanese. In 1992 AJALT was awarded the Japan Foundation Special Prize. AJALT maintains a website at www.ajalt.org, through which they can be contacted with questions regarding this book or any of their other publications.

Illustrations by Shinsaku Sumi.

CD narration by Yuki Minatsuki, Aya Ogawa, Yuri Haruta, Koji Yoshida, Tatsuo Endo, Sosei Shinbori, and Howard Colefield.

CD recording and editing by the English Language Education Council, Inc.

PHOTO CREDITS: © Sachiyo Yasuda, 1, 19, 47, 87, 159 (timetable only), 177, 203, 221. © Sebun Photo, 67. © JTB Photo Communications, Inc., 69 (top). © Orion Press, 109. © Ben Simmons, 139. © iStockphoto.com/ Lawrence Karn, 159. Tokyo National Museum (Image: TNM Image Archives; Source: http://TnmArchives.jp/), 188.

Distributed in the United States by Kodansha America, LLC, and in the United Kingdom and continental Europe by Kodansha Europe Ltd.

Published by Kodansha International Ltd., 17–14 Otowa 1-chome, Bunkyo-ku, Tokyo 112–8652.

Copyright © 2006 by the Association for Japanese-Language Teaching. All rights reserved. Printed in Japan.

First published 1984
Second edition 1994
Second edition, Kana Version 1995
Third edition 2006
20 19 18 17 16 15 14 13 12 11 10 09   15 14 13 12 11 10 9 8 7 6 5

Library of Congress Cataloging-in-Publication Data

Japanese for busy people. I, Kana version / Association for
  Japanese-Language Teaching.—Rev. 3rd ed.
        p. cm.
    Includes index.
    ISBN 978–4–7700–3009–2
    1. Japanese language—Textbooks for foreign speakers—English.
  2. Japanese language—Spoken Japanese. I. Kokusai Nihongo Fukyu
  Kyokai (Japan). II. Title

  PL539.5.J3J358 2006
  495.6'83421—dc22
                                        2006045244

CONTENTS

UNIT 1   MEETING PEOPLE   1

GRAMMAR   2

LESSON 1 3	■ Talk about nationalities and occupations	
INTRODUCTIONS	■ Introduce yourself and others, at your workplace or at a party	

LESSON 2 9	■ Talk about a nearby object and its owner	
EXCHANGING BUSINESS CARDS	■ Ask for telephone numbers	

UNIT 2   SHOPPING   19

GRAMMAR   20

LESSON 3 21	■ Talk about the times of meetings and parties	
ASKING ABOUT BUSINESS HOURS	■ Ask the hours of services in stores and hotels	

LESSON 4 28	■ Ask the prices of items in a store and make a purchase	
SHOPPING, PART I		

LESSON 5 37	■ Ask what the size, color, and country of origin of an item is, and buy the item	
SHOPPING, PART II	■ Buy one or more of an item, telling the clerk how many you need	

QUIZ 1 (UNITS 1–2)   45

UNIT 3   GETTING AROUND   47

GRAMMAR   48

LESSON 6 49	■ Talk about where you will go, when, and with whom	
CONFIRMING SCHEDULES		

LESSON 7 59	■ Talk about travel destinations, places and people to visit, dates and times, and means of transportation	
VISITING ANOTHER COMPANY		

PREFACE TO THE REVISED 3RD EDITION

The new *Japanese for Busy People* is made up of three volumes: Book I (available in both romanized and *kana* editions), Book II, and Book III. *Japanese for Busy People I* was first published in 1984. It was based on materials used by AJALT teachers with more than ten years of experience teaching Japanese at every level from beginning to advanced.

The series was first revised in 1994, when *Japanese for Busy People II* was divided into two volumes, Book II and Book III. Only a minimum number of modifications were made to Book I at that time. This 3rd Edition, then, constitutes the first major revision of Book I. It involves a wide variety of changes, including the adoption of a unit-based structure, notes about Japanese culture, new and expanded exercises, and updated dialogues. The authors have made every effort to apply the results of the most recent research in Japanese-language education to ensure that learners acquire a clearer understanding of the situations in which Japanese is actually used, and gain increased confidence in their communicative abilities.

It is our fervent hope that this book will inspire people to learn more about Japan and the Japanese language.

Acknowledgments for *Japanese for Busy people I* (1st edition, 1984)

Compilation of this textbook has been a cooperative endeavor, and we deeply appreciate the collective efforts and individual contributions of Mss. Sachiko Adachi, Nori Ando, Haruko Matsui, Shigeko Miyazaki, Sachiko Okaniwa, Terumi Sawada, and Yuriko Yobuko. For English translations and editorial assistance, we wish to thank Ms. Dorothy Britton.

Acknowledgments for *Japanese for Busy People I, Revised Edition* (1994)

We would like to express our gratitude to the following people: Mss. Haruko Matsui, Junko Shinada, Keiko Ito, Mikiko Ochiai, and Satoko Mizoguchi.

Acknowledgments for the *Kana Version* of *Japanese for Busy People I, Revised Edition* (1995)

We would like to express our gratitude to the following people: Mss. Haruko Matsui, Junko Shinada, Mikiko Ochiai, and Satoko Mizoguchi.

Acknowledgments for *Japanese for Busy People I, Revised 3rd Edition*

Six AJALT teachers have written this textbook. They are Mss. Yoko Hattori, Sakae Tanabe, Izumi Sawa, Motoko Iwamoto, Shigeyo Tsutsui, and Takako Kobayashi. They were assisted by Ms. Reiko Sawane.

INTRODUCTION

Aims

This first volume of *Japanese for Busy People, Revised 3rd Edition* has been developed to meet the needs of busy beginning learners seeking an effective method of acquiring a natural command of spoken Japanese in a limited amount of time. The book is suitable for both those studying with a teacher and those studying on their own. In order to minimize the burden on busy learners, the vocabulary and grammar items presented have been narrowed down to about a third of those introduced in a typical first-year course. However, the textbook is set up so that learners can use the material they have learned right away in conversations with speakers of Japanese. In other words, *Japanese for Busy People I* is a textbook for learning "survival Japanese."

Despite this, *Japanese for Busy People I* does not present simple, childish Japanese. That is, we do not focus on mere grammatical correctness. Instead, we place our emphasis on conversational patterns that actually occur. Thus, by studying with this book, learners will acquire the most essential language patterns for everyday life, and be able to express their intentions in uncomplicated adult-level Japanese. They will also start to build a basis for favorable relations with the people around them by talking about themselves and their surroundings and circumstances, and asking about those of others.

This book is intended for beginners, but it can also provide a firm foundation for more advanced study. Learners can acquire a general idea of the nature of the Japanese language as they study the dialogues and notes in it. For this reason, *Japanese for Busy People I* is suitable as a review text for those who already know a certain amount of Japanese but want to confirm that they are using the language correctly.

Major features of *Japanese for Busy People I, Revised 3rd Edition*

In this newly revised version of *Japanese for Busy People I*, we have made the following modifications to ensure that those studying Japanese for the first time will have an enjoyable and effective learning experience.

Adoption of a unit structure. The content of the thirty lessons that made up the previous editions of *Japanese for Busy People I* has been reedited into eleven units, each consisting of two or three lessons linked by a single theme. The reason for this new design is that we believe learning sociocultural information, linguistic information, and communication strategies in an interrelated way is important for producing natural and appropriate Japanese.

Culture notes. We have placed culture notes at the beginning of each unit. These notes describe Japanese customs and events, as well as features of Japan itself. Here our intention is to get learners interested in the lives and customs of the Japanese people, in order to increase their desire to learn Japanese and deepen their understanding of it. We hope that as readers come into contact with the social and cultural information presented in these notes, they will gain an awareness of cultural diversity and acquire specific mental images of the themes introduced in the units.

Practice. In this section we have drawn on our classroom experience as well as recent thinking in Japanese-language education to reconstruct and revise the exercises to emphasize both language production and comprehension. Recognizing the importance of vocabulary acquisition at the beginning stages, for example, we have added a "Word Power" subsection that presents the major vocabulary that forms the basis for learning in the lesson. Here we have taken great pains with the presentation of the vocabulary, grouping similar items together to make them easier for learners to memorize. In addition, we have stated and highlighted in italics the intention of each exercise so that learners can understand it at a glance. The exercises themselves incorporate drawings, charts, tables, and other illustrations that we hope will make for a stimulating learning experience. Finally, we have added brief listening exercises to each lesson.

Other features. A 70-minute CD containing the Target Dialogues, Word Power sections, listening exercises, and Short Dialogues is attached to the inside back cover of this book. Additional features of this textbook include profiles of the characters who appear in it and an expanded contents page that lets learners see at a glance the goals to be achieved in each unit. We have also added quizzes every few units, so that learners can consolidate their understanding of recently introduced language.

The structure of the unit

A unit is made up of a culture note, a page on grammar, and two or three lessons. The culture notes are designed to stimulate interest in the themes of each unit and help learners construct a mental image of what they are going to learn. The grammar page, appearing right after the culture note, provides simple explanations of the basic grammatical items introduced in the unit. To the extent possible, the explanations here do not cover knowledge or information beyond that which pertains to the usage of the grammatical items in the unit.

The twenty-five lessons in Book I are each composed of the following four elements:

Target Dialogue. The Target Dialogues, which appear at the beginning of each lesson, indicate specifically what kinds of things the learner will be able to talk about after studying the lesson. We have limited these dialogues to practical expressions and grammatical items necessary for everyday conversation. Vocabulary lists, as well as notes that explain particularly difficult expressions, accompany the dialogues.

Practice. The Practice section consists of Word Power, Key Sentences, and Exercises. Word Power introduces basic vocabulary that learners should memorize before moving on to the other exercises. The words in this section are introduced with the aid of illustrations and charts, and all are available on the CD. The Key Sentences demonstrate the grammatical items from the lesson by using them in simple sentences. Finally, the Exercises consist of five different types of practice activities:

(1) Exercises that consist of repeating vocabulary or the conjugations of verbs or adjectives.

(2) Basic sentence-pattern exercises that aim to help learners comprehend the sentence structures of Japanese and gain an idea of their meanings.

(3) Substitution drills and drills in the form of dialogues that lead to conversation practice.

(4) Conversation practice created with an awareness of the situations and circumstances in which Japanese is actually used.

(5) Listening exercises in which learners listen to the CD and answer questions about what they hear.

Practicing exercise types (1), (2), and (3) allows learners to make a smooth transition to type (4), the conversation practice, and finally to move on to the Target Dialogue.

Short Dialogue(s). These are relatively short conversations that demonstrate helpful expressions, ways of getting people's attention, and ways of acknowledging what people have said. Like the Target Dialogues, they are often accompanied by notes that explain points to be aware of when using certain phrases and expressions.

Active Communication. This section, coming at the very end of the lesson, presents one or two tasks for which the learners themselves select the vocabulary, grammar, and expressions they need from the material in the lesson and use them in actual situations or classroom-based communication activities.

Using *Japanese for Busy People I*

We recommend the following methods of use, both for those who use *Japanese for Busy People I* as teachers and for self-taught learners. Materials should be adapted flexibly, depending on the learner's circumstances, but as a rule it should take about sixty hours to finish *Japanese for Busy People I.* We suggest learners proceed through the lessons as follows, with each lesson taking about two hours.

CULTURE NOTE — This section touches on the social and cultural background of the themes covered in the unit and is meant to expand the learner's awareness of the material to be learned.

GRAMMAR — This page is an overview of the grammatical concepts introduced in the unit. One should read it to get an idea of the kinds of grammatical items one will be learning in the unit.

LESSON

TARGET DIALOGUE — The Target Dialogue demonstrates what one will be able to say after finishing the lesson. Read the text of the dialogue while listening to the CD, and then scan the text to check the meaning against the English translation. It is important that one not get bogged down in the dialogue at this stage, since one will return to it at the end of the lesson (see below), after completing the Exercises.

PRACTICE

WORD POWER — This is a warm-up exercise. Learners should listen to the CD and practice pronouncing the words until they have memorized them. English translations of the words appear in a gray box at the bottom of the page.

KEY SENTENCES — Learners can gain an understanding of the lesson's grammatical structures by memorizing these useful sentences. New vocabulary items appear in a gray box at the bottom of the page.

EXERCISES — Here, learners absorb the lesson's grammatical structures through exercises that ask one to apply them. The exercises usually begin with vocabulary repetition or conjugation practice, then move on to tasks in which one is asked to make up sentences or dialogues and, finally, to full-fledged conversation reenactment. The last exercise, recorded on the CD, is intended to help learners hone their listening skills.

SHORT DIALOGUE(S)	One should thoroughly practice these short dialogues that contain handy, frequently used expressions. If one practices them so thoroughly that they begin to come naturally, one will be able to use them in a variety of situations.
▼ ▼	
TARGET DIALOGUE	The Target Dialogue is the culmination of one's study of the lesson. After learners have finished the exercises, they should return to the Target Dialogue and practice it.
▼ ▼	
ACTIVE COMMUNICATION	If the learner is in an environment that allows him or her to perform linguistic tasks, he or she should test himself or herself with the challenges presented here.

The *Kana* Version

The *Kana Version* is a basic textbook for students who intend to master the native *hiragana* and *katakana* scripts early on in their studies. The *Kana Version* assumes that the learner is thoroughly familiar with both *hiragana* and *katakana*, or is currently working through a textbook for learning *kana*. In any case, the learner should be able to read *kana* by the time he or she begins using this book.

Introducing the characters

The following characters feature in this textbook. Since they often appear in the exercises, it is a good idea to remember their names, faces, and relationships.

スミス

Mike Smith (32 years old), an American, is an attorney for ABC Foods. He is single.

チャン

Mei Chan (30 years old) is from Hong Kong. She works in ABC Foods' sales department. She is single.

グリーン

Frank Green (56 years old), an American, is the president of the Tokyo branch of ABC Foods. He lives in Tokyo, with his wife.

ささき

Keiko Sasaki (53 years old), a Japanese, is the department manager of ABC Foods' sales department. She is married.

かとう

Akira Kato (46 years old), a Japanese, is the section chief of ABC Foods' sales department. He is married.

なかむら

Mayumi Nakamura (26 years old), a Japanese, works as a secretary to Ms. Sasaki. She is single.

すずき

Daisuke Suzuki (24 years old), a Japanese, is a member of ABC Foods' sales staff. He is single.

たかはし

Shingo Takahashi (48 years old), a Japanese, works for Nozomi Department Store, where he is the division chief of the sales department. His wife's name is Junko.

やまもと

Ichiro Yamamoto (45 years old), a Japanese, is the president of the Kyoto branch of ABC Foods.

In addition to the above, the following people also appear in this book: Hideo Ogawa (male, 49 years old, a friend of Mr. Green), Taro Yamada (male, a banker and a friend of Mr. Smith), and Ayako Matsui (female, the Greens' next-door neighbor).

CHARACTERISTICS OF JAPANESE GRAMMAR

The grammar in this text is derived from a natural analysis of the Japanese language, rather than being an interpretation adapted to the syntax of Western languages. We have given as few technical terms as possible, choosing ones that will make for a smooth transition from the basic level to more advanced study.

The following points are basic and in most cases reflect differences between the grammars of Japanese and English.

1. Japanese nouns have neither gender nor number. But plurals of certain words can be expressed by the use of suffixes.

2. The verb (or the copula です) comes at the end of the sentence or clause.

    ex. わたしは　にほんじんです。 "I am a Japanese."
    　　わたしは　きょうとに　いきます。 "I go (or *will go*) to Kyoto."

3. The gender, number, or person of the subject does not affect the other parts of the sentence.

4. Verb conjugation shows only two tenses, the "present form" and the "past form." Whether use of the "present form" refers to habitual action or the future, and whether the "past form" is equivalent to the English past tense, present perfect, or past perfect can usually be determined from the context.

5. Japanese adjectives, unlike English ones, inflect for tense (present and past) and mood (for example, to show whether the word is negative).

6. The grammatical function of nouns is indicated by particles. Their role is similar to English prepositions, but since they always come after the word, they are sometimes referred to as *postpositions*.

    ex. とうきょうで, "at Tokyo"
    　　１５にちに, "on the 15th (of the month)"

7. Many degrees of politeness are expressible in Japanese. In this book the style is one that anyone may use without being rude.

NOTE: The following abbreviations are used in this book:

aff.	affirmative
neg.	negative
A*a*:	answer, affirmative
A*n*:	answer, negative
ex.	example
ー い adj.	ー い adjective
ー な adj.	ー な adjective

USEFUL DAILY EXPRESSIONS

1. おはようございます。"Good morning." Used until about 10:00 a.m.

2. こんにちは。"Hello." A rather informal greeting used from about 10:00 a.m. until sundown.

3. こんばんは。"Good evening."

4. おやすみなさい。"Good night." Said at night before going to bed and when parting at night during late hours outside the home.

5. さようなら。"Good-bye." On more formal occasions one uses しつれいします.

6. では／じゃ　また。"Well then . . ." Said informally when parting from relatives or friends.

7. おさきに　しつれいします。Said when leaving the office or a meeting before other people.

8. いってらっしゃい。"So long." (*lit.*, "Go and come back.") Said to members of a household as they leave the house. Occasionally it is used at work.

9. いってきます。"So long." (*lit.*, "[I'm] going and coming back.") This expression forms a pair with いってらっしゃい. (See 8 above.) Occasionally it is used at work. A politer form is いってまいります.

10. ただいま。"I'm back." (*lit.*, "[I have returned] just now.") Said by a person on returning home. Occasionally it is used at work.

11. おかえりなさい。"Welcome home." This expression forms a pair with ただいま. (See 10 above.) Occasionally it is used at work.

12. いただきます。Said before eating a meal.

13. ごちそうさまでした。Said after eating a meal.

14. おめでとうございます。"Congratulations."

15. どうも　ありがとうございます。"Thank you very much."

16. どういたしまして。"You're welcome."

17. すみません。"Excuse me," "I'm sorry."

18. ちょっと　まってください。"Wait just a moment, please."

19. もう　いちど　おねがいします。"Once more, please."

20. どうぞ　おさきに。"Please, go ahead."

21. きをつけて。"Take care," "Be careful."

22. おだいじに。"Take care of yourself." Used toward an ill or injured person.

MEETING PEOPLE

In Japan, people bow rather than shake hands, hug, or kiss, when they meet for the first time. A typical bow is performed with both feet together, the hands flat on the thighs (for men) or crossed in front (for women), and the torso inclined at a 15- to 45-degree angle. The eyes remain open during the bow, and the bowing person's line of sight moves with his or her torso rather than staying fixed on the other person. Generally, the deeper and slower the bow, the politer it is. Bowing properly is essential to making a good first impression, so we recommend practicing it until you become comfortable with it.

UNIT 1 GRAMMAR

Identifying People and Things

> **noun 1 は noun 2 です**

>   ex. グレイさんは　べんごしです。"Mr. Grey is an attorney."

■ The particle は—the topic marker
は ("as for . . .") follows noun 1, singling it out as the "topic" of the sentence. Noun 2 is then identi-fied, and the phrase is concluded with です. The topic is the person or thing that the sentence is about. The topic is often the same as the subject but not necessarily.

> noun 1 は noun 2 ですか
> はい、(noun 1 は) noun 2 です
> いいえ、(noun 1 は) noun 2 ではありません／じゃありません

>   ex. グレイさんは　べんごしですか。"Is Mr. Grey an attorney?"
>   はい、べんごしです。"Yes, (he) is an attorney."
>   いいえ、べんごしではありません。"No, (he) isn't an attorney."

■ The particle か—the question marker
It is easy to make questions in Japanese. Simply place the particle か at the end of the sentence. No change in word order is required even when the question contains interrogatives like "who," "what," "when," etc.
NOTE: Intonation normally rises on か, i.e., . . .ですか. ♪

■ はい／いいえ
はい is virtually the same as "yes," and いいえ is virtually the same as "no."

■ Omission of the topic (noun 1)
When it is obvious to the other person what the topic is, it is generally omitted.
>   ex. （わたしは）グレイです。"(As for me) I'm Grey."

But when it is necessary to make clear what the topic is, it is not omitted.
>   ex. こちらは　グレイさんです。"This is Mr. Grey."

Often the topic is omitted in answers to questions.
>   ex. グレイさんは　べんごしですか。"Is Mr. Grey an attorney?"
>   はい、べんごしです。"Yes, (he) is an attorney."
>   いいえ、べんごしでは　ありません。"No, (he) isn't an attorney."

■ ではありません／じゃありません
ではありません or じゃありません is the negative form of です。じゃ is more informal than では; otherwise they are the same. The chart below summarizes the forms of です。

PRESENT FORM		PAST FORM	
aff.	*neg.*	*aff.*	*neg.*
です	ではありません	でした	ではありませんでした
is	is not	was	was not

TARGET DIALOGUE

Ms. Sasaki introduces Mr. Smith to Mr. Takahashi.

ささき：たかはしさん、こちらは　スミスさんです。

スミスさんは　ＡＢＣフーズの　べんごしです。

スミス：はじめまして。スミスです。よろしく　おねがいします。

たかはし：はじめまして。のぞみデパートの　たかはしです。

よろしく　おねがいします。

Sasaki: Mr. Takahashi, this is Mr. Smith. Mr. Smith is an attorney with ABC Foods.
Smith: How do you do. My name is Smith. Pleased to meet you.
Takahashi: How do you do. I'm Takahashi from Nozomi Department Store. Pleased to meet you.

VOCABULARY

～さん	Mr., Mrs., Ms., Miss (see Note 1 below)
こちら	this one (polite for "this person"; see Note 2 below)
は	(particle that denotes the topic of a sentence)
です	be
ＡＢＣフーズ	ABC Foods (fictitious company name)
の	's, of (particle indicating belonging; see Note 4 below)
べんごし	attorney, lawyer
はじめまして	how do you do
よろしく　おねがいします	pleased to meet you (see Note 5 below)
のぞみデパート	Nozomi Department Store (fictitious company name)
デパート	department store

NOTES

1. たかはしさん
   さん is a title of respect added to a person's name, so it cannot be used after one's own name. さん may be used with both male and female names, and with either surnames or given names.

2. こちらは　スミスさんです。
   こちら ("this one") implies "this person here" and is a polite way of saying "this person." It is used when introducing one person to another.

3. （わたしは）スミスです。
   Especially in conversational Japanese, わたし ("I") is hardly ever used. あなた ("you") is similarly avoided, especially when addressing superiors, in which case the person's surname followed by さん is used.

4. のぞみデパートの　たかはしです。

The particle の attaches to nouns, and the noun-の combination modifies the word that comes after it. の expresses belonging or affiliation. Here it shows that Mr. Takahashi belongs to, in the sense that he works for, Nozomi Department Store. Japanese customarily give their company name and position when being introduced.

5. よろしく　おねがいします。

A phrase used when being introduced, よろしく　おねがいします is usually combined with はじめまして. It is also used when taking one's leave after having asked a favor. よろしく means "well" and is a request for the other person's favorable consideration in the future.

PRACTICE

WORD POWER

I. Countries and nationalities:

1. にほん	5. アメリカ	9. ちゅうごくじん	13. オーストラリアじん
2. ちゅうごく	6. オーストラリア	10. ドイツじん	14. タイじん
3. ドイツ	7. タイ	11. イギリスじん	
4. イギリス	8. にほんじん	12. アメリカじん	

VOCABULARY				
にほん	Japan	アメリカ	the United States
ちゅうごく	China	オーストラリア	Australia
ドイツ	Germany	タイ	Thailand
イギリス	the United Kingdom	～じん	-ese, -ian (person from)

II. Occupations:

1. べんごし   2. ひしょ   3. がくせい   4. エンジニア

KEY SENTENCES

1. (わたしは) スミスです。
2. スミスさんは　ＡＢＣフーズの　べんごしです。
3. こちらは　のぞみデパートの　たかはしさんです。

1. I am Smith.
2. Mr. Smith is an attorney with ABC Foods.
3. This is Mr. Takahashi from Nozomi Department Store.

EXERCISES

 I. Make up sentences following the patterns of the examples. Substitute the underlined words with the words in parentheses.

   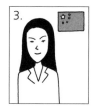 

| Mr. Smith, attorney | Ms. Hoffman, engineer | Ms. Brown, secretary | Ms. Lin, student | Mr. Takahashi |

A. *State someone's nationality.*

ex. スミスさんは　アメリカじんです。

1. .... (ホフマンさん、ドイツじん)

2. .... (ブラウンさん、イギリスじん)

3. .... (リンさん、ちゅうごくじん)

4. .... (たかはしさん、にほんじん)

VOCABULARY			
べんごし	attorney, lawyer	ホフマン	Hoffman (surname)
ひしょ	secretary	ブラウン	Brown (surname)
がくせい	student	リン	Lin (surname)
エンジニア	engineer		

B. *State someone's occupation.*

ex. <u>スミスさん</u>は <u>べんごし</u>です。

1. .... (ホフマンさん、エンジニア)

2. .... (ブラウンさん、ひしょ)

3. .... (リンさん、がくせい)

II. Make up dialogues following the patterns of the examples. Substitute the underlined words with the words in parentheses.

A. *Ask and answer what someone's nationality is.*

ex. A: <u>スミスさん</u>は <u>アメリカじん</u>ですか。
B: はい、<u>アメリカじん</u>です。

1. A: .... (ホフマンさん、ドイツじん)

B: .... (ドイツじん)

2. A: .... (ブラウンさん、イギリスじん)

B: .... (イギリスじん)

3. A: .... (リンさん、ちゅうごくじん)

B: .... (ちゅうごくじん)

4. A: .... (たかはしさん、にほんじん)

B: .... (にほんじん)

B. *Ask and answer what someone's occupation is.*

ex. A: <u>スミスさん</u>は <u>エンジニア</u>ですか。
B: いいえ。<u>べんごし</u>です。

1. A: .... (ブラウンさん)

B: .... (ひしょ)

2. A: .... (リンさん)

B: .... (がくせい)

C. *Ask and answer whether someone is of one nationality/occupation or another.*

ex. A: <u>スミスさん</u>は <u>アメリカじん</u>ですか、<u>イギリスじん</u>ですか。
B: <u>アメリカじん</u>です。

1. A: .... (たかはしさん、にほんじん、ちゅうごくじん)

B: .... (にほんじん)

VOCABULARY	か	(particle that denotes question)
	はい	yes
	いいえ	no

2. A: .... (ブラウンさん、イギリスじん、ドイツじん)

   B: .... (イギリスじん)

3. A: .... (ホフマンさん、エンジニア、べんごし)

   B: .... (エンジニア)

III. ***Respond to a self-introduction.*** Make up dialogues following the pattern of the example, assuming the roles indicated in parentheses.

ex. スミス: はじめまして、ＡＢＣフーズの　スミスです。よろしく　おねがいします。
あなた: はじめまして。<u>ベルリンモーターズ</u>の　<u>ホフマン</u>です。よろしく　おねがいします。

1. スミス: ....

   あなた: .... (ロンドンぎんこう、ブラウン)

2. スミス: ....

   あなた: .... (のぞみデパート、たかはし)

IV. ***Introduce people.*** Look at the illustrations and pretend you are B. Introduce A and C to each other, as in the example.

| ex. A　　B　　C | 1. A　　B　　C | 2. A　　B　　C |

A: ベルリンモーターズ、
　　ホフマンさん
C: ＡＢＣフーズ、
　　スミスさん

A: ロンドンぎんこう、
　　ブラウンさん
C: とうきょうだいがく、
　　リンさん

A: のぞみデパート、
　　たかはしさん
C: ベルリンモーターズ、
　　ホフマンさん

ex. B: こちらは　<u>ベルリンモーターズ</u>の　<u>ホフマンさん</u>です。こちらは <u>ＡＢＣ　フーズ</u>の　<u>スミスさん</u>です。

1. B: ....

2. B: ....

V. Listen to the CD and fill in the blank based on the information you hear.

スミスさんは .... です。

VOCABULARY			
あなた	you	とうきょうだいがく	Tokyo University
ベルリンモーターズ	Berlin Motors (fictitious company name)	とうきょう	Tokyo
ロンドンぎんこう	Bank of London (fictitious bank name)	だいがく	university, college
ロンドン	London		
ぎんこう	bank		

SHORT DIALOGUES

TRACK 4

I. At the reception desk of a company:

スミス：　ＡＢＣフーズの　スミスです。たかはしさんを　おねがいします。
うけつけ: はい。

Smith:　　　I'm Smith from ABC Foods. (I'd like to see) Mr. Takahashi, please.
receptionist: All right.

VOCABULARY

を	(particle; see Note 1 below)
おねがいします	please (get me . . .)
うけつけ	reception desk, receptionist

II. The buzzer on a home security intercom system sounds.

チャン：　はい、どなたですか。
なかむら:なかむらです。
チャン：　はい、どうぞ。

Chan:　　　Yes? Who is it?
Nakamura: It's Nakamura.
Chan:　　　All right. Please (come in).

VOCABULARY

どなた	who
はい、どうぞ	please go ahead, please feel free

NOTES

1. たかはしさんを　おねがいします。
Use "(person)を　おねがいします" when asking a receptionist to summon somebody you want to see. おねがいします is a very convenient phrase often used in making polite requests.

2. どなた
The basic word for "who" is だれ, but どなた is more polite.

3. はい、どうぞ。
This expression is used when granting a visitor permission to enter a room or an office. It can also be used when handing over something that another person has asked for.

Active Communication

1. Introduce yourself to a classmate. Then introduce two classmates to each other.

2. If you're in Japan, try introducing yourself to a Japanese person. State who you are and what your occupation is.

EXCHANGING BUSINESS CARDS

TARGET DIALOGUE

TRACK 5

Mr. Takahashi gives Mr. Smith his business card. Mr. Smith cannot read *kanji*.

たかはし：わたしの　めいしです。どうぞ。

スミス：どうも　ありがとうございます。*(flipping over Takahashi's business card to examine the other side)* これは　たかはしさんの　なまえ ですか。

たかはし：ええ、そうです。たかはし　しんごです。

スミス：これは？

たかはし：かいしゃの　なまえです。のぞみデパートです。

Takahashi: This is my business card. Here.
　　Smith: Thank you very much. Is this your name?
Takahashi: Yes that's right. It's Shingo Takahashi.
　　Smith: What about this?
Takahashi: It's the name of (my) company. It's "Nozomi Department Store."

VOCABULARY

わたしの	my
めいし	business card
どうぞ	please; if you please
どうも　ありがとうございます	thank you very much
これ	this one
なまえ	name
ええ	yes (less formal than はい)
そうです	that's right
これは？	what about this?
かいしゃ	company, the office

NOTES

1. （これは）わたしの　めいしです。
   わたしの　めいし means "my business card." The particle の here expresses possession.

2. どうも　ありがとうございます。
   This is an expression of gratitude. There are several levels of politeness in Japanese, and どうも ありがとうございます is an example of the most polite level. More casual are, in descending order or politeness, ありがとうございます, どうも　ありがとう, and ありがとう.

9

3. これは　たかはしさんの　なまえですか。

Note that although addressing Mr. Takahashi, Mr. Smith uses his name rather than saying あなたの, "your." (See Note 3, p. 3.)

4. そうです。

When replying to questions that end with ですか, そう can be used instead of repeating the noun.

5. これは？

A rising intonation on the particle は makes this informal phrase a question without using the question marker か.

PRACTICE

WORD POWER

I. Numbers:

0	1	2	3	4	5	6	7	8	9
ゼロ／れい	いち	に	さん	よん／し	ご	ろく	なな／しち	はち	きゅう／く

II. Business vocabulary:

① のぞみデパート

② 高橋真吾

③ 東京都港区虎ノ門 3–25–2
④ (03) 3459-9620*
⑤ s.takahashi@nozomidpt.com

Nozomi Department Store

Shingo Takahashi

3–25–2 Toranomon, Minato-ku, Tokyo
(03) 3459-9620
E-MAIL: s.takahashi@nozomidpt.com

1. めいし　　　4. でんわばんごう
2. なまえ　　　5. メールアドレス
3. じゅうしょ

*The area code for Tokyo is 03. When saying a phone number aloud, put の between the area code (e.g., 03) and the exchange, and between the exchange and the last four numbers. The phone number here is pronounced ゼロ　さんの　さん　よん　ご　きゅうの　きゅう　ろく　に　ゼロ.

NOTE: The 0 used in telephone numbers is pronounced ゼロ instead of れい.

VOCABULARY			
めいし	business card	でんわ	telephone
なまえ	name	ばんごう	number
じゅうしょ	address	メールアドレス	e-mail address
でんわばんごう	telephone number		

III. Personal belongings:

1. けいたい　　2. かさ　　3. ほん　　4. しんぶん　　5. かぎ　　6. とけい

KEY SENTENCES

1. これは　めいしです。
2. これは　めいしではありません。
3. これは　ささきさんの　かさです。
4. たかはしさんの　でんわばんごうは　０３-３４５９-９６２０です。

1. This is a business card.
2. This is not a business card.
3. This is Ms. Sasaki's umbrella.
4. Mr. Takahashi's telephone number is 03-3459-9620.

VOCABULARY			
けいたい	cell/mobile phone	かぎ	key
かさ	umbrella	とけい	watch, clock
ほん	book	ではありません	is/are not
しんぶん	newspaper		

11

EXERCISES

I. Make up sentences following the patterns of the examples. Substitute the underlined words with the words in parentheses.

A. *State what an object is.*

ex. これは　ほんです。

1. .... （かぎ）

2. .... （とけい）

B. *State what an object is not.*

ex. これは　ほんではありません。

1. .... （かぎ）

2. .... （とけい）

II. Make up dialogues following the patterns of the examples and based on the information in the illustrations.

A. *Ask and answer whether an object is what it appears to be.*

ex. A: これは　しんぶんですか。
B: はい、しんぶんです。

1. A: ....

B: ....

2. A: ....

B: ....

3. A: ....

B: ....

B. *Negate the identity of an object.*

ex. A: これは　ほんですか。
B: いいえ、ほんではありません。

1. A: これは　かさですか。

B: ....

2. A: これは　とけいですか。

   B: ....

3. A: これは　かぎですか。

   B: ....

 III. *Ask and answer what an object is.* Look at the illustrations and make up dialogues following the pattern of the example.

ex. A: これは　なんですか。
   B: しんぶんです。

1. A: ....

   B: ....

2. A: ....

   B: ....

3. A: ....

   B: ....

 IV. *State who the owner of an object is.* Make up sentences following the pattern of the example and based on the information in the illustrations.

 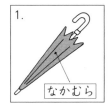  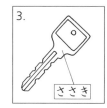

ex. これは　スミスさんの　ほんです。

1. ....

2. ....

3. ....

VOCABULARY　　なん　　　　　　　　what

13

V. Make up dialogues following the patterns of the examples and based on the information in the illustrations.

A. *Ask and answer whether an object belongs to someone.*

ex. A: これは　<u>ささきさんの</u>　<u>かさ</u>ですか。
B: はい、<u>ささきさんの</u>です。

1. A: ....

   B: ....

2. A: ....

   B:..

3. A: ....

   B: ....

B. *Deny that an object belongs to someone.*

ex. A: これは　なかむらさんの　かさですか。
B: いいえ、<u>なかむらさんの</u>ではありません。

1. A: これは　ささきさんの　ほんですか。

   B: ....

2. A: これは　チャンさんの　かぎですか。

   B: ....

3. A: これは　スミスさんの　けいたいですか。

   B: ....

C. *Ask and answer who an object's owner is.*

ex. A: これは　だれの　<u>かさ</u>ですか。
B: <u>ささきさんの</u>です。

1. A: ....

   B: ....

2. A: ....

   B: ....

3. A: ....

   B: ....

VI. Use the information in the table to make up sentences or dialogues as in the examples.

NAME	TELEPHONE NUMBER
ex. スミス	03-3459-9660
1. ささき	03-3298-7748
2. たいしかん	03-3225-1116
3. ぎんこう	03-5690-3111
4. たかはし	03-3459-9620

A. *State someone's phone number.*

ex. スミスさんの　でんわばんごうは　ゼロ　さんの　さん　よん　ご
　　きゅうの　きゅう　ろく　ろく　ゼロです。

1. ....

2. ....

3. ....

4. ....

B. *Ask for and provide someone's phone number.*

ex. A: スミスさんの　でんわばんごうは　なんばんですか。
　　B: ゼロ　さんの　さん　よん　ご　きゅうの　きゅう　ろく　ろく
　　　　ゼロです。

1. A: ....

   B: ....

2. A: ....

   B: ....

3. A: ....

   B: ....

4. A: ....

   B: ....

VOCABULARY		
	たいしかん	embassy
	なんばん	what number

VII. **Talk about who an object's owner is.** Make up dialogues following the pattern of the example. Substitute the underlined words with the words in parentheses.

ex. Ms. Nakamura is cleaning up the meeting room after a meeting. Mr. Smith comes into the room.

スミス： これは　なかむらさんの　<u>ほん</u>ですか。
なかむら：(looking at the book) いいえ、わたしのではありません。
スミス： だれの　<u>ほん</u>ですか。
なかむら：チャンさんのです。

1. スミス： .... （かさ）

   なかむら： ....

   スミス： .... （かさ）

   なかむら： ....

2. スミス： .... （かぎ）

   なかむら： ....

   スミス： .... （かぎ）

   なかむら： ....

3. スミス： .... （けいたい）

   なかむら： ....

   スミス： .... （けいたい）

   なかむら： ....

VIII. Listen to the CD and fill in the blank based on the information you hear.

スミスさんの　でんわばんごうは .... です。

SHORT DIALOGUES

I. After Mr. Takahashi leaves the room, Mr. Smith finds a datebook on the sofa.

スミス：　これは　なかむらさんの　てちょうですか。
なかむら：いいえ、わたしのではありません。
スミス：　だれのですか。

Ms. Nakamura notices the name "Takahashi" on the datebook, so she runs after him.

なかむら：これは　たかはしさんの　てちょうですか。
たかはし：ええ、そうです。どうも　ありがとうございます。

Smith: Ms. Nakamura, is this your datebook?
Nakamura: No, it's not mine.
Smith: Whose is it?

. . . .

Nakamura: Is this your datebook, Mr. Takahashi?
Takahashi: Yes, it is. Thank you very much.

VOCABULARY

てちょう   datebook, small notebook, planner

II. Ms. Chan meets Mrs. Matsui at a party and asks her for her telephone number.

チャン：まついさんの　でんわばんごうは　なんばんですか。
まつい：０３-３４５９-９６３０です。
　　　　けいたいは　０９０-１２３４-５６７８です。
チャン：すみません。もう　いちど　おねがいします。

Chan: What is your phone number, Mrs. Matsui?
Matsui: It's 03-3459-9630. My mobile phone number is 090-1234-5678.
Chan: I'm sorry, could you repeat that?

VOCABULARY

すみません	I'm sorry; excuse me
もう　いちど　おねがいします	one more time, please
もう　いちど	one more time
もう	more
いちど	one time

Active Communication

1. Ask the people around you what their phone numbers are and make a list.

2. If you're in Japan, ask an employee of a restaurant or store what the establishment's phone number is.

SHOPPING

Japan is a shopper's paradise. From large and lavish department stores to small, hole-in-the-wall establishments in shopping arcades, the country abounds with shops. For the most part, price labels are attached to goods, although sometimes when the prices are not given or are written in *kanji* it is necessary to ask how much an item costs. Salesclerks are generally polite and helpful; upon entering a store or restaurant, a customer will almost always be greeted. The greeting is *irasshaimase*!

UNIT ■
2 GRAMMAR

Pronouns and Noun Modifiers

これ／それ／あれは noun です

    ex. これは　ほんです。"This is a book."

■ これ／それ／あれ

Whereas English has only "this" and "that," Japanese has three separate demonstrative pronouns: これ, それ, and あれ. これ (see ① below) indicates something near the speaker, それ (see ② below) something near the listener, and あれ (see ③ below) something not near either person.

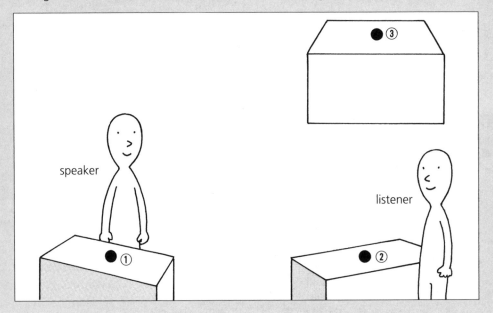

この／その／あの noun 1 は noun 2 です

    ex. この　ほんは　わたしのです。"This book is mine."

■ この／その／あの

この, その, and あの have similar meanings to これ, それ, and あれ, but they modify nouns.

LESSON 3

ASKING ABOUT BUSINESS HOURS

 TARGET DIALOGUE

Mr. Smith goes to the department store, but it isn't open yet.

スミス：すみません、いま　なんじですか。

おんなの　ひと：９じ５０ぷんです。

スミス：デパートは　なんじからですか。

おんなの　ひと：１０じからです。

スミス：なんじまでですか。

おんなの　ひと：ごご　８じまでです。

スミス：ありがとうございます。

おんなの　ひと：どういたしまして。

■デパートは　１０じから　８じまでです。

    Smith: Excuse me. What time is it?
woman: It's 9:50.
    Smith: What time does the department store open?
woman: It opens at 10:00.
    Smith: Until what time is it open?
woman: It's open till 8:00 p.m.
    Smith: Thank you.
woman: You're welcome.

■The department store is open from 10:00 to 8:00.

VOCABULARY

すみません	excuse me
いま	now
なんじ	what time
〜じ	o'clock (counter)
おんなの　ひと	woman
おんな	female, woman
ひと	person
９じ（くじ）	nine o'clock
５０ぷん（ごじゅっぷん）	fifty minutes
５０（ごじゅう）	fifty
〜ふん／ぷん	minute
から	from (particle)

21

１０じ	ten o'clock
まで	until (particle)
ごご	p.m., in the afternoon
８じ	eight o'clock
どういたしまして	you're welcome; don't mention it

NOTES

1. （デパートは）１０じからです。／（デパートは）ごご　８じまでです。

When stating the hours that a business is open, use the "noun 1 は noun 2 です" pattern. However, if the topic of the sentence is clear from the context, it may be omitted, as it has been here. (See "Omission of the topic (noun 1)" in Unit 1 Grammar, p. 2.) The time the business opens is followed by から, and the time that it closes is followed by まで.

PRACTICE

WORD POWER

I. Services and activities:

  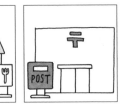

1. デパート　　2. スーパー　　3. レストラン　　4. ゆうびんきょく　5. ぎんこう

6. しごと　　　7. かいぎ　　　8. ひるやすみ　　9. パーティー　　10. えいが

VOCABULARY					
デパート	department store	ぎんこう	bank	ひる	noon
スーパー	supermarket	しごと	work, job	やすみ	break, rest
レストラン	restaurant	かいぎ	meeting, conference	パーティー	party
ゆうびんきょく	post office	ひるやすみ	lunch break	えいが	movie

II. Numbers:

10	じゅう	20	にじゅう	30	さんじゅう
11	じゅういち	21	にじゅういち	40	よんじゅう
12	じゅうに	22	にじゅうに	50	ごじゅう
13	じゅうさん	23	にじゅうさん	60	ろくじゅう
14	じゅうよん／じゅうし	24	にじゅうよん／にじゅうし	70	ななじゅう
15	じゅうご	25	にじゅうご	80	はちじゅう
16	じゅうろく	26	にじゅうろく	90	きゅうじゅう
17	じゅうなな／じゅうしち	27	にじゅうなな／にじゅうしち		
18	じゅうはち	28	にじゅうはち	100	ひゃく
19	じゅうく／じゅうきゅう	29	にじゅうく／にじゅうきゅう		

III. Times:

1:00 いちじ	3:05 さんじ　ごふん	3:10 さんじ　じゅっぷん	
2:00 にじ	3:15 さんじ　じゅうごふん	3:20 さんじ　にじゅっぷん	
3:00 さんじ	3:25 さんじ　にじゅうごふん	3:30 さんじ　さんじゅっぷん／はん	
4:00 よじ	3:35 さんじ　さんじゅうごふん	3:40 さんじ　よんじゅっぷん	
5:00 ごじ	3:45 さんじ　よんじゅうごふん	3:50 さんじ　ごじゅっぷん	
6:00 ろくじ	3:55 さんじ　ごじゅうごふん		
7:00 しちじ			
8:00 はちじ		4:00 a.m.　ごぜん　よじ	
9:00 くじ		9:00 p.m.　ごご　くじ	
10:00 じゅうじ			
11:00 じゅういちじ			
12:00 じゅうにじ			

NOTE: Hours and minutes are written in hiragana here, but throughout the rest of the book they are written with numerals, e.g., １じ for "1:00," １０じ２０ぷん for "10:20," etc.

KEY SENTENCES

1. いま　３じです。
2. しごとは　９じから　５じまでです。

1. It's 3:00.
2. Work is from 9:00 to 5:00.

VOCABULARY　はん　　half past (of time)
ごぜん　　a.m., in the morning

23

EXERCISES

 I. *State the time.* Practice telling the times indicated below.

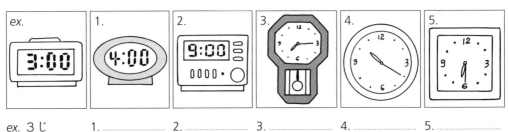

| ex. | 1. | 2. | 3. | 4. | 5. |

ex. 3 じ   1. .... 2. .... 3. .... 4. .... 5. ....

 II. *Ask and give the time.* Make up dialogues following the pattern of the example. Substitute the underlined word with the times indicated in exercise I.

ex. A: いま　なんじですか。
B: <u>3じ</u>です。

1. A: ....
   B: ....

2. A: ....
   B: ....

3. A: ....
   B: ....

4. A: ....
   B: ....

5. A: ....
   B: ....

III. Make up sentences following the patterns of the examples. Substitute the underlined word(s) with the alternatives given.

A. *State a department store's opening time.*

ex. デパートは　１０じからです。

1. .... （９：００）

2. .... （１１：００）

B. *State what time work will finish.*

ex. しごとは　５じまでです。

1. .... （７：００）

2. .... （６：３０）

C. *State what work hours are, from what time until what time.*

ex. しごとは　９じから　５じまでです。

1. .... （９：３０、６：００）

2. .... （１０：００、７：００）

IV. Make up dialogues following the patterns of the examples. Substitute the underlined words with the alternatives given.

A. *Ask and answer what time a business will open.*

ex. A: ぎんこうは　なんじからですか。
B: ９じからです。

1. A: .... （スーパー）

   B: .... （１１：００）

2. A: .... （ゆうびんきょく）

   B: .... （９：００）

B. *Ask and answer what time something will end or close.*

ex. A: パーティーは　なんじまでですか。
B: ごご　９じまでです。

1. A: .... （レストラン）

   B: .... （ごご　１１：３０）

2. A: .... （かいぎ）

   B: .... （１０：３０）

C. *Ask and answer what an event's hours are.*

ex. A: <u>かいぎ</u>は　なんじから　なんじまでですか。
　　B: <u>１じ</u>から　<u>３じ</u>までです。

1. A: .... (ひるやすみ)

　　B: .... （１２：３０、１：３０）

2. A: .... (えいが)

　　B: .... （４：１５、６：３０）

V. ***Find out when a service will begin or when a facility will open.*** Make up dialogues following the pattern of the example. Substitute the underlined words with the alternatives given.

ex. Mr. Smith is at a resort hotel. He asks the front desk when meals are served and when the hotel's facilities open.

　　スミス：　すみません。<u>あさごはん</u>は　なんじからですか。
　　フロント：<u>７じ</u>からです。
　　スミス：　どうも　ありがとう。

1. スミス： .... （ばんごはん）

　　フロント： .... （６：００）

　　スミス： ....

2. スミス： .... （プール）

　　フロント： .... （８：００ a.m.）

　　スミス： ....

3. スミス： .... （ジム）

　　フロント： .... （9：００ a.m.）

　　スミス： ....

VI. Listen to the CD and fill in the blank based on the information you hear.

　　ジムは .... からです。

VOCABULARY					
あさごはん	breakfast	フロント	the front desk (of a hotel)	プール	pool
あさ	morning	どうも　ありがとう	thank you	ジム	gym
ごはん	meal	ばんごはん	dinner		
		ばん	evening		

26

SHORT DIALOGUE

TRACK 12

Ms. Sasaki wants to call the London branch of her company.

ささき: なかむらさん、いま なんじですか。
なかむら: 4じはんです。
ささき: ロンドンは いま なんじですか。
なかむら: ごぜん 8じはんです。
ささき: そうですか。どうも ありがとう。

Sasaki: Ms. Nakamura, what time is it?
Nakamura   It's 4:30.
Sasaki: What time is it in London?
Nakamura: It's 8:30 in the morning.
Sasaki: Is that so? Thank you very much.

VOCABULARY

そうですか   I see

NOTES

1. そうですか。
   This expression, meaning "I see" or "is that so?" is used as a comment on what someone else has said.
   It is spoken with falling intonation.

Active Communication

1. Ask someone for the time.

2. If you're in Japan, try asking for the business hours of a restaurant or other facilities you are interested in.

SHOPPING, PART I

TARGET DIALOGUE

TRACK 13

Mr. Smith is shopping in a department store.

みせの　ひと：いらっしゃいませ。

スミス：*(pointing)* それを　みせてください。

みせの　ひと：はい、どうぞ。

スミス：ありがとう。これは　いくらですか。

みせの　ひと：3,000えんです。

スミス：*(pointing)* それは　いくらですか。

みせの　ひと：これも　3,000えんです。

スミス：じゃ、それを　ください。

みせの　ひと：はい、ありがとうございます。

salesperson: May I help you?
    Smith: Please show me that one.
salesperson: Yes, here it is.
    Smith: Thank you. How much is this?
salesperson: It's 3,000 yen.
    Smith: How much is that one?
salesperson: This is also 3,000 yen.
    Smith: I'll take that one, then.
salesperson: All right. Thank you.

VOCABULARY

みせ	shop, store, restaurant
いらっしゃいませ	may I help you?; welcome
それ	that one
みせてください	please show me
いくら	how much
3,000えん（さんぜんえん）	3,000 yen
〜えん	yen
も	also, too, either (particle)
じゃ	well then
ください	please give me

NOTES

1. それを　みせてください。

When you want to take a closer look at an item in a store, use "(something)を　みせてください" ("please show me . . .").

2. さんぜんえん

The system of counting large numbers is different in Japanese and English. The chart below shows how to count from a thousand to a trillion.

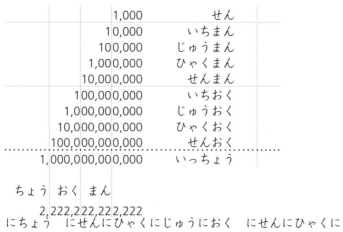

1,000	せん
10,000	いちまん
100,000	じゅうまん
1,000,000	ひゃくまん
10,000,000	せんまん
100,000,000	いちおく
1,000,000,000	じゅうおく
10,000,000,000	ひゃくおく
100,000,000,000	せんおく
1,000,000,000,000	いっちょう

ちょう　おく　まん

2,222,222,222,222

にちょう　にせんにひゃくにじゅうにおく　にせんにひゃくにじゅうにまん
にせんにひゃくにじゅうに

Decimals. (The word for "decimal point" is てん.)

0	れい
0.7	れいてんなな
0.29	れいてんにきゅう
0.538	れいてんごさんはち

Fractions. (ぶん means "part.")

1/2	にぶんの　いち	2/3	さんぶんの　に
1/4	よんぶんの　いち		

3. これも　3,000えんです。

The particle も means "too," "also," "either," etc. It is used in both affirmative and negative sentences.

ex. それは　さんぜんえんです。これも　さんぜんえんです。
"That one is 3,000 yen. This one is 3,000 yen, too."
これは　わたしの　かさではありません。それも　わたしのではありません。
"This is not my umbrella. That's not mine either."

4. じゃ、これを　ください。

じゃ and では correspond to "well" or "well then," interjections that express conclusion or resignation. これを　ください means "I'll take this one" and is the phrase to use when you have decided what you want to buy.

PRACTICE

WORD POWER

I. Electronic appliances:

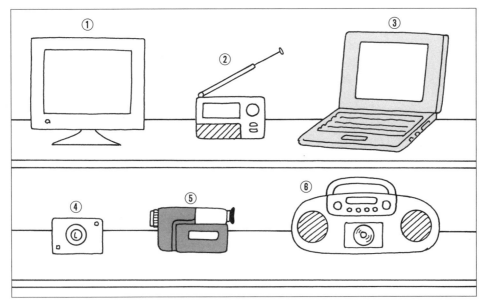

1. テレビ　2. ラジオ　3. パソコン　4. デジカメ　5. ビデオカメラ　6. ＣＤプレーヤー

II. Numbers:

100	ひゃく	1,000	せん	10,000	いちまん
200	にひゃく	2,000	にせん	20,000	にまん
300	さんびゃく	3,000	さんぜん	30,000	さんまん
400	よんひゃく	4,000	よんせん	40,000	よんまん
500	ごひゃく	5,000	ごせん	50,000	ごまん
600	ろっぴゃく	6,000	ろくせん	60,000	ろくまん
700	ななひゃく	7,000	ななせん	70,000	ななまん
800	はっぴゃく	8,000	はっせん	80,000	はちまん
900	きゅうひゃく	9,000	きゅうせん	90,000	きゅうまん

Intermediate numbers are made by combining the numbers composing them.
　ex. 135 ひゃくさんじゅうご　　1,829 せんはっぴゃくにじゅうきゅう

NOTE: Large numbers are written in hiragana here, but throughout the rest of the book, numerals are used to write them, e.g., ３，０００えん for "3,000 yen."

VOCABULARY					
テレビ	television	ビデオカメラ	video camera	ＣＤプレーヤー	CD player
ラジオ	radio	ビデオ	video	ＣＤ（シーディー）	CD
パソコン	(personal) computer	カメラ	camera		
デジカメ	digital camera				

III. Japanese currency:

1. 1えん　　2. 5えん　　3. 10えん　　4. 50えん　　5. 100えん　　6. 500えん

7. 1,000えん

8. 2,000えん

9. 5,000えん

10. 10,000えん

KEY SENTENCES

1. それは　テレビです。
2. あれは　パソコンです。
3. これは　3,000えんです。あれも　3,000えんです。

1. That is a television set.
2. That over there is a personal computer.
3. This is 3,000 yen. That, too, is 3,000 yen.

VOCABULARY　　あれ　　　that one over there

EXERCISES

 I. *State an item's price*. Look at the illustrations and state the price of each item.

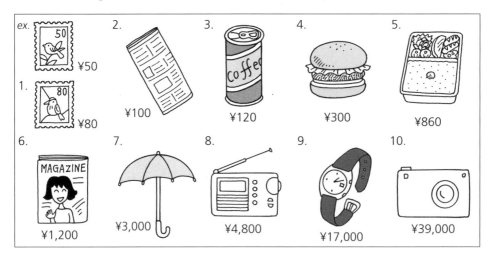

ex. ごじゅうえん   3. ....   6. ....   9. ....

1. ....   4. ....   7. ....   10. ....

2. ....   5. ....   8. ....

II. *Ask and give an item's price.* Make up dialogues following the pattern of the example and based on the information in the illustrations.

ex. A: これは　いくらですか。
    B: ５００えんです。

1. A: ....

   B: ....

2. A: ....

   B: ....

3. A: ....

   B: ....

 III. _Identify objects in different locations._ Look at the illustration and make up sentences like the examples. Substitute the underlined words with the alternatives given.

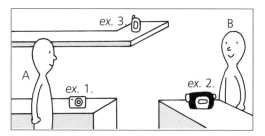 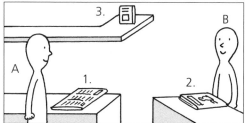

ex. 1. A: これは　<u>デジカメ</u>です。
ex. 2. A: それは　<u>ビデオカメラ</u>です。
ex. 3. A: あれは　<u>けいたい</u>です。

1. A: .... （しんぶん）

2. A: .... （ざっし）

3. A: .... （ほん）

 IV. _Ask and give an item's price._ Use the information in the illustrations to make appropriate questions for each of the answers given.

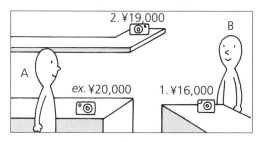 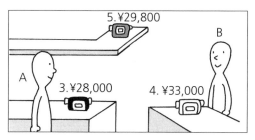

ex. A: <u>これは</u>　いくらですか。
   B: ２０，０００えんです。

1. A: ....
   B: １６，０００えんです。

2. A: ....
    B: １９，０００えんです。

3. A: ....
    B: ２８，０００えんです。

4. A: ....
    B: ３３，０００えんです。

5. A: ....
    B: ２９，８００えんです。

V. ***State that two things cost the same or are the same thing***. Make up sentences following the pattern of the example. Substitute the underlined words with the alternatives given.

ex. これは　<u>８００えん</u>です。それも　<u>８００えん</u>です。

1. .... (１，５００えん)

2. .... (とけい)

3. .... (スミスさんの　ほん)

VI. ***Ask the price of more than one item.*** Make up dialogues following the pattern of the example. Substitute the underlined words with the alternatives given.

ex. スミス:　　　　これは　いくらですか。
    みせの　ひと:<u>8,000えん</u>です。
    スミス:　　　　あれも　<u>8,000えん</u>ですか。
    みせの　ひと:いいえ、<u>8,000えん</u>では
    　　　　　　　ありません。7,500えんです。

1. スミス:　　　...
    みせの　ひと:... (７，０００えん)
    スミス:　　　.. (７，０００えん)
    みせの　ひと:... (７，０００えん)

2. スミス:　　　...
    みせの　ひと:... (９，０００えん)
    スミス:　　　.. (９，０００えん)
    みせの　ひと:... (９，０００えん)

3. スミス　　　...
    みせの　ひと:... (６，５００えん)
    スミス:　　　.. (６，５００えん)
    みせの　ひと:... (６，５００えん)

VII. ***Confirm what an item is.*** Make up dialogues following the pattern of the example. Substitute the underlined words with the alternatives given.

ex. Mr. Smith comes to a store.

スミス: 　　　あれは　<u>ＤＶＤ</u>ですか。
みせの　ひと: いいえ、<u>ＣＤ</u>です。
スミス: 　　　それは　<u>ＤＶＤ</u>ですか。
みせの　ひと: はい、<u>ＤＶＤ</u>です。

1. スミス: .... (シャープペンシル)

　みせの　ひと: .... (ボールペン)

　スミス: .... (シャープペンシル)

　みせの　ひと: .... (シャープペンシル)

2. スミス: .... (フランスごの　じしょ)

　みせの　ひと: .... (えいごの　じしょ)

　スミス: .... (フランスごの　じしょ)

　みせの　ひと: .... (フランスごの　じしょ)

VIII. ***Buy something at a store.*** Make up dialogues following the pattern of the example. Substitute the underlined words with the alternatives given.

ex. スミス: 　　　すみません。あれは　<u>ビデオカメラ</u>ですか。
みせの　ひと: いいえ、<u>デジカメ</u>です。
スミス: 　　　それは　<u>ビデオカメラ</u>ですか。
みせの　ひと: はい、そうです。
スミス: 　　　いくらですか。
みせの　ひと: <u>５０，０００えん</u>です。
スミス: 　　　じゃ、それを　ください。

1. スミス: .... (ＣＤプレーヤー)

　みせの　ひと: .... (ラジオ)

　スミス: .... (ＣＤプレーヤー)

　みせの　ひと: ....

　スミス: ....

　みせの　ひと: .... (１５，０００えん)

　スミス: ....

VOCABULARY	ＤＶＤ（ディーブイディー）	DVD	フランスご	French (language)
	シャープペンシル	mechanical pencil	フランス	France
	ボールペン	ballpoint pen	〜ご	language
			じしょ	dictionary
			えいご	English (language)

2. スミス: .... (テレビ)

みせの　ひと: .... (パソコン)

スミス: .... (テレビ)

みせの　ひと: ....

スミス: ....

みせの　ひと: .... (１８０，０００えん)

スミス: ....

IX. Listen to the CD and fill in the blank based on the information you hear.

ビデオカメラは .... えんです。

SHORT DIALOGUE

Mr. Smith is at a store, shopping.

スミス: これを　ください。
みせの　ひと: ４，３００えんです。
スミス: カードでも　いいですか。
みせの　ひと: はい、けっこうです。

Smith: I'll take this.
salesperson: It's 4,300 yen.
Smith: Is it all right to use a credit card?
salesperson: Yes, it's fine.

VOCABULARY

カード	(credit) card
〜でも　いいですか	is . . . all right?
はい、けっこうです	yes, it's fine

NOTES

1. カードでも　いいですか。
   The phrase でも　いいですか is used to ask if something is permissible. It means "is . . . all right?"

Active Communication

If you're in Japan, try asking the prices of items at vendors where prices are not listed or are written in *kanji*.

SHOPPING, PART II

TARGET DIALOGUE

TRACK 17

Mr. Smith buys a T-shirt.

スミス：すみません。あの　Ｔシャツは　いくらですか。

みせの　ひと：どれですか。

スミス：あの　あおい　Ｔシャツです。

みせの　ひと：あれは　１，５００えんです。

スミス：その　あかい　Ｔシャツは　いくらですか。

みせの　ひと：１，０００えんです。

スミス：じゃ、それを　２まい　ください。

■ あかい　Ｔシャツは　１，０００えんです。

Smith: Excuse me. How much is that T-shirt over there?
salesperson: Which one?
Smith: That blue T-shirt.
salesperson: That's 1,500 yen.
Smith: How much is that red T-shirt?
salesperson: It's 1,000 yen.
Smith: Well then, give me two of those.

■ The red T-shirt is 1,000 yen.

VOCABULARY

あの	that over there (used before a noun)
Ｔシャツ	T-shirt
どれ	which one
あおい	blue
その	that (used before a noun)
あかい	red
２まい	two (shirts or other flat objects)
〜まい	(counter for flat objects)

NOTES

1. それを　２まい　ください。
   まい is a unit for counting thin, flat objects like shirts and pieces of paper. Japanese has two numerical systems: the ひとつ, ふたつ, みっつ system and the abstract いち, に, さん system. Counting things can be done in two ways: (1) using the ひとつ, ふたつ, みっつ system independently (see Word Power

II, p. 39), or (2) using the いち, に, さん system combined with a counter such as まい or ほん (ぼん, ぽん), the latter for long, slender objects like pencils and bottles.

　ex. りんごを　ふたつ　ください。 "Please give me two apples."

The ひとつ, ふたつ, みっつ system, however, only goes as far as とお (10), after which the いち, に, さん system is used: じゅういち, じゅうに, じゅうさん, etc.

Note the word order here: thing + を + number (or number and counter) + ください。

PRACTICE

WORD POWER

I. Items for sale:

1. はがき	4. あかい	7. ビール	10. ちいさい
2. きって	5. あおい	8. りんご	
3. Ｔシャツ	6. くろい	9. おおきい	

VOCABULARY	はがき	postcard	あおい	blue	おおきい	large, big
	きって	stamp	くろい	black	ちいさい	small, little
	Ｔシャツ	T-shirt	ビール	beer		
38	あかい	red	りんご	apple		

II. Numbers and counters:

	📄 👕 etc.	🍾 ☂ etc.	🍎 🍔 etc.
1	いちまい	いっぽん	ひとつ
2	にまい	にほん	ふたつ
3	さんまい	さんぼん	みっつ
4	よんまい	よんほん	よっつ
5	ごまい	ごほん	いつつ
6	ろくまい	ろっぽん	むっつ
7	ななまい	ななほん	ななつ
8	はちまい	はっぽん	やっつ
9	きゅうまい	きゅうほん	ここのつ
10	じゅうまい	じゅっぽん	とお
11	じゅういちまい	じゅういっぽん	じゅういち
12	じゅうにまい	じゅうにほん	じゅうに

KEY SENTENCES

1. この　Ｔシャツは　２，０００えんです。
2. あの　ちいさい　カメラは　５，０００えんです。
3. これは　スイスの　とけいです。
4. その　りんごを　ふたつ　ください。

1. This T-shirt is 2,000 yen.
2. That little camera over there is 5,000 yen.
3. This is a Swiss watch.
4. Give me two of those apples.

VOCABULARY

この	this (used before a noun)
スイス	Switzerland

EXERCISES

I. *Single out a specific item and state its price.* Look at the illustration and state how much the umbrellas cost, following the pattern of the example.

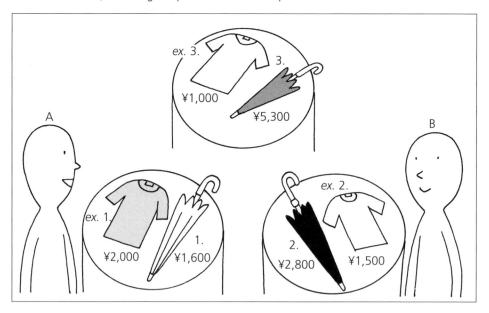

ex. 1. A: この　Tシャツは　2,000えんです。
ex. 2. A: その　Tシャツは　1,500えんです。
ex. 3. A: あの　Tシャツは　1,000えんです。

1.　A: ....

2.　A: ....

3.　A: ....

II. *Ask and give a specific item's price.* Make up dialogues following the pattern of the example and based on the information in the illustration.

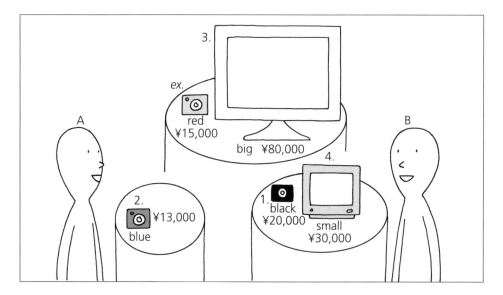

ex. A: あの　あかい　カメラは　いくらですか。
B: １５，０００えんです。

1. A: ....

   B: ....

2. A: ....

   B: ....

3. A: ....

   B: ....

4. A: ....

   B: ....

III. Make up dialogues following the patterns of the examples. Substitute the underlined parts with the alternatives given.

A. *Ask and answer whether an item is from a given country.*

　ex. A: これは　スイスの　とけいですか。
　　　B: いいえ、スイスのではありません。フランスのです。

1. A: .... (イギリスの　くるま)

   B: .... (イギリスの、イタリアの)

2. A: .... (にほんの　カメラ)

   B: .... (にほんの、ドイツの)

B. *Ask and answer what an item's country of origin is.*

　ex. A: これは　どこの　パソコンですか。
　　　B: かんこくのです。

1. A: .... (デジカメ)

   B: .... (にほんの)

2. A: .... (ビール)

   B: .... (ドイツの)

VOCABULARY		
くるま	car	
イタリア	Italy	
どこ	where, which place	
かんこく	South Korea	

IV. ***Ask an item's price and whether it is a product of Japan.*** Make up dialogues following the pattern of the example. Substitute the underlined parts with the alternatives given.

ex. Mr. Smith has gone to a store to shop.

スミス: <u>あの カメラ</u>は いくらですか。
みせの ひと: <u>２０，０００えん</u>です。
スミス: <u>あれ</u>は にほんの <u>カメラ</u>ですか。
みせの ひと: はい、にほんのです。

1. スミス: .... (その とけい)

　 みせの ひと: .... (１５，０００えん)

　 スミス: .... (それ、とけい)

　 みせの ひと: ....

2. スミス: .... (この テレビ)

　 みせの ひと: .... (４３，０００えん)

　 スミス: .... (これ、テレビ)

　 みせの ひと: ....

3. スミス: .... (この くるま)

　 みせの ひと: .... (１，５００，０００えん)

　 スミス: .... (これ、くるま)

　 みせの ひと: ....

V. ***Ask for more than one of an item at a store.*** Make up sentences following the pattern of the example and based on the information in the illustration.

VOCABULARY	みかん	tangerine
	キロ	kilogram

ex. スミス: その　りんごを　ふたつ　ください。

1. スミス: ....

2. スミス: ....

3. スミス: ....

4. スミス: ....

 VI. ***Talk about an item's price and country of origin.*** Make up dialogues following the pattern of the example. Substitute the underlined words with the words in parentheses.

ex. スミス:　　　すみません。その　<u>ワイン</u>は　いくらですか。
みせの　ひと: 1,200えんです。
スミス:　　　それは　どこの　<u>ワイン</u>ですか。
みせの　ひと: <u>フランス</u>のです。
スミス:　　　じゃ、それを　<u>2ほん</u>　ください。

1. スミス:　　　... (コーヒーカップ)

   みせの　ひと: ....

   スミス:　　　... (コーヒーカップ)

   みせの　ひと: .... (イタリア)

   スミス:　　　... (むっつ)

2. スミス:　　　... (タオル)

   みせの　ひと: ....

   スミス:　　　... (タオル)

   みせの　ひと: .... (イギリス)

   スミス:　　　... (4まい)

VII. Listen to the CD and choose the correct answers.

TRACK 19

1. Where is the beer from?

   a) にほん　　　　b) アメリカ　　　c) ドイツ

2. How much does the beer cost?

   a) 300えん　　b) 200えん　　c) 100えん

VOCABULARY				
ワイン	wine		タオル	towel
コーヒーカップ	coffee cup			
コーヒー	coffee			
カップ	cup			

SHORT DIALOGUE

At a confectionary:

みせの　ひと: いらっしゃいませ。
チャン:　　　シュークリームを　みっつ　ください。
みせの　ひと: はい、６３０えんです。

salesperson: May I help you?
Chan:　　　　I'd like three cream puffs, please.
salesperson: All right. That will be 630 yen.

VOCABULARY

シュークリーム　　　cream puff

Active Communication

1. Ask your classmates or colleagues where an item they own is from (i.e., what its country of origin is).

2. If you're in Japan, go shopping and buy more than one of an item. Be sure to use the pattern "number of items + ください."

Quiz 1 (Units 1–2)

I Fill in the blank(s) in each sentence with the appropriate particle. Where a particle is not needed, write in an *X*.

1. こちら（　　　　）ささきさんです。

2. スミスさんは　ＡＢＣフーズ（　　　　）べんごしです。

3. ブラウンさんは　エンジニアです（　　　　）、べんこしです（　　　　）。
   エンジニアです。

4. これは　わたし（　　　　）ほんではありません。
   すずきさん（　　　　）です。

5. かいぎは　9じ（　　　　）11じ（　　　　）です。

6. それ（　　　　）いくらですか。
   3,000えんです。
   あれ（　　　　）3,000えんですか。
   いいえ、3,000えんではありません。3,800えんです。

7. そのビール（　　　　）5ほん（　　　　）ください。

8. それは　どこ（　　　　）カメラですか。
   ドイツ（　　　　）です。

II Complete each sentence by filling in the blank(s) with the appropriate word.

1. ホフマンさんは（　　　　）ですか。
   はい、ドイツじんです。

2. それは（　　　　）ですか。
   とけいです。

3. これは（　　　　）の　かさですか。
   いいえ、たかはしさんのではありません。
   （　　　　）のですか。
   スミスさんのです。

4. スミスさんの　うちの　でんわばんごうは（　　　　）ですか。
   03-3459-9660です。

5. ひるやすみは（　　　　）から（　　　　）までですか。
   12じから　1じまでです。

6. その　あかい　Ｔシャツは（　　　　）ですか。
   2,300えんです。

7. あの　パソコンは（　　　　）のですか。
   にほんのです。

GETTING AROUND

Japan boasts one of the most convenient transportation systems in the world. All major cities from Fukuoka in southern Japan to Tokyo in the east and Hachinohe in the north are connected by bullet train. Other train systems connect towns and outlying suburbs of cities. In large metropolitan areas such as Tokyo, Nagoya, and Osaka, there are also extensive subway systems. To an astounding degree of accuracy, these modes of transportation depart and arrive as scheduled.

Motion Verbs

| noun は place に　いきます |

> *ex.* グレイさんは　あした　きょうとに　いきます。 "Mr. Grey will go to Kyoto tomorrow."

■ Verbs

Japanese sentences end with a verb (or some other element followed by です, which behaves like a verb). The endings of verbs show the tense and whether the verb is affirmative or negative.

Tenses of Japanese verbs can be divided roughly into two large categories:

(1) The present form. The present, or ーます form—so called because verbs in this tense end in ーます—encompasses both the simple present (used for expressing habitual action) and future tenses.

> *ex.* グレイさんは　まいにち　かいしゃに　いきます。
> "Mr. Grey goes to the office (*lit.*, 'company') every day."
> （わたしは）あした　かえります。
> "(I) return/am returning/will return tomorrow."

(2) The past form. The past, or ーました form, on the other hand, includes not only the simple past tense but also the present perfect.

> *ex.* （わたしは）せんしゅう　きょうとに　いきました。 "Last week (I) went to Kyoto."
> グレイさんは　もう　うちに　かえりました。 "Mr. Grey has already gone home."

The chart below summarizes the tenses of Japanese verbs and shows the endings—affirmative and negative—that correspond to each.

PRESENT FORM		PAST FORM	
aff.	*neg.*	*aff.*	*neg.*
ーます	ーません	ーました	ーませんでした

■ The particle に

The role of the preposition "to" in English is played by the particle に in Japanese. に is placed after a noun that denotes a place. It indicates the direction of movement with motion verbs such as いきます ("go"), きます ("come"), and かえります ("return").

> *ex.* とうきょうに　いきます。 "I am going to Tokyo." (*lit.*, "'Tokyo-ward' I am going.")

In this pattern, the particle へ can also be used in place of に.

| noun は place に いきますか
はい、(noun は place に) いきます
いいえ、(noun は place に) いきません |

> *ex.* グレイさんは　あした　きょうとに　いきますか。 "Mr. Grey, will you go to Kyoto tomorrow?"
> はい、いきます。 "Yes, (I) will go."
> いいえ、いきません。 "No, (I) will not go."

■ Questions that contain verbs

To ask a question like "will you go?" that contains a verb, simply add か to the verb. Answers to such questions can be brief, as in the examples above.

CONFIRMING SCHEDULES

TARGET DIALOGUE

Mr. Smith phones Mr. Takahashi of Nozomi Department Store to confirm the time of Friday's meeting.

スミス：もしもし、ＡＢＣの　スミスです。

たかはし：たかはしです。おはようございます。

スミス：あした　そちらに　いきます。かいぎは　３じからですね。

たかはし：はい、３じからです。ひとりで　きますか。

スミス：いいえ、かいしゃの　ひとと　いきます。

たかはし：そうですか。では、あした。

スミス：しつれいします。

■スミスさんは　あした　かいしゃの　ひとと　のぞみデパートに
いきます。

    Smith: Hello, this is Smith from ABC.
Takahashi: This is Takahashi. Good morning.
    Smith: I'll go to your company (*lit.*, "there") tomorrow. The meeting is from 3:00, right?
Takahashi: Yes, it starts at 3:00. Are you coming alone?
    Smith: No, I'll go with someone from the company.
Takahashi: Is that so? Well then, till tomorrow . . .
    Smith: Good-bye.

■ Mr. Smith is going to Nozomi Department Store with a colleague tomorrow.

VOCABULARY

もしもし	hello (on the telephone)
おはようございます	good morning
あした	tomorrow
そちら	there (where your listener is)
に	to (particle; see Unit 3 Grammar at left)
いきます	go
ね	right?; isn't it? (particle)
ひとりで	alone (*lit.*, "by one person")
きます	come
と	with, together with (particle)
では	well then, in any case (formal way of saying じゃ)
しつれいします	good-bye (*lit.*, "I'm going to be rude.")

NOTES

1. **もしもし**
   This is the conventional beginning of a telephone conversation and may be repeated during the call to confirm whether the other party is still on the line.

2. **あした そちらに いきます。**
   Relative time expressions like あした ("tomorrow"), らいしゅう ("next week"), こんげつ ("this month"), and きょねん ("last year") generally do not take particles.

3. **かいぎは 3じからですね。**
   The particle ね comes at the end of a sentence or phrase and, like "isn't it?" in English, seeks confirmation and agreement from the other person. It is spoken with rising intonation.

4. **ひとりで きますか。**
   いいえ、かいしゃの ひとと いきます。
   The phrase かいしゃの ひとと いきます means "I'll go with someone from the company." The Japanese verbs いきます and きます are always used from the point of view of the speaker. いきます expresses the idea of moving from where the speaker is now to some other place. きます, on the other hand, expresses the idea of moving toward the place where the speaker is now. Therefore, unlike in English, a speaker talking about going to the place where the listener is located, as in the above exchange, uses いきます rather than きます.
   The particle と ("with") in かいしゃの ひとと いきます is used to indicate accompaniment.

5. **しつれいします。**
   This expression is used as a form of "good-bye" when hanging up the phone or leaving a house or room. It is also used when entering a house or room, passing in front of someone, leaving in the middle of a gathering, and so on to mean "excuse me."

PRACTICE

WORD POWER

 I. Destinations:

| 1. くうこう | 2. えき | 3. ししゃ | 4. こうえん | 5. ともだちの うち |

VOCABULARY

くうこう	airport	ともだち	friend
えき	station	うち	house
ししゃ	branch office		
こうえん	park		

II. Verbs:

1. いきます 2. きます 3. かえります

III. Time expressions:

	LAST	THIS	NEXT
day	きのう	きょう	あした
week	せんしゅう	こんしゅう	らいしゅう
month	せんげつ	こんげつ	らいげつ
year	きょねん	ことし	らいねん

KEY SENTENCES

1. スミスさんは　あした　ぎんこうに　いきます。
2. スミスさんは　せんしゅう　ホンコンに　いきました。
3. チャンさんは　きのう　ともだちと　レストランに　いきました。
4. チャンさんは　きょねん　にほんに　きました。
5. スミスさんは　らいねん　アメリカに　かえります。

1. Mr. Smith is going to the bank tomorrow.
2. Mr. Smith went to Hong Kong last week.
3. Ms. Chan went to a restaurant with a friend yesterday.
4. Ms. Chan came to Japan last year.
5. Mr. Smith will return to the United States next year.

VOCABULARY							
いきます	go	きょう	today	らいしゅう	next week	きょねん	last year
きます	come	あした	tomorrow	せんげつ	last month	ことし	this year
かえります	return, go home	せんしゅう	last week	こんげつ	this month	らいねん	next year
きのう	yesterday	こんしゅう	this week	らいげつ	next month	ホンコン	Hong Kong

EXERCISES

I. **Practice conjugating verbs.** Repeat the verbs below and memorize their forms—present and past, affirmative and negative.

	PRESENT FORM		PAST FORM	
	aff.	*neg.*	*aff.*	*neg.*
go	いきます	いきません	いきました	いきませんでした
come	きます	きません	きました	きませんでした
return, go home	かえります	かえりません	かえりました	かえりませんでした

II. Make up sentences following the patterns of the examples. Substitute the underlined words with the alternatives given.

A. **State where someone will go.**

　ex. スミスさんは　ぎんこうに　いきます。

　1. .... （くうこう）

　2. .... （とうきょうえき）

　3. .... （おおさかししゃ）

　4. .... （ぎんざの　デパート）

B. **State when someone will go to Kyoto.**

　ex. スミスさんは　あした　きょうとに　いきます。

　1. .... （らいしゅう）

　2. .... （らいげつ）

　3. .... （あさって）

C. **State when someone went to Hong Kong.**

　ex. スミスさんは　きのう　ホンコンに　いきました。

　1. .... （せんしゅう）

　2. .... （せんげつ）

　3. .... （きょねん）

VOCABULARY				
	とうきょうえき	Tokyo Station	きょうと	Kyoto
	おおさかししゃ	Osaka (branch) office	あさって	the day after tomorrow
	おおさか	Osaka		
52	ぎんざ	Ginza (famous shopping district in Tokyo)		

III. Make up dialogues following the patterns of the examples. Substitute the underlined words with the alternatives given.

A. *Ask and answer whether someone will go to a particular place.*

ex. A: スミスさんは　あした　<u>きょうと</u>に　いきますか。
　　B: はい、いきます。

1. A: .... (ゆうびんきょく)

　　B: ....

2. A: .... (ぎんざの　デパート)

　　B: ....

B. *Ask and answer whether someone will go to a particular place.*

ex. A: スミスさんは　あした　<u>ぎんこう</u>に　いきますか。
　　B: いいえ、いきません。

1. A: .... (おおさかししゃ)

　　B: ....

2. A: .... (くうこう)

　　B: ....

C. *Ask and answer whether someone went to a particular place.*

ex. A: スミスさんは　きのう　<u>ホンコン</u>に　いきましたか。
　　B: はい、いきました。

1. A: .... (こうえん)

　　B: ....

2. A: .... (ともだちの　うち)

　　B: ....

D. *Ask and answer whether someone went to a particular place.*

ex. A: スミスさんは　きのう　<u>たいしかん</u>に　いきましたか。
　　B: いいえ、いきませんでした。

1. A: .... (のぞみデパート)

　　B: ....

2. A: .... (ぎんこう)

　　B: ....

IV. Make up dialogues following the patterns of the examples. Substitute the underlined words with the alternatives given.

A. ***Ask and answer where someone will go.***

ex. A: スミスさんは　あした　どこに　いきますか。
B: <u>のぞみデパート</u>に　いきます。

1. A: ....

   B: .... （きょうと）

2. A: ....

   B: .... （ともだちの　うち）

B. ***Ask and answer when someone will go to a particular place.***

ex. A: かとうさんは　いつ　おおさかししゃに　いきますか。
B: <u>らいしゅう</u>　いきます。

1. A: ....

   B: .... （あした）

2. A: ....

   B: .... （らいげつ）

V. ***State whom someone will go somewhere with.*** Make up sentences following the pattern of the example. Substitute the underlined word with the alternatives given.

ex. チャンさんは　<u>ともだち</u>と　レストランに　いきます。

1. .... （なかむらさん）

2. .... （すずきさん）

3. .... （スミスさん）

VI. ***Ask and answer whom someone will go somewhere with.*** Make up dialogues following the pattern of the example. Substitute the underlined word with the alternatives given.

ex. A: スミスさんは　あした　だれと　のぞみデパートに　いきますか。
B: <u>かとうさん</u>と　いきます。

1. A: ....

   B: .... （チャンさん）

2. A: ....

   B: .... （ささきさん）

| VOCABULARY | いつ | when |

54

VII. Make up sentences following the patterns of the examples. Substitute the underlined words with the alternatives given.

A. *State who came to Japan.*

ex. <u>スミスさん</u>は　きょねん　にほんに　きました。

1. .... （チャンさん）

2. .... （グリーンさん）

B. *State who will return to America.*

ex. <u>スミスさん</u>は　らいねん　アメリカに　かえります。

1. .... （グリーンさん）

2. .... （スミスさんの　ともだち）

VIII. *State when, where, and with whom someone will travel.* Make up sentences following the pattern of the example and based on the information in the illustration.

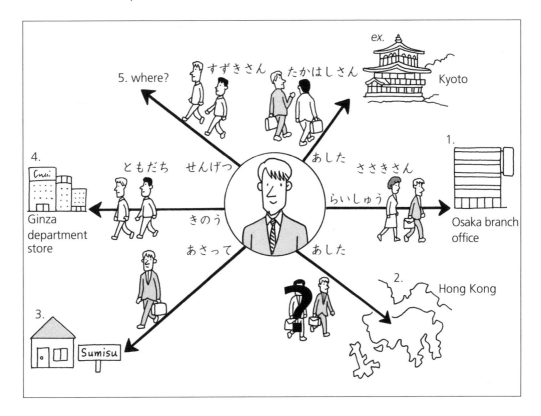

ex. スミスさんは　<u>あした</u>　<u>たかはしさんと</u>　<u>きょうとに</u>　いきます。

1. ....

2. ....

3. ....

4. ....

5. ....

IX. *Talk about a plan.* Make up dialogues following the pattern of the example. Substitute the underlined words with the words in parentheses.

ex. Mr. Smith is talking on the phone with a person from the Yokohama branch office.

よこはまししゃの　ひと: スミスさんは　いつ　よこはまししゃに
　　　　　　　　　　　きますか。
スミス:　　　　　　　　<u>あした</u>　いきます。
よこはまししゃの　ひと: だれと　きますか。
スミス:　　　　　　　　<u>チャンさんと</u>　いきます。
よこはまししゃの　ひと: そうですか。

1. よこはまししゃの　ひと: ....

　 スミス: .... （らいしゅう）

　 よこはまししゃの　ひと: ....

　 スミス: .... （かとうさん）

　 よこはまししゃの　ひと: ....

2. よこはまししゃの　ひと: ....

　 スミス: .... （あさって）

　 よこはまししゃの　ひと: ....

　 スミス: .... （ささきさん）

　 よこはまししゃの　ひと: ....

X. Listen to the CD and fill in the blanks based on the information you hear.

スミスさんは　あさって .... と .... に
いきます。

| VOCABULARY | よこはまししゃ | Yokohama (branch) office |
| | よこはま | Yokohama (port city southwest of Tokyo) |

SHORT DIALOGUES

I. Ms. Chan sees Mr. Suzuki in front of ABC Foods carrying a large piece of luggage.

チャン: あ、すずきさん、しゅっちょうですか。
すずき: ええ、おおさかししゃに いきます。あさって とうきょうに
　　　　 かえります。
チャン: そうですか。いってらっしゃい。

Chan:　　Oh, Mr. Suzuki, are you going on a business trip?
Suzuki:　Yes, I'm going to the Osaka branch office. I'll come back to Tokyo the day after
　　　　　tomorrow.
Chan:　　Really? Have a good trip.

VOCABULARY

あ	oh (interjection used to get someone's attention)
しゅっちょう	business trip
いってらっしゃい	good-bye, have a nice trip

II. At a bus stop, Mr. Smith asks the driver a question before boarding.

スミス:　　　　　　　　すみません。この バスは しぶやに いきますか。
バスの うんてんしゅ: いいえ、いきません。
スミス:　　　　　　　　どの バスが いきますか。
バスの うんてんしゅ: 88ばんの バスが いきます。
スミス:　　　　　　　　ありがとうございます。

Smith:　　　Excuse me. Does this bus go to Shibuya?
bus driver: No, it doesn't.
Smith:　　　Which bus goes there?
bus driver: The number 88 bus goes there.
Smith:　　　Thank you.

VOCABULARY

バス	bus
しぶや	Shibuya (district in Tokyo)
うんてんしゅ	driver
どの	which (used before a noun)
が	(particle that marks the subject of a sentence; see Note 2 below)
～ばん	number . . . (counter; used as a suffix after a number)

1. どの　バス
   どれ is used alone to mean "which," but if "which" is to be followed by a noun, then どの is used.
   > *ex.* どれ, "which one"
   >   どの　バス, "which bus"

2. どの　バスが　いきますか。
   ８８ばんの　バスが　いきます。
   The particle が is used instead of the topic marker は after interrogatives like どれ and どの. In the case of どの, it follows the noun: どの　バスが. が is repeated in replies to questions of the どれが or どの . . . が pattern, as in the exchange here.

Active Communication

Ask someone where they are going tomorrow, next week, next month, and so on.

VISITING ANOTHER COMPANY

TARGET DIALOGUE

Mr. Smith goes to Nozomi Department Store on business with Ms. Chan on Friday.

たかはし：スミスさん、チャンさん、どうぞ　おはいりください。

スミス：しつれいします。

チャン：しつれいします。

たかはし：どうぞ　こちらへ。

スミス、チャン：ありがとうございます。

たかはし：くるまで　きましたか。

スミス：いいえ、ちかてつで　きました。

■スミスさんは　きんようびに　チャンさんと　ちかてつで　のぞみ
デパートに　いきました。

Takahashi: Mr. Smith, Ms. Chan, please come in.
    Smith: Excuse me.
     Chan: Excuse me.
Takahashi: Come right this way.
Smith, Chan: Thank you.
Takahashi: Did you come by car?
    Smith: No, we came by subway.

■ On Friday, Mr. Smith went with Ms. Chan to Nozomi Department Store by subway.

VOCABULARY

おはいりください	please come in
どうぞ　こちらへ	come right this way
で	by means of (particle indicating means)
ちかてつ	subway
きんようび	Friday
に	at, on, in (particle indicating time; see Note 2 below)

NOTES

1. くるまで きましたか。

The function of the particle で ("by means of"), which follows nouns, is to express means of conveyance.

  ex. バスで, "by bus"
  タクシーで, "by taxi"

But to say "by foot," use あるいて, e.g., あるいて きました, "(I) walked here."

To ask the means by which someone will go somewhere, use なんで:

  ex. なんで いきますか。 "How will you go?"
  バスで いきます。 "I'll go by bus."

2. きんようびに . . . いきました。

Unlike relative time expressions (see Note 2, p. 50), specific time expressions take the particle に.

  ex. 5じに, "at 5:00"
  どようびに, "on Saturday"
  12にちに, "on the twelfth"
  2006ねんに, "in 2006"

PRACTICE

WORD POWER

I. Dates:

YEARS		
1998ねん	せん きゅうひゃく きゅうじゅう はち ねん	the year 1998
2006ねん	にせん ろく ねん	the year 2006

7

SUN	MON	TUE	WED	THU	FRI	SAT
						1
2	3	4	5	6	7	8
9	10	11	12	13	14	15
16	17	18	19	20	21	22
23	24	25	26	27	28	29
30	31					

DAYS OF THE WEEK	
にちようび	Sunday
げつようび	Monday
かようび	Tuesday
すいようび	Wednesday
もくようび	Thursday
きんようび	Friday
どようび	Saturday

VOCABULARY

〜ねん   year (counter)
〜ようび   day (of the week)

MONTHS		DAYS OF THE MONTH			
いちがつ	January	ついたち	1st	じゅうしちにち	17th
にがつ	February	ふつか	2nd	じゅうはちにち	18th
さんがつ	March	みっか	3rd	じゅうくにち	19th
しがつ	April	よっか	4th	はつか	20th
ごがつ	May	いつか	5th	にじゅういちにち	21st
ろくがつ	June	むいか	6th	にじゅうににち	22nd
しちがつ	July	なのか	7th	にじゅうさんにち	23rd
はちがつ	August	ようか	8th	にじゅうよっか	24th
くがつ	September	ここのか	9th	にじゅうごにち	25th
じゅうがつ	October	とおか	10th	にじゅうろくにち	26th
じゅういちがつ	November	じゅういちにち	11th	にじゅうしちにち	27th
じゅうにがつ	December	じゅうににち	12th	にじゅうはちにち	28th
		じゅうさんにち	13th	にじゅうくにち	29th
		じゅうよっか	14th	さんじゅうにち	30th
		じゅうごにち	15th	さんじゅういちにち	31st
		じゅうろくにち	16th		

NOTE: Months and dates are written in hiragana here, but elsewhere in the book numerals are used to write them, e.g., １がつ for "January," １１にち for "the eleventh," etc.

II. Means of transportation:

1. でんしゃ   2. ちかてつ   3. くるま   4. タクシー   5. しんかんせん 6. ひこうき

KEY SENTENCES

1. かいぎは すいようびです。
2. ブラウンさんは ３がつ ２６にちに イギリスから にほんに きました。
3. ジョンソンさんは らいしゅうの きんようびに にほんに きます。
4. スミスさんは しんかんせんで おおさかに いきます。

1. The meeting is Wednesday.
2. Ms. Brown came to Japan from the United Kingdom on March 26.
3. Mr. Johnson will come to Japan next Friday.
4. Mr. Smith is going to Osaka on the Shinkansen.

VOCABULARY					
～がつ	month	くるま	car	ひこうき	airplane
～にち	day (of the month) (counter)	タクシー	taxi	から	from (particle indicating origin or point of departure)
でんしゃ	train	しんかんせん	the Shinkansen (Japan's bullet train)	ジョンソン	Johnson (surname)
ちかてつ	subway				

EXERCISES

 I. *State when a meeting will be held.* Make up sentences following the pattern of the example. Substitute the underlined word with the alternatives given.

ex. かいぎは <u>すいようび</u>です。

1. .... (げつようび)

2. .... (4がつ　はつか)

 II. Make up dialogues following the patterns of the examples. Substitute the underlined parts with the alternatives given.

A. *Ask and answer when a festival will be held.*

ex. A: おまつりは <u>なんがつ</u>ですか。
　　B: <u>9がつ</u>です。

1. A: .... (なんにち)

   B: .... (17にち)

2. A: .... (なんようび)

   B: .... (かようび)

B. *Ask and answer when an event will take place.*

ex. A: <u>たんじょうび</u>は　いつですか。
　　B: <u>8がつ　19にち</u>です。

1. A: .... (かいぎ)

   B: .... (7がつ　ついたち)

2. A: .... (パーティー)

   B: .... (らいしゅうの　どようび)

C. *Ask and answer when an event will take place, from when until when.*

ex. A: <u>なつやすみ</u>は　いつから　いつまでですか。
　　B: <u>8がつ　みっか</u>から　<u>28にち</u>までです。

1. A: .... (しゅっちょう)

   B: .... (げつようび, もくようび)

2. A: .... (りょこう)

   B: .... (4がつ　29にち、5がつ　いつか)

VOCABULARY	おまつり	festival	なんにち	what day (of the month)	なつやすみ	summer vacation
	お〜	(polite prefix)	なんようび	what day (of the week)	なつ	summer
	なんがつ	what month	たんじょうび	birthday	りょこう	trip, travel

III. *State when someone came to a place.* Make up sentences following the pattern of the example. Substitute the underlined word with the alternatives given.

ex. ブラウンさんは　<u>4がつ</u>に　イギリスから　きました。

1. ....　（１１がつ）

2. ....　（３がつ　２６にち）

3. ....　（２００４ねん）

 IV. *Ask and answer when someone will come to Japan.* Make up dialogues following the pattern of the example. Substitute the underlined word with the alternatives given.

ex. A: ジョンソンさんは　いつ　にほんに　きますか。
　　B: <u>すいようび</u>に　きます。

1. A: ....

　　B: ....　（にちようび）

2. A: ....

　　B: ....　（らいしゅうの　きんようび）

 V. *State how someone got home.* Make up sentences following the pattern of the example. Substitute the underlined part with the alternatives given.

ex. スミスさんは　<u>ちかてつで</u>　うちに　かえりました。

1. ....　（タクシーで）

2. ....　（でんしゃで）

3. ....　（あるいて）

 VI. *Ask and answer how someone will get to Osaka.* Make up dialogues following the pattern of the example. Substitute the underlined word with the words in parentheses.

ex. A: スミスさんは　なんで　おおさかに　いきますか。
　　B: <u>くるまで</u>　いきます。

1. A: ....

　　B: ....　（しんかんせん）

2. A: ....

　　B: ....　（ひこうき）

| VOCABULARY | あるいて | by foot, by walking |
| | なんで | by what means |

VII. *State when and how someone will reach his destination.* Look at the illustration and make up sentences following the pattern of the example.

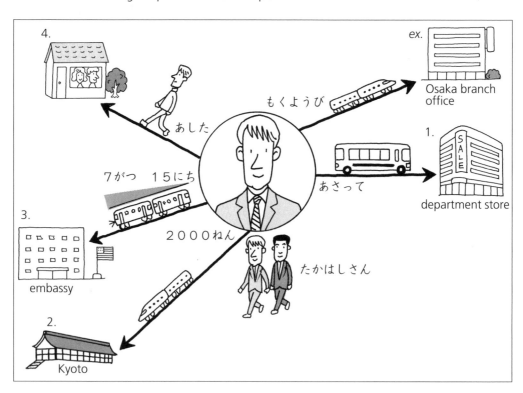

ex. スミスさんは　もくようびに　しんかんせんで　おおさかししゃに　いきます。

1. ....

2. ....

3. ....

4. ....

VIII. **Describe a schedule.** Look at the page from Mr. Smith's weekly planner and make up sentences following the pattern of the example and based on the information provided.

ex.	Mon.	12:00	Go to Tokyo Hotel (by taxi, with Mr. Suzuki)
	Tue.		
1.	Wed.		Go to Osaka branch office (by airplane, alone)
	Thu.		
2.	Fri.	12:00	Go to the restaurant (with my secretary)
		4:00	Go to Yokohama branch office (with Ms. Sasaki)
		6:00	Go to the American Embassy
	Sat.		
3.	Sun.	9:00 a.m.	Go to the park (with friends)
		7:00 p.m.	Go to a friend's house (with Mr. Suzuki)

ex. スミスさんは　げつようびの　１２じに　すずきさんと　タクシーで
とうきょうホテルに　いきます。

1. ....

2. ....

 ....

 ....

3. ....

 ....

IX. **Talk about a plan.** Make up dialogues following the pattern of the example. Substitute the underlined words with the words in parentheses.

ex. おおさかししゃの　ひと: らいしゅうの　げつようびに　そちらに
　　　　　　　　　　　　　　　　いきます。
　　　スミス:　　　　　　　　　なんじに　きますか。
　　　おおさかししゃの　ひと: １０じに　いきます。
　　　スミス:　　　　　　　　　なんで　きますか。
　　　おおさかししゃの　ひと: しんかんせんで　いきます。
　　　スミス:　　　　　　　　　そうですか。

1. おおさかししゃの　ひと: ....

 スミス: ....

 おおさかししゃの　ひと: .... (９じ)

 スミス: ....

 おおさかししゃの　ひと: .... (ひこうき)

 スミス: ....

VOCABULARY　　とうきょうホテル　　Tokyo Hotel (fictitious hotel name)
　　　　　　　　　　ホテル　　　　　　　hotel

2. おおさかししゃの　ひと: ....

スミス: ....

おおさかししゃの　ひと: .... （１１じ）

スミス: ....

おおさかししゃの　ひと: .... （しんかんせん）

スミス: ....

TRACK 27

X. Listen to the CD and choose the correct answers to the questions asked.

1. a) げつようび　　b) もくようび　　c) すいようび

2. a) 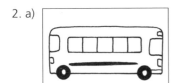　　b) 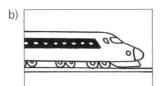　　c)

SHORT DIALOGUE

TRACK 28

A conversation while drinking tea at Nozomi Department Store:

たかはし: チャンさんは　いつ　にほんに　きましたか。
チャン: 　きょねんの　１０がつに　ホンコンから　きました。
たかはし: そうですか。なつやすみに　ホンコンに　かえりますか。
チャン: 　いいえ、かえりません。ともだちと　おきなわに　いきます。

Takahashi: Ms. Chan, when did you come to Japan?
Chan: I came in October of last year, from Hong Kong.
Takahashi: Really? Will you go back to Hong Kong for summer vacation?
Chan: No, I won't. I'm going to Okinawa with a friend.

VOCABULARY

おきなわ   Okinawa (islands on the southwestern tip of Japan)

Active Communication

1. Ask people when their birthdays are.

2. Ask people when their summer vacations are.

A WEEKEND EXCURSION

In the vicinity of Tokyo lie a number of places to visit for pleasure. From the historical sites of Nikko in the north to the gorgeous lakes surrounding Mt. Fuji in the southwest, these locations are only about two hours away from the city. Other popular places include Kamakura, a historical town that dates back to the twelfth century; Okutama, a region abound with rivers, gorges, and mountains; and Hakone, an attractive place to enjoy *onsen*. *Onsen* are Japanese spas, and to visit one is a small luxury that the Japanese enjoy tremendously.

UNIT ■
4 GRAMMAR

Existence of People and Things

■ place に noun が　あります／います

    ex. 1かいに　レストランが　あります。"There is a restaurant on the first floor."
    うけつけに　おんなの　ひとが　います。"There is a woman at the reception desk."

■ The verbs あります and います

Both verbs express "being." あります is used for inanimate things (books, buildings, trees), and います for animate things (people, animals, insects).

■ The particle に

Existence in or at a place is indicated by the particle に.

■ The subject marker が

When a subject is introduced for the first time, or when the speaker believes the information to be new to the listener, the subject marker が is used after the noun. が should be used, for instance, when stating that someone or something unknown to your listener is in or at a particular place.

■ noun は place に あります／います

    ex. レストランは　1かいに　あります。"The restaurant is on the first floor."

■ が → は

To state that a thing or person exists in a particular location, use があります／います, as in 1かいに　レストランが　あります. But if you want to comment about that thing or person—even to say where it or he/she exists—use は instead of が, as in レストランは　1かいに　あります, where "the restaurant" is the topic of the sentence. Note the difference in translation: "There is a restaurant on the first floor" for the first sentence, versus "The restaurant is on the first floor" for the second.

GOING TO NIKKO

💿 TARGET DIALOGUE

Mr. Kato and Ms. Chan are talking about Nikko.

かとう：どようびに　かぞくと　にっこうに　いきます。

チャン：そうですか。にっこうに　なにが
　　　　　ありますか。

かとう：おおきい　おてらや　じんじゃが
　　　　　あります。おんせんも　あります。

チャン：おんせんって　なんですか。

かとう：(shows her a pamphlet and points) これです。にほんの　スパですよ。

チャン：いいですね。

■ かとうさんは　どようびに　かぞくと
　　にっこうに　いきます。にっこうに
　　おおきい　おてらや　じんじゃが　あります。

The Toshogu Shrine (Nikko)

Kato: On Saturday I'm going to Nikko with my family.
Chan: Really? What is there in Nikko?
Kato: There are large temples and shrines. There are also *onsen*.
Chan: What are *onsen*?
Kato: These. Japanese spas.
Chan: That's nice.

Nikko

■ Mr. Kato will go to Nikko with his family on Saturday. There are large temples and shrines (and other such things) in Nikko.

VOCABULARY

かぞく	family
にっこう	Nikko (scenic area north of Tokyo)
なに	what
あります	be, exist
おてら	Buddhist temple
や	and, and so on (particle; see Note 1 below)
じんじゃ	Shinto shrine
おんせん	hot spring (resort)
～って　なんですか	what is a/an . . . ?
スパ	spa
よ	(particle; see Note 2 below)
いいですね	that's nice

NOTES

1. （にっこうに）おてらや　じんじゃが　あります。

The particle や is used for "and" when listing two or more things or people and implying the existence of others. Another particle, と, also means "and," but it does not imply the existence of other people or things.

    ex. 1かいに　ぎんこうと　コンビニが　あります。

      "There is a bank and a convenience store on the first floor (and nothing else)."

Note that unlike "and" in English, both や and と are used only to connect nouns. They cannot be used to connect verbs or clauses.

2. にほんの　スパですよ。

The particle よ is added to the end of a sentence to call attention to information the speaker thinks the other person does not know.

PRACTICE

WORD POWER

I. Parts of a building:

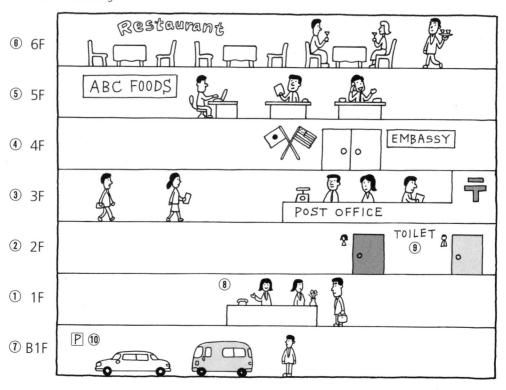

1. いっかい	3. さんがい	5. ごかい	7. ちか　いっかい	9. おてあらい
2. にかい	4. よんかい	6. ろっかい	8. うけつけ	10. ちゅうしゃじょう

VOCABULARY

いっかい	first floor, ground floor		うけつけ	reception desk
～かい／がい	floor, story (counter)		おてあらい	restroom, lavatory
ちか　いっかい	first basement floor (of several)		ちゅうしゃじょう	parking lot
ちか	basement			

70

NOTE: Floors are written in hiragana here, but elsewhere in the book they are written with numerals, e.g., 1 かい for "first floor," 3 がい for "third floor," etc.

II. Things in a hotel room:

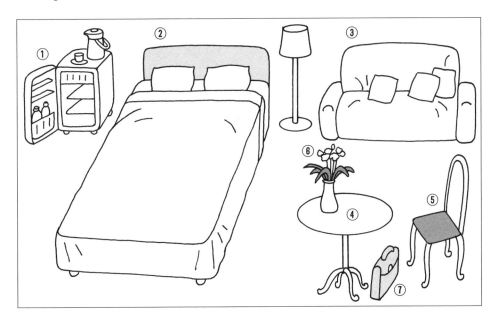

1. れいぞうこ　　2. ベッド　　3. ソファー　4. テーブル　5. いす　　6. はな　　7. かばん

III. Positions:

1. うえ

2. した

3. まえ

4. うしろ

5. なか

6. となり

7. ちかく

VOCABULARY					
れいぞうこ	refrigerator	はな	flower	うしろ	back, behind
ベッド	bed	かばん	briefcase, tote bag	なか	inside, middle
ソファー	sofa	うえ	top, above	となり	next to
テーブル	table	した	bottom, below, under	ちかく	vicinity, nearby
いす	chair	まえ	front, before		

KEY SENTENCES

1. 1かいに ぎんこうが あります。
2. うけつけに おんなの ひとが います。
3. テーブルの うえに しんぶんと はなが あります。
4. かばんの なかに かぎや ほんが あります。
5. テーブルの うえに なにも ありません。
6. 2かいに だれも いません。

1. There is a bank on the first floor.
2. There is a woman at the reception desk.
3. There is a newspaper and some flowers on the table.
4. Inside the briefcase there are keys and books and so on.
5. There is nothing on the table.
6. There is no one on the second floor.

EXERCISES

I. *Practice conjugating verbs.* Repeat the verbs below and memorize their forms—present and past, affirmative and negative.

	PRESENT FORM		PAST FORM	
	aff.	*neg.*	*aff.*	*neg.*
be	あります	ありません	ありました	ありませんでした
be	います	いません	いました	いませんでした

II. Make up sentences following the patterns of the examples. Substitute the underlined words with the words in the parentheses.

A. *State what is in or at a particular place.*

ex. にっこうに <u>おてら</u>が あります。

1. .... (じんじゃ)

2. .... (みずうみ)

B. *State who is at a particular place.*

ex. うけつけに <u>おんなの ひと</u>が います。

1. .... (おとこの ひと)

2. .... (たかはしさん)

VOCABULARY				
	います	be, exist (only of animate objects)	みずうみ	lake
	と	and (particle; see Note 1, p. 70)	おとこの ひと	man
	なにも ...—ません	nothing	おとこ	male, man
72	だれも ...—ません	no one		

III. Make up dialogues following the patterns of the examples. Substitute the underlined words with the words in parentheses.

A. *Ask and answer what is at a particular place.*

ex. A: <u>１かいに</u>　なにが　ありますか。
B: <u>ぎんこう</u>が　あります。

1. A: .... （２かい）

   B: .... （ゆうびんきょく）

2. A: .... （３がい）

   B: .... （たいしかん）

B. *Ask and answer who is at a particular place.*

ex. A: <u>うけつけに</u>　だれが　いますか。
B: <u>たかはしさん</u>が　います。

1. A: .... （ちゅうしゃじょう）

   B: .... （おとこの　ひと）

2. A: .... （３がい）

   B: .... （スミスさん）

IV. *State where a thing is located.* Make up sentences following the pattern of the example. Substitute the underlined part with the alternatives given.

ex. <u>テーブルの　うえ</u>に　さいふが　あります。

1. .... （かばんの　なか）

2. .... （しんぶんの　した）

V. Make up dialogues following the patterns of the examples. Substitute the underlined part(s) with the alternatives given.

A. *Ask and answer what is inside another thing.*

ex. A: <u>かばんの　なかに</u>　なにが　ありますか。
B: <u>ペン</u>が　あります。

1. A: ....

   B: .... （かぎ）

2. A: ....

   B: .... （けいたい）

| **VOCABULARY** | さいふ | wallet |
| | ペン | pen |

3. A: ....

B: .... (さいふ)

4. A: ....

B: .... (にほんごの　ほん)

B. *Ask and answer what is on, in, or nearby another thing.*

ex. A: <u>テーブルの　うえに</u>　なにが　ありますか。
B: <u>しんぶんと　はなが</u>　あります。

1. A: .... (ソファーの　うえ)

B: .... (ほんと　セーター)

2. A: .... (れいぞうこの　なか)

B: .... (みずや　ビール)

3. A: .... (ベッドの　ちかく)

B: .... (でんわ)

C. *Ask and answer what is in or on another thing.*

ex. A: <u>ひきだしの　なかに</u>　なにが　ありますか。
B: なにも　ありません。

1. A: .... (いすの　うえ)

B: ....

2. A: .... (ポケットの　なか)

B: ....

D. *Ask and answer who is at a particular place.*

ex. A: <u>２かいに</u>　だれが　いますか。
B: だれも　いません。

1. A: .... (５かい)

B: ....

2. A: .... (うけつけ)

B: ....

VOCABULARY	にほんご	Japanese (language)	ひきだし	drawer
	セーター	sweater	ポケット	pocket
	みず	(cold) water		

74

VI. **State or ask where someone or something is located.** Make up sentences following the pattern of the example and based on the information in the illustrations.

ex. ２かいに　ぎんこうが　あります。

1. ....   5. ....

2. ....   6. ....

3. ....   7. ....

4. ....   8. ....

VII. **Talk about a tourist destination.** Make up dialogues following the pattern of the example. Substitute the underlined parts with the alternatives given.

ex. かとう: にちようびに　くるまで　はこねに　いきます。
スミス: そうですか。はこねに　なにが　ありますか。
かとう: みずうみや　おんせんが　あります。
スミス: いいですね。

1. かとう: .... (かまくら)

   スミス: .... (かまくら)

   かとう: .... (じんじゃや　おてら)

   スミス: ....

VOCABULARY　　はこね　　Hakone (national park southwest of Tokyo)
かまくら　　Kamakura (historic town southwest of Tokyo)

2.　かとう: ....　(おだいば)

　　　スミス: ....　(おだいば)

　　　かとう: ....　(ホテルや　おんせん)

　　　スミス: ....

VIII. Listen to the CD and fill in the blanks based on the information you hear.

1.　１かいに .... が　あります。

2.　２かいに .... が　あります。

3.　３がいに .... が　あります。

SHORT READING

Mr. Kato stays at a famous inn in Nikko.

りょかんの　ちかくに　おおきい　みずうみや　たきが　あります。
りょかんの　となりに　そばやが　あります。りょかんの　まえに
ちいさい　こうえんが　あります。

Near the inn are things like a large lake and waterfalls. Next to the inn is a buckwheat noodle shop. In front of the inn is a small park.

VOCABULARY

りょかん	traditional Japanese inn
たき	waterfall
そばや	buckwheat noodle shop
〜や	shop (suffix)

Active Communication

Using the vocabulary you have learned so far, ask someone what is in his or her hometown or nearby his or her house.

VOCABULARY　おだいば　Odaiba (new town with a shopping center, built on reclaimed land in Tokyo Bay)

LOOKING FOR A PARKING LOT

 TARGET DIALOGUE

Mr. Kato has come to Nikko. He asks a salesperson at a store where to find a parking lot.

かとう：すみません。この　ちかくに　ちゅうしゃじょうが
　　　　ありますか。

みせの　ひと：ええ、ありますよ。

かとう：どこですか。

みせの　ひと：あそこに　コンビニが　ありますね。
　　　　　　ちゅうしゃじょうは　あの　コンビニの　となりです。

かとう：どうも　ありがとう。

■ ちゅうしゃじょうは　コンビニの　となりに　あります。

Kato: Excuse me. Is there a parking lot in the vicinity?
salesperson: Yes, there is.
Kato: Where is it?
salesperson: There's a convenience store over there, right? The parking lot is next to the convenience store.
Kato: Thank you.

■ The parking lot is next to the convenience store.

VOCABULARY

あそこ	over there
コンビニ	convenience store

NOTES

1. ちゅうしゃじょうは　コンビニの　となりです。
When the verb is understood, です sometimes takes its place at the end of the sentence.
　　ex. テレビは　どこに　ありますか。 "Where is the TV set?"
　　　　テーブルの　うえです (instead of テーブルの　うえに　あります)。 "It's on the table."
If it is uncertain whether there is a TV set, です cannot be substituted, and あります must be repeated to make the meaning clear.
　　ex. テーブルの　うえに　テレビが　ありますか。 "Is there a TV set on the table?"
　　　　はい、あります。／はい、テレビが　あります。 "Yes, there is./Yes, there is a TV set."

PRACTICE

WORD POWER

I. Things near a train station:

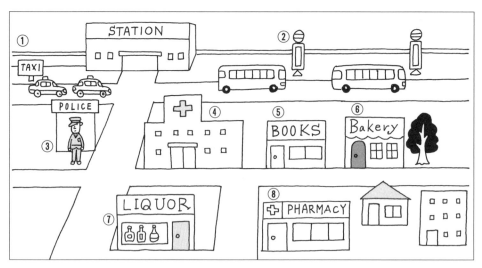

| 1. タクシーのりば | 3. こうばん | 5. ほんや | 7. さかや |
| 2. バスのりば | 4. びょういん | 6. パンや | 8. くすりや |

II. Office supplies:

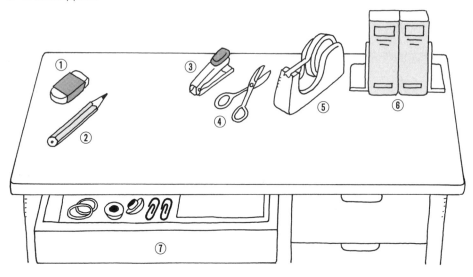

| 1. けしゴム | 3. ホッチキス | 5. セロテープ | 7. ひきだし |
| 2. えんぴつ | 4. はさみ | 6. ファイル | |

VOCABULARY							
タクシーのりば	taxi stand	パンや	bakery	けしゴム	eraser	ファイル	file
バスのりば	bus terminal	パン	bread	えんぴつ	pencil		
こうばん	police box	さかや	liquor store	ホッチキス	stapler		
びょういん	hospital, clinic	くすりや	drugstore	はさみ	scissors		
ほんや	bookstore	くすり	medicine	セロテープ	Scotch tape		

III. Numbers of people:

	ひとり
	ふたり
	さんにん
	よにん
	ごにん
?	なんにん

NOTE: Other than ひとり and ふたり, numbers of people from now on will be expressed with numerals: 3にん, 4にん, etc.

KEY SENTENCES

1. テーブルの　うえに　ビールが　2ほん　あります。
2. コンビニの　まえに　おとこの　ひとが　ふたり　います。
3. タクシーのりばは　えきの　ちかくに　あります。
4. ゆうびんきょくは　あの　ビルの　なかです。

1. There are two bottles of beer on the table.
2. There are two men in front of the convenience store.
3. The taxi stand is in the vicinity of the station.
4. The post office is inside that building over there.

VOCABULARY				
ひとり	one person		なんにん	how many people
ふたり	two people			
さんにん	three people			
～にん	person (counter)			79

EXERCISES

I. Make up sentences following the patterns of the examples. Substitute the underlined words with the words in parentheses.

A. *State how many of a certain object are in a drawer.*

ex. ひきだしの　なかに　<u>ペン</u>が　<u>5ほん</u>　あります。

1. .... （めいし、3まい）

2. .... （けしゴム、ふたつ）

3. .... （ファイル、たくさん）

B. *State how many people are in front of a building.*

ex. コンビニの　まえに　<u>おとこの　ひと</u>が　<u>ふたり</u>　います。

1. .... （おんなの　ひと、3にん）

2. .... （おとこの　こ、ひとり）

3. .... （おんなの　こ、たくさん）

II. Make up dialogues following the patterns of the examples. Substitute the underlined words with the words in parentheses.

A. *Ask and answer how many of a certain object are on a table.*

ex. A:テーブルの　うえに　<u>りんご</u>が　<u>いくつ</u>　ありますか。
B:<u>みっつ</u>　あります。

1. A: .... （きって、なんまい）

B: .... （5まい）

2. A: .... （ビール、なんぼん）

B: .... （2ほん）

3. A: .... （コーヒーカップ、いくつ）

B: .... （よっつ）

VOCABULARY	たくさん	a lot, many, much	いくつ	how many (small objects)
	おとこの　こ	boy	なんまい	how many (flat objects)
	こ	child	なんぼん	how many (long, thin objects)
80	おんなの　こ	girl		

B. *Ask and answer how many people are in front of a building.*

ex. A: ぎんこうの　まえに　<u>おとこの　ひと</u>が　なんにん　いますか。
　　B: <u>ひとり</u>　います。

1.　A: .... （おんなの　ひと）

　　B: .... （４にん）

2.　A: .... （おとこの　こ）

　　B: .... （ふたり）

3.　A: .... （がくせい）

　　B: .... （たくさん）

 III. *Indicate where a facility or store is located.* Make up sentences following the pattern of the example and based on the information in the illustrations.

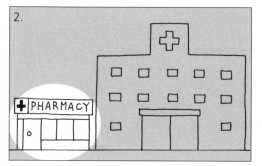 

ex. <u>ちゅうしゃじょう</u>は　<u>コンビニの　となり</u>に　あります。

1. .... （タクシーのりば、えきの　まえ）

2. .... （くすりや、びょういんの　となり）

3. .... （こうばん、あそこ）

IV. Make up dialogues following the patterns of the examples. Substitute the underlined parts with the alternatives given.

A. *Ask and answer where something is.*

ex. A: <u>ちゅうしゃじょう</u>は　どこに　ありますか。
　　B: <u>コンビニの　となり</u>に　あります。

1. A: .... （タクシーのりば）

   B: .... （えきの　まえ）

2. A: .... （ほんや）

   B: .... （デパートの　となり）

3. A: .... （きょうの　しんぶん）

   B: .... （ここ）

4. A: .... （くるまの　かぎ）

   B: .... （かばんの　なか）

B. *Ask and answer where someone is.*

ex. A: <u>スミスさん</u>は　どこに　いますか。
　　B: <u>2かい</u>に　います。

1. A: .... （たかはしさん）

   B: .... （にわ）

2. A: .... （グリーンさん）

   B: .... （3がい）

3. A: .... （ささきさん）

   B: .... （かいぎしつ）

C. *Ask and answer where something or someone is.*

ex. A: <u>こうばん</u>は　どこですか。
　　B: <u>えきの　まえ</u>です。

1. A: .... （おてあらい）

   B: .... （あそこ）

2. A: .... （はさみ）

   B: .... （テーブルの　うえ）

VOCABULARY	ここ	here
	にわ	garden
	かいぎしつ	conference room

3.　A: .... （ビール）

　　B: .... （れいぞうこの　なか）

4.　A: .... （スミスさん）

　　B: .... （２かい）

 V. ***Ask where a facility or store at an airport is located.*** Make up sentences following the pattern of the example and based on the information in the illustration.

ex. チャン: <u>チェックインカウンター</u>は　どこに　ありますか。

1.　チャン: ....

2.　チャン: ....

3.　チャン: ....

4.　チャン: ....

5.　チャン: ....

6.　チャン: ....

VOCABULARY	カート	cart (for luggage)
	チェックインカウンター	check-in counter

VI. *Talk about where a facility is located.* Make up dialogues following the pattern of the example. Substitute the underlined parts with the alternatives given.

ex. おとこの　ひと: すみません。この　ちかくに　<u>タクシーのりば</u>が
　　　　　　　　　　ありますか。
　　チャン:　　　　　ええ、ありますよ。
　　おとこの　ひと: どこですか。
　　チャン:　　　　　<u>タクシーのりば</u>は　<u>えきの　まえ</u>です。
　　おとこの　ひと: どうも　ありがとうございます。

1.　おとこの　ひと: .... （バスてい）

　　チャン: ....

　　おとこの　ひと: ....

　　チャン: .... （コンビニの　まえ）

　　おとこの　ひと: ....

2.　おとこの　ひと: .... （ゆうびんきょく）

　　チャン: ....

　　おとこの　ひと: ....

　　チャン: .... （あのビルの　なか）

　　おとこの　ひと: ....

3.　おとこの　ひと: .... （ちかてつの　いりぐち）

　　チャン: ....

　　おとこの　ひと: ....

　　チャン: .... （あそこ）

　　おとこの　ひと: ....

VII. Listen to the CD and fill in the blank based on the information you hear.

　　ちゅうしゃじょうは .... です。

VOCABULARY　バスてい　bus stop
　　　　　　　いりぐち　entrance

SHORT DIALOGUES

I. Mr. Kato is looking for today's newspaper.

かとう: きょうの　しんぶんは　どこに　ありますか。
チャン: ここに　あります。はい、どうぞ。

Kato:　　Where is today's paper?
Chan:　It's here. Here you go.

II. Mr. Kato calls Mr. Suzuki on his cell phone while Mr. Suzuki is out on a sales visit.

かとう: すずきさん。いま　どこですか。
すずき: いま　のぞみデパートに　います。
かとう: なんじごろ　かいしゃに　かえりますか。
すずき: ３じに　かえります。

Kato:　　　Mr. Suzuki, where are you now?
Suzuki:　I'm at Nozomi Department Store.
Kato:　　　About what time are you coming back to the office?
Suzuki:　I'll be back at 3:00.

VOCABULARY

なんじごろ	about/approximately what time
ごろ	about (used of time; see Note 1 below)

NOTES

1. なんじごろ . . .
The suffix ごろ is used to indicate an approximate point in time. Unlike "about" in English, however, it cannot be used to express an approximate period.

Active Communication

If you're in Japan, go out on the street and ask various people if there is a station, department store, post office, etc. in the vicinity.

5

DINING OUT

Japanese cuisine is not just sushi and tempura; in fact, most Japanese people only have these dishes occasionally. There are many different kinds of foods in Japan and, consequently, many specialty restaurants. The inexpensive restaurants typically showcase their dishes—sometimes the real thing, but more often than not plastic replicas—in their front windows. Among the most expensive establishments are sushi bars and tempura restaurants. Ginza, an upscale shopping district in Tokyo that features in this unit, is famous for its restaurants and bars.

UNIT

5 GRAMMAR

Verbs That Take a Grammatical Object

person は noun を verb

    ex. グレイさんは　えいがを　みます。"Mr. Grey will see a movie."

■ The particle を

Placed after a noun, を indicates that the noun is the object of the sentence. を is used with verbs like みます ("see"), よみます ("read"), のみます ("drink"), かいます ("buy"), and a host of others.

person 1 は person 2 に verb

    ex. グレイさんは　よしださんに　あいます。"Mr. Grey will meet Mr. Yoshida."

■ The particle に

The particle に can also serve as an object marker, as in the example here, where Mr. Yoshida is the object of the verb あいます ("meet"). Essentially, に indicates the person or thing an action is directed at.

person 1 は person 2/place に noun を verb

    ex. グレイさんは　よしださんに　てがみを　かきました。
    "Mr. Grey wrote a letter to Mr. Yoshida."
    グレイさんは　たいしかんに　てがみを　かきました。
    "Mr. Grey wrote a letter to the embassy."

■ The particle に

With verbs like てがみを　かきます ("write a letter"), にもつを　おくります ("send luggage"), and でんわを　します ("telephone"), に indicates the receiver of the action. In English, the receiver corresponds to the indirect object.

LESSON 10
MAKING PLANS FOR THE WEEKEND

TARGET DIALOGUE

TRACK 36

Ms. Sasaki and Mr. Smith are talking about their plans for the weekend.

スミス：しゅうまつに　なにを　しますか。

ささき：どようびに　ともだちと　かぶきを　みます。

スミス：そうですか。

ささき：スミスさんは？

スミス：にちようびに　ぎんざで　すずきさんと　てんぷらを
　　　　たべます。

ささき：いいですね。

■　ささきさんは　どようびに　ともだちと　かぶきを　みます。
　　スミスさんは　にちようびに　ぎんざで　すずきさんと　てんぷらを
　　たべます。

　Smith: What are you going to do during the weekend?
Sasaki: I'm going to see Kabuki with a friend on Saturday.
　Smith: Oh, really.
Sasaki: What about you?
　Smith: I'm going to eat tempura in Ginza with Mr. Suzuki on Sunday.
Sasaki: Sounds good.

■ Ms. Sasaki is going to see Kabuki with a friend on Saturday. Mr. Smith is going to eat tempura in Ginza with Mr. Suzuki on Sunday.

VOCABULARY

しゅうまつ	weekend
します	do
かぶき	Kabuki (a traditional form of theater)
みます	see
で	(particle indicating the location where an action takes place)
てんぷら	tempura (deep-fried seafood/vegetables)
たべます	eat

NOTES

1. ぎんざで　すずきさんと　てんぷらを　たべます。

Nouns and place names concerned with actions such as where things are bought, seen, eaten, sold and so on take the particle で.

PRACTICE

WORD POWER

I. Food:

1. あさごはん	4. コーヒー	7. さけ	10. ジュース
2. ひるごはん	5. こうちゃ	8. スープ	11. サンドイッチ
3. ばんごはん	6. おちゃ	9. ミルク	12. サラダ

VOCABULARY

あさごはん	breakfast	こうちゃ	tea	ミルク	milk
ひるごはん	lunch	おちゃ	green tea	ジュース	juice
ばんごはん	dinner	さけ	sake (Japanese rice wine)	サンドイッチ	sandwich
コーヒー	coffee	スープ	soup	サラダ	salad

II. Verbs:

1. たべます   2. のみます   3. かいます   4. よみます   5. ききます

6. みます   7. テニスを します   8. べんきょうを します   9. かいものを します   10. しごとを します

NOTE: For more on the "noun を します" verb type, see p. 246.

III. Time expressions:

	DAY	MORNING	EVENING	WEEK
every	まいにち	まいあさ	まいばん	まいしゅう

KEY SENTENCES

1. スミスさんは　あした　えいがを　みます。
2. スミスさんは　まいにち　ジョギングを　します。
3. スミスさんは　きのう　レストランで　ばんごはんを　たべました。

1. Mr. Smith is going to see a movie tomorrow.
2. Mr. Smith jogs every day.
3. Mr. Smith ate dinner at a restaurant yesterday.

VOCABULARY

たべます	eat	みます	see	まいにち	every day	
のみます	drink	テニスを します	play tennis	まいあさ	every morning	
かいます	buy	べんきょうを します	study	まいばん	every evening	
よみます	read	かいものを します	shop	まいしゅう	every week	
ききます	listen (to)	しごとを します	work	ジョギングを します	jog	91

EXERCISES

I. *Practice conjugating verbs.* Repeat the verbs below and memorize their forms—present and past, affirmative and negative.

	PRESENT FORM		PAST FORM	
	aff.	*neg.*	*aff.*	*neg.*
eat	たべます	たべません	たべました	たべませんでした
drink	のみます	のみません	のみました	のみませんでした
buy	かいます	かいません	かいました	かいませんでした
read	よみます	よみません	よみました	よみませんでした
listen (to)	ききます	ききません	ききました	ききませんでした
see	みます	みません	みました	みませんでした
do	します	しません	しました	しませんでした

II. Make up sentences following the patterns of the examples. Substitute the underlined words with the words in parentheses.

A. *State what someone will see.*

ex. すずきさんは　<u>テレビ</u>を　みます。

1. .... （えいが）

2. .... （かぶき）

B. *State what someone will listen to.*

ex. すずきさんは　<u>おんがく</u>を　ききます。

1. .... （ＣＤ）

2. .... （ラジオ）

III. Make up sentences or dialogues following the patterns of the examples and based on the information in the illustrations.

A. *State what someone will do.*

ex. スミスさんは　ステーキを　たべます。

1. ....

2. ....

3. ....

4. ....

B. *Ask and answer what someone will do.*

ex. A: スミスさんは　なにを　たべますか。
B: ステーキを　たべます。

1. A: ....

B: ....

2. A: ....

B: ....

3. A: ....

B: ....

4. A: ....

B: ....

IV. Make up sentences following the patterns of the examples. Substitute the underlined words with the alternatives given.

A. *State where someone will drink beer.*

ex. すずきさんは　うちで　ビールを　のみます。

1. .... (レストラン)

2. .... (ホテルの　バー)

| VOCABULARY | ステーキ | steak |
| | バー | bar |

B. *State where someone will buy a magazine.*

   ex. すずきさんは <u>ほんや</u>で ざっしを かいます。

    1. .... (コンビニ)

    2. .... (くうこう)

V. Make up sentences following the patterns of the examples and based on the information in the illustrations.

ex. レストラン	1. としょかん	2. かいしゃ	3. ゆうびんきょく	4. スポーツクラブ

A. *State where someone will do something.*

   ex. スミスさんは レストランで ばんごはんを たべます。

    1. ....

    2. ....

    3. ....

    4. ....

B. *Ask and answer where someone will do something.*

   ex. A: スミスさんは どこで ばんごはんを たべますか。
       B: レストランで たべます。

    1. A: ....

       B: ....

    2. A: ....

       B: ....

    3. A: ....

       B: ....

    4. A: ....

       B: ....

VOCABULARY		
	としょかん	library
	スポーツクラブ	gym, fitness/sports club
	スポーツ	sport(s)
94	クラブ	club

VI. **State what someone does regularly.** Make up sentences following the pattern of the example and based on the information in the illustrations.

ex. every day	1. every morning	2. every evening	3. every week

ex. かとうさんは　まいにち　いぬと　さんぽを　します。

1. ....

2. ....

3. ....

VII. **Talk about the events of a weekend.** Make up dialogues following the pattern of the example. Substitute the underlined words with the alternatives given.

ex. かとう: しゅうまつに　なにを　しましたか。
スミス: <u>ともだちと　ゴルフを</u>　しました。
かとう: どこで　しましたか。
スミス: <u>はこね</u>で　しました。
かとう: そうですか。

1. かとう: ....
   スミス: .... （グリーンさん、テニス）
   かとう: ....
   スミス: .... （ホテルの　テニスコート）
   かとう: ....

2. かとう: ....
   スミス: .... （すずきさん、かいもの）
   かとう: ....
   スミス: .... （ぎんざの　デパート）
   かとう: ....

VOCABULARY			
いぬ	dog	さんぽを　します	go for a walk
やさいジュース	vegetable juice	ゴルフを　します	play golf
やさい	vegetable	テニスコート	tennis court
おくさん	(another person's) wife		

95

VIII. Listen to the CD and fill in the blanks based on the information you hear.

TRACK 38

1. チャンさんは　かまくらで ....を　みました。

2. チャンさんは ....ひるごはんを　たべました。

SHORT DIALOGUE

 Mr. Suzuki phones the tempura specialty restaurant Tenmasa to make a reservation.

TRACK 39

みせの　ひと: てんまさでございます。
すずき:　　　よやくを　おねがいします。
みせの　ひと: はい、ありがとうございます。
すずき:　　　にちようびの　7じに　おねがいします。ふたりです。
みせの　ひと: はい、わかりました。では、おなまえと　おでんわばんごうを
　　　　　　　おねがいします。

restaurant employee: This is Tenmasa.
Suzuki:　　　　　　 I'd like to make a reservation.
restaurant employee: All right. Thank you.
Suzuki:　　　　　　 Sunday at seven o'clock, please, for two people.
restaurant employee: Yes. Well, then, please give me your name and telephone number.

VOCABULARY

てんまさでございます	this is Tenmasa (speaking on the phone)
てんまさ	Tenmasa (fictitious restaurant name)
でございます	(humble form of です)
よやく	reservation
わかりました	understood; I see; I understand
わかります	understand
おなまえ	(another person's) name (polite word for なまえ)

NOTES

1. よやくを　おねがいします。

This is the phrase to use when you want to make a reservation. おねがいします can be used to order food or drink, too.

ex. コーヒーを　おねがいします。"I'll have (a cup of) coffee, please."

Active Communication

1. Talk to someone about your plans for the weekend.

2. Tell someone about what you did the previous weekend.

AT A TEMPURA RESTAURANT

 TARGET DIALOGUE

Mr. Smith and Mr. Suzuki have arrived at a tempura restaurant in Ginza.

みせの　ひと：いらっしゃいませ。

　　すずき：すずきです。

みせの　ひと：すずきさまですね。どうぞ　こちらへ。

　　スミス：(*a few moments later, at the table*) いい　みせですね。

　　　　　　すずきさんは　よく　この　みせに　きますか。

　　すずき：ええ、ときどき　きます。おいしいですから。

　　スミス：(*fifteen minutes later, after their dishes have arrived*) すずきさん、

　　　　　　この　さかなは　なんですか。

　　すずき：キスです。

　　スミス：おいしいですね。

■スミスさんは　すずきさんと　ぎんざの　てんぷらやに　いきました。
　スミスさんは　すずきさんに　さかなの　なまえを　ききました。

restaurant employee: Welcome.
　　　　　　Suzuki: I'm Suzuki.
restaurant employee: Oh, Mr. Suzuki. Right this way, please.
　　　　　　　Smith: This is a nice restaurant, isn't it? Do you come to this restaurant often, Mr. Suzuki?
　　　　　　Suzuki: Yes, I come sometimes. Because (this restaurant's tempura) is so delicious.
　　　　　　　Smith: Mr. Suzuki, what's this fish?
　　　　　　Suzuki: It's whiting.
　　　　　　　Smith: It's delicious, isn't it?

■ Mr. Smith went to a tempura restaurant in Ginza with Mr. Suzuki. Mr. Smith asked Mr. Suzuki the name of the fish.

VOCABULARY

すずきさま	Mr. Suzuki
〜さま	Mr., Ms., Mrs., Miss (more polite than さん)
よく	often (see Appendix I, p. 248)
ときどき	sometimes (see Appendix I, p. 248)
おいしいです	be delicious, be tasty

から	because (particle)
さかな	fish
キス	whiting (kind of fish) (NOTE: Names of fish, fruits, vegetables, etc. are sometimes written in *katakana*.)
てんぷらや	tempura restaurant
ききます	ask

NOTES

1. (この　みせの　てんぷらは) おいしいですから。

   から follows a sentence or clause that explains the reason for something. Here, the topic phrase この　みせの　てんぷらは is being omitted. (For more on から, see Note 3, p.142.)

PRACTICE

WORD POWER

I. Verbs:

1. でんわを　します   2. かきます   3. おくります   4. あいます

VOCABULARY	でんわを　します	telephone
	かきます	write
	おくります	send
	あいます	meet

II. Family:

1. たかはしさんの　おとうさん
2. たかはしさんの　おかあさん
3. たかはしさんの　おくさん
4. ちち

5. はは
6. つま／かない
7. ささきさんの　ごしゅじん
8. おっと／しゅじん

KEY SENTENCES

1. スミスさんは　ともだちに　でんわを　します。
2. スミスさんは　あした　たかはしさんに　あいます。
3. チャンさんは　よく　おかあさんに　てがみを　かきます。
4. チャンさんは　あまり　テレビを　みません。

1. Mr. Smith is going to phone a friend.
2. Mr. Smith is going to see Mr. Takahashi tomorrow.
3. Ms. Chan often writes letters to her mother.
4. Ms. Chan doesn't watch television very much.

VOCABULARY

おとうさん	(another person's) father	つま／かない	(my) wife	あまり ...	not much
おかあさん	(another person's) mother	ごしゅじん	(another person's) husband	ーません	(see Appendix I, p. 248.)
おくさん	(another person's) wife	ご〜	(honorific prefix)		
ちち	(my) father	おっと／しゅじん	(my) husband		
はは	(my) mother	てがみ	letter		

EXERCISES

I. *Practice conjugating verbs.* Repeat the verbs below and memorize their forms—present and past, affirmative and negative.

	PRESENT FORM		PAST FORM	
	aff.	*neg.*	*aff.*	*neg.*
telephone	でんわを します	でんわを しません	でんわを しました	でんわを しませんでした
write	かきます	かきません	かきました	かきませんでした
send	おくります	おくりません	おくりました	おくりませんでした
meet	あいます	あいません	あいました	あいませんでした

II. Make up sentences following the patterns of the examples. Substitute the underlined words with the words in parentheses.

A. *State whom someone will write to.*

ex. スミスさんは <u>ともだち</u>に てがみを かきます。

1. .... （おとうさん）

2. .... （たかはしさん）

3. .... （たいしかん）

B. *State whom someone will telephone.*

ex. スミスさんは <u>レストラン</u>に でんわを します。

1. .... （おかあさん）

2. .... （かいしゃの　ひと）

3. .... （のぞみデパート）

III. Make up sentences or dialogues following the patterns of the examples and based on the information in the illustration.

1.

2.

3. メール
SEND

ex. 1. たかはしさん

1) ともだち

2) のぞみデパートのしゃちょう

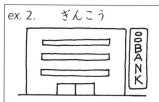
ex. 2. ぎんこう
〇〇BANK

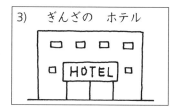
3) ぎんざの ホテル
HOTEL

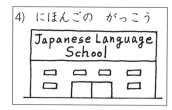
4) にほんごの がっこう
Japanese Language School

A. *State who will write to, call, or e-mail whom.*

ex. 1. スミスさんは　たかはしさんに　てがみを　かきます。
ex. 2. スミスさんは　ぎんこうに　てがみを　かきます。

1. 1) ....

　　2) ....

　　3) ....

　　4) ....

2. 1) ....

　　2) ....

　　3) ....

　　4) ....

3. 1) ....

　　2) ....

　　3) ....

　　4) ....

VOCABULARY	がっこう	school
	しゃちょう	president (of a company)
	メール	e-mail

B. *Ask and answer who will write to, call, or e-mail whom.*

ex. 1. A: スミスさんは　だれに　てがみを　かきますか。
B: たかはしさんに　かきます。
ex. 2. A: スミスさんは　どこに　てがみを　かきますか。
B: ぎんこうに　かきます。

1. 1) A: ....

   B: ....

   2) A: ....

   B: ....

   3) A: ....

   B: ....

   4) A: ....

   B: ....

2. 1) A: ....

   B: ....

   2) A: ....

   B: ....

   3) A: ....

   B: ....

   4) A: ....

   B: ....

3. 1) A: ....

   B: ....

   2) A: ....

   B: ....

   3) A: ....

   B: ....

   4) A: ....

   B: ....

IV. **Describe a schedule.** Make up sentences following the pattern of the example and based on the information in the planner.

ex.	Mon.	4:00	とうきょうえき	すずきさん
1.	Tue.	10:00	のぞみデパート	たかはしさん
2.	Wed.	7:00	レストランローマ	ささきさんの　ごしゅじん
3.	Thu.	11:00	さっぽろししゃ	ししゃの　ひと
4.	Fri.	6:30	ホテルの　ロビー	なかむらさん

ex. スミスさんは　げつようびの　4じに　とうきょうえきで　すずきさんに
あいます。

1. ....

2. ....

3. ....

4. ....

V. **Give a qualified answer in response to a question.** Answer the questions below using the words in parentheses and the appropriate verb.

ex. A: スミスさんは　よく　ビールを　のみますか。
B: はい、よく　のみます。

1. A: たかはしさんは　よく　すしを　たべますか。

B: .... (はい、ときどき)

2. A: すずきさんは　よく　ともだちに　でんわを　しますか。

B: .... (いいえ、あまり . . . ーません)

3. A: チャンさんは　よく　えいがを　みますか。

B: .... (いいえ、ぜんぜん . . . ーません)

VI. **Give a reason for an answer.** Answer the questions below using the example as a guide. Substitute the underlined word with the words in parentheses.

ex. A: スミスさんは　よく　テニスを　しますか。
B: はい。うちの　ちかくに　テニスコートが　ありますから。

1. A: ささきさんは　よく　さんぽを　しますか。

B: はい。.. (こうえん)

2. A: チャンさんは　よく　すしを　たべますか。

B: はい。.. (すしや)

VOCABULARY			
レストランローマ	Restaurant Roma (fictitious restaurant name)	ロビー	lobby
ローマ	Rome	すし	sushi
さっぽろししゃ	Sapporo (branch) office	ぜんぜん . . . ーません	not at all (see Appendix I, p. 248.)
さっぽろ	Sapporo (city on the island of Hokkaido)	すしや	sushi restaurant

VII. *Order at a restaurant.* Make up dialogues following the pattern of the example and based on the information in the illustration.

ex. スミス:　　　　ビールを　2ほん　おねがいします。
　　みせの　ひと: はい。

1. スミス:　...
　　みせの　ひと: ....

2. スミス:　...
　　みせの　ひと: ....

3. スミス:　...
　　みせの　ひと: ....

VOCABULARY　　アイスクリーム　　ice cream

VIII. ***Talk about a weekend plan.*** Make up dialogues following the pattern of the example. Substitute the underlined parts with the alternatives given.

ex. すずき: こんどの　しゅうまつに　なにを　しますか。
チャン: <u>しぶやとしょかん</u>に　いきます。
すずき: チャンさんは　よく　<u>しぶやとしょかん</u>に　いきますか。
チャン: ええ、<u>えいごの　ビデオ</u>が　たくさん　ありますから。

1. すずき: ....
   チャン: .... （ＡＢＣスポーツクラブ）
   すずき: .... （ＡＢＣスポーツクラブ）
   チャン: .... （マシーン）

2. すずき: ....
   チャン: .... （レストランドラゴン）
   すずき: .... （レストランドラゴン）
   チャン: .... （くにの　りょうり）

IX. Listen to the CD and fill in the blank based on the information you hear.

チャンさんは　よく　おかあさんに .... ます。

SHORT DIALOGUES

I. Mr. Green comes to the restaurant Tenmasa with his wife.

グリーン:　　すみません。まつコースを　ふたつ　おねがいします。
みせの　ひと: はい。おのみものは？
グリーン:　　なまビールを　ふたつ　おねがいします。
みせの　ひと: はい。

Green:　　　　　　　Excuse me, two "pine" meals please.
restaurant employee: All right. What about a beverage?
Green:　　　　　　　Two draft beers, please.
restaurant employee: All right.

VOCABULARY

まつコース　　　"pine" meal (the most expensive set meal at a traditional restaurant)
おのみもの　　　beverage
なまビール　　　draft beer

VOCABULARY	こんど	this coming	くに	(my) country
	マシーン	machine	りょうり	cooking, cuisine
	レストランドラゴン	Restaurant Dragon (fictitious restaurant name)		

II. Mr. Green pays for his meal at Tenmasa. He needs a receipt.

グリーン:　　すみません。おかんじょうを　おねがいします。
みせの ひと: はい。
グリーン:　　すみません。りょうしゅうしょを　おねがいします。
みせの ひと: はい。おなまえは？

Green:　　　　　　　　Excuse me, I'd like the check, please.
restaurant employee: All right.
Green:　　　　　　　　Excuse me. I'd like a receipt.
restaurant employee: All right. What is your name?

VOCABULARY

おかんじょう　　　　　bill, check

りょうしゅうしょ　　　receipt (requiring signature from the restaurant or store
where the purchase was made and usually necessary
when appling for reimbursement of expenses incurred)

Active Communication

Go to a restaurant and try ordering food
and a beverage in Japanese.

I Fill in the blank(s) in each sentence with the appropriate particle. Where a particle is not needed, write in an *X*.

1. テーブルの　うえに　はな（　　　　　）しんぶんが　あります。
   (Hint: There are other things in addition to these two.)

2. ゆうびんきょくの　まえ（　　　　　）おんなの　ひと（　　　　　）おとこの　こが
   います。(Hint: No one else is there.)

3. １かいに　だれ（　　　　　）いますか。
   スミスさん（　　　　　）います。

4. バスのりば（　　　　　）どこ（　　　　　）ありますか。
   デパート（　　　　　）まえです。

5. たかはしさんは　あした　かいしゃの　ひと（　　　　　）おおさか（　　　　　）い
   きます。

6. スミスさんは　ささきさん（　　　　　）でんわを　しました。

7. たかはしさんは　かいしゃの　ちかくの　レストラン（　　　　　）ひるごはん
   （　　　　　）たべました。

8. わたしは　バス（　　　　　）うち（　　　　　）かえります。

9. わたしは　まいあさ（　　　　　）うち（　　　　　）しんぶん（　　　　　）よみます。

10. スミスさんは　いつ（　　　　　）にほんに　きましたか。
    ５がつ　１８にち（　　　　　）きました。

11. よく　テニスを　しますか。
    ええ、うちの　ちかくに　テニスコートが　あります（　　　　　）。
    (Hint: This sentence is giving the reason.)

II Complete each question by filling in the blank(s) with the appropriate word.

1. ほんやの　まえに（　　　　　）がいますか。
   たかはしさんの　おくさんが　います。

2. タクシーのりばは（　　　　　）ですか。
   あそこです。

3. えきの　ちかくに（　　　　　）が　ありますか。
   バスのりばや　ゆうびんきょくや　デパートが　あります。

4. テーブルの　うえに　りんごが（　　　　　）ありますか。
   みっつ　あります。

5. えきの　まえに　おとこの　ひとが（　　　　　）いますか。
   ふたり　います。

6. チャンさんの　たんじょうびは（　　　　　）ですか。
   １がつ　２９にちです。

7. （　　　　　）が　きょうとししゃに　でんわを　しましたか。
   スミスさんが　しました。

8. たかはしさんは きのう(　　　　)に いきましたか。
   くうこうに いきました。

9. (　　　　)に ブラウンさんに あいましたか。
   ３じに あいました。

10. ブラウンさんは(　　　　)アメリカに かえりましたか。
    せんしゅうの どようびに かえりました。

11. きのう(　　　　)を しましたか。
    てがみを かきました。
    (　　　　)に かきましたか。
    ははに かきました。

III Choose one of the two words in parentheses to complete the sentence in a way that makes sense in the context.

1. テーブルの うえに しゃしんや ほんが (あります、います)。

2. いすの うえに なにも (あります、ありません)。

3. よく レストラン さくらに いきますか。
   いいえ、あまり (いきます、いきません)。

4. ときどき テレビを (みます、みません)か。
   いいえ、ぜんぜん (みます、みません)。

5. チャンさんは (よく、あまり) ともだちに でんわを します。

VISITING A JAPANESE HOME

In Japan, it is usual to offer guests green tea and Japanese sweets, or *wagashi*. *Wagashi* convey a sense of the seasons. The soft, moist sweets given in spring, for example, are modeled on cherry blossom flowers, while summer *wagashi* take the form of refreshing jellies made from adzuki beans and agar. *Wagashi* are perfect for both entertaining guests and appreciating the seasons. They also make nice gifts. Throughout Japan there are confectionaries that specialize in these unique treats. Some of the oldest and most successful ones have been in business for centuries.

UNIT 6 GRAMMAR

Adjectives

adjective + noun

> *ex.* さくらは　きれいな　はなです。"Cherry blossoms are pretty flowers."

noun は adjective です

> *ex.* グレイさんの　うちは　おおきいです。"Mr. Grey's house is big."

Japanese adjectives can either modify nouns by directly preceding them, or act as predicates. In this they resemble English adjectives. There are two kinds of adjectives: －い adjectives and －な adjectives.

MODIFYING NOUN: ADJECTIVE + NOUN		
－い ADJ.	おおきい　こうえん	big park
－な ADJ.	きれいな　はな	pretty flower

Unlike English adjectives, Japanese adjectives are inflected for tense and mood as shown below.

	AS PREDICATE: ADJECTIVE + です			
	PRESENT FORM		PAST FORM	
	aff.	*neg.*	*aff.*	*neg.*
－い ADJ.	おおきいです	おおきくないです	おおきかったです	おおきくなかったです
－な ADJ.	きれいです	きれいではありません	きれいでした	きれいではありませんでした

Giving and Receiving

person 1 は person 2 に noun を　あげます

> *ex.* おかださんは　グレイさんに　とけいを　あげました。"Ms. Okada gave Mr. Grey a watch."

person 1 は person 2 に noun を　もらいます

> *ex.* グレイさんは　おかださんに　とけいを　もらいました。
> "Mr. Grey received a watch from Ms. Okada."

The sentence pattern used with the verbs あげます ("give") and もらいます ("receive") is the same as the one introduced in Unit 5: "person 1 は person 2 に noun を verb." With あげます, the person who is given something is marked by the particle に, and the thing he or she is given is marked by を. But with もらいます, に indicates the giver rather than the receiver. Here に corresponds to "from." **NOTE:** あげます cannot be used in the sense of "someone gives something to me (the speaker)." For this meaning, the verb くれます is used.

LESSON 12
RECEIVING HOSPITALITY

TARGET DIALOGUE

TRACK 44

Mr. Smith has been invited to the home of his client Mr. Takahashi for the first time.

たかはし：おちゃを　どうぞ。

スミス：ありがとうございます。

たかはし：おかしは　いかがですか。

スミス：はい、　いただきます。　きれいな　おかしですね。

　　　　　にほんの　おかしですか。

たかはし：ええ、そうです。

スミス：とても　おいしいです。

たかはし：おちゃを　もう　1ぱい　いかがですか。

スミス：いいえ、　もう　けっこうです。

■スミスさんは　たかはしさんの　うちで　きれいな　にほんの
おかしを　たべました。おちゃを　1ぱい　のみました。

Takahashi: Have some tea.
    Smith: Thank you.
Takahashi: How about some sweets?
    Smith: Yes, I'll have some. These are pretty sweets. Are they Japanese sweets?
Takahashi: Yes, they are.
    Smith: They're very tasty.
Takahashi: How about another cup of tea?
    Smith: No thanks, I'm fine.

■ Mr. Smith ate some pretty Japanese sweets at Mr. Takahashi's home. He drank one cup of tea.

VOCABULARY

どうぞ	please (see Note 1 below)
おかし	sweets
いかがですか	how about . . . ? (see Note 2 below)
いただきます	(said before eating; see Note 3 below)
きれい（な）	pretty
とても	very
1ぱい（いっぱい）	one cup
〜はい／ばい／ぱい	cupful, glassful (counter)

いいえ、もう　けっこうです　　　no thank you, I'm fine (see Note 4 below)
けっこうです　　　　　　　　　　　no thank you

NOTES

1. おちゃを　どうぞ。
   "(Thing) を　どうぞ" ("please help yourself to . . .") is used to offer something to someone.

2. おかしは　いかがですか。
   いかがですか is often used when politely offering things like food or drink. It means "would you like one?" or "how about some?"

3. はい、いただきます。
   This phrase is spoken when taking something that is offered. It implies both acceptance and grati-tude.

4. いいえ、もう　けっこうです。
   This is a polite way of refusing a second helping of food or drink. If you want to refuse the first time you are offered something, say いいえ、けっこうです。

PRACTICE

WORD POWER

TRACK 45

I. ー い adjectives:

1. おおきいです

2. ちいさいです

3. たかいです

4. やすいです

5. あたらしいです

6. ふるいです

7. ちかいです

8. とおいです

VOCABULARY			
おおきいです	big	あたらしいです	new, fresh
ちいさいです	small	ふるいです	old (not used of people)
たかいです	expensive	ちかいです	near
やすいです	inexpensive	とおいです	far

 9. むずかしいです

 10. やさしいです

 11. あまいです

 12. からいです

 13. あついです

 14. さむいです

 15. いいです

 16. おもしろいです

 17. いそがしいです

 18. おいしいです

II. ー な adjectives:

 1. にぎやかです

 2. しずかです

 3. べんりです

 4. ゆうめいです

 5. きれいです

 6. しんせつです

 7. ひまです

VOCABULARY							
むずかしいです	difficult	さむいです	cold	にぎやかです	lively	しんせつです	kind, helpful
やさしいです	easy	いいです	good, nice	しずかです	quiet	ひまです	free, not busy
あまいです	sweet	おもしろいです	interesting	べんりです	convenient		
からいです	hot, spicy	いそがしいです	busy	ゆうめいです	famous		
あついです	hot	おいしいです	delicious	きれいです	pretty, clean		113

KEY SENTENCES

1. たかはしさんの　うちは　あたらしいです。
2. これは　おもしろい　ほんです。
3. とうきょうの　ちかてつは　べんりです。
4. スミスさんは　せんしゅう　ゆうめいな　レストランで　しょくじを
   しました。

1. Mr. Takahashi's house is new.
2. This is an interesting book.
3. The Tokyo subway is convenient.
4. Mr. Smith had a meal at a famous restaurant last week.

EXERCISES

I. *Practice conjugating* ー\\ *adjectives.* Repeat the adjectives below and memorize their forms.

	AS PREDICATE: PRESENT FORM		MODIFYING NOUN
	aff.	*neg.*	
big	おおきいです	おおきくないです	おおきい
small	ちいさいです	ちいさくないです	ちいさい
expensive	たかいです	たかくないです	たかい
cheap	やすいです	やすくないです	やすい
new, fresh	あたらしいです	あたらしくないです	あたらしい
old	ふるいです	ふるくないです	ふるい
near	ちかいです	ちかくないです	ちかい
far	とおいです	とおくないです	とおい
difficult	むずかしいです	むずかしくないです	むずかしい
easy	やさしいです	やさしくないです	やさしい
sweet	あまいです	あまくないです	あまい
hot, spicy	からいです	からくないです	からい
hot	あついです	あつくないです	あつい
cold	さむいです	さむくないです	さむい
good, nice	いいです	よくないです	いい
interesting	おもしろいです	おもしろくないです	おもしろい
busy	いそがしいです	いそがしくないです	いそがしい
delicious	おいしいです	おいしくないです	おいしい

II. *State a thing's characteristic.* Make up sentences following the pattern of the example. Substitute the underlined parts with the alternatives given.

ex. <u>この くるまは おおきいです</u>。

1. .... （この カメラ、やすいです）

2. .... （たかはしさんの うち、あたらしいです）

III. Make up dialogues following the patterns of the examples. Substitute the underlined parts with the alternatives given. Be sure to use the same grammatical forms as in the examples.

A. *Ask and answer how something tastes.*

ex. A: <u>すきやきは おいしいです</u>か。
　　B: はい、<u>おいしいです</u>。

1. A: .... （この ケーキ、あまいです）

　 B: .... （あまいです）

2. A: .... （この カレー、からいです）

　 B: .... （からいです）

B. *Ask and give one's opinion about something.*

ex. A: <u>にほんごは むずかしいです</u>か。
　　B: いいえ、<u>むずかしくないです</u>。

1. A: .... （この ゲーム、おもしろいです）

　 B: .... （おもしろいです）

2. A: .... （あの じしょ、いいです）

　 B: .... （いいです）

VOCABULARY		
すきやき	sukiyaki	
ケーキ	cake	
カレー	curry	
ゲーム	game	

IV. *Describe something.* Make up sentences following the pattern of the example and based on the information in the illustrations.

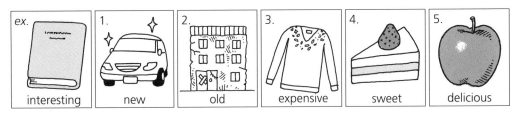

ex.	1.	2.	3.	4.	5.
interesting	new	old	expensive	sweet	delicious

ex. これは　おもしろい　ほんです。

1. ....

2. ....

3. ....

4. ....

5. ....

V. *Practice conjugating* － な *adjectives.* Repeat the adjectives below and memorize their forms.

	AS PREDICATE: PRESENT FORM		MODIFYING NOUN
	aff.	*neg.*	
lively	にぎやかです	にぎやかではありません	にぎやかな
quiet	しずかです	しずかではありません	しずかな
convenient	べんりです	べんりではありません	べんりな
famous	ゆうめいです	ゆうめいではありません	ゆうめいな
pretty, clean	きれいです	きれいではありません	きれいな
kind, helpful	しんせつです	しんせつではありません	しんせつな
free, not busy	ひまです	ひまではありません	ひまな

VI. *Describe someone or something.* Make up sentences following the pattern of the example. Substitute the underlined parts with the alternatives given.

ex. ホワイトさんは　しんせつです。

1. .... （グリーンさんの　おくさん、きれいです）

2 .... （とうきょうの　ちかてつ、べんりです）

VOCABULARY	ホワイト	White (surname)

VII. Make up dialogues following the patterns of the examples. Substitute the underlined part(s) with the alternatives given.

A. *Ask and give one's opinion about a place.*

ex. A: あの　レストランは　しずかですか。
B: はい、しずかです。

1. A: .... (ろっぽんぎ、にぎやかです)

   B: .... (にぎやかです)

2. A: .... (あの　こうえん、きれいです)

   B: .... (きれいです)

B. *Ask and answer whether one is free.*

ex. A: あした　ひまですか。
B: いいえ、ひまではありません。いそがしいです。

1. A: .... (あしたの　ごご)

   B: ....

2. A: .... (あさっての　ばん)

   B: ....

VIII. *Describe a restaurant where someone had a meal.* Make up sentences following the pattern of the example and based on the information in the illustrations.

famous

quiet

pretty

ex. スミスさんは　せんしゅう　ゆうめいな　レストランで　しょくじを　しました。

1. ....

2. ....

VOCABULARY　　ろっぽんぎ　　　　Roppongi (district in Tokyo)

IX. Make up dialogues following the patterns of the examples. Substitute the underlined words with the words in parentheses.

A. *Ask and give one's opinion about a hotel.*

ex. A: とうきょうホテルは <u>きれいな</u> ホテルですか。
B: はい、<u>きれいな</u> ホテルです。

1. A: .... (あたらしい)

   B: .... (あたらしい)

2. A: .... (おおきい)

   B: .... (おおきい)

B. *Ask and give one's opinion about a restaurant.*

ex. A: レストランぎんざは <u>ゆうめいな</u> レストランですか。
B: いいえ、<u>ゆうめいな</u> レストランではありません。

1. A: .... (しずかな)

   B: .... (しずかな)

2. A: .... (いい)

   B: .... (いい)

C. *Ask and give one's opinion about a place.*

ex. A: しゅうまつに <u>にっこう</u>に いきます。
B: <u>にっこう</u>は どんな ところですか。
A: <u>きれいな</u> ところですよ。

1. A: .... (あさくさ)

   B: .... (あさくさ)

   A: .... (にぎやかな)

2. A: .... (おだいば)

   B: .... (おだいば)

   A: .... (おもしろい)

VOCABULARY	どんな	what kind of
	ところ	place
	あさくさ	Asakusa (district in Tokyo)

X. *Compliment someone's possessions.* Mr. Smith is visiting Mr. Takahashi's house. Compliment Mr. Takahashi's house and the things (numbered in the picture) he owns, assuming the role of Mr. Smith. Make up sentences following the pattern of the example.

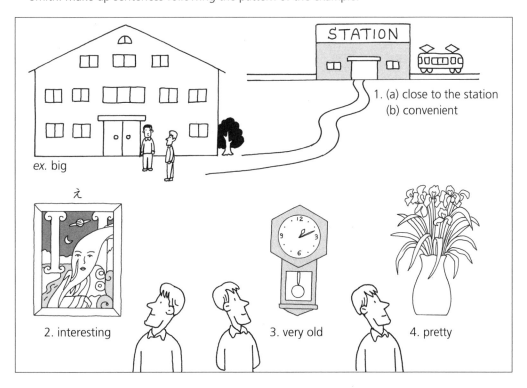

ex. スミス: <u>おおきい うち</u>ですね。

1. スミス: (a) ....

          (b) ....

2. スミス: ....

3. スミス: ....

4. スミス: ....

XI. Make up dialogues following the patterns of the examples. Substitute the underlined parts with the alternatives given.

A. *Talk about the weather.*

ex. スミス: 　きょうは　<u>いい</u>　てんきですね。
たかはし: ええ、ほんとうに　<u>いい</u>　てんきですね。

1. スミス: .... （あつい）

　たかはし: .... （あつい）

2. スミス: .... （さむい）

　たかはし: .... （さむい）

B. *Ask and answer whether a facility is far from where one is.*

ex. チャン: 　　　すみません。<u>ちかてつの　えき</u>は　ここから　とおいですか。
おとこの　ひと: いいえ、とおくないです。あるいて　5ふんぐらいですよ。
チャン: 　　　そうですか。ありがとうございます。

1. チャン: .... （バスてい）

　おとこの　ひと: ....

　チャン: ....

2. チャン: .... （こうえん）

　おとこの　ひと: ....

　チャン: ....

 XII. Listen to the CD and fill in the blank based on the information you hear.

はこねは .... ところです。

VOCABULARY			
てんき	weather	5ふんぐらい	about five minutes
ほんとうに	really	5ふん	for five minutes
		ぐらい	about, approximately (particle; used of a period, price, amout, etc., but not of a specific point in time)

120

SHORT DIALOGUES

I. Mr. Smith visits Mr. Takahashi's home. He rings the security system intercom.

たかはし: はい。
スミス:　スミスです。
たかはし: あ、ちょっと　まってください。(Takahashi *goes to answer the door*.)
たかはし: よく　いらっしゃいました。
スミス:　おじゃまします。

Takahashi:　Yes?
Mr. Smith:　It's me, Smith.
Takahashi:　Oh, please wait a minute. (Takahashi *goes to answer the door*.)
Takahashi:　Welcome!
Mr. Smith:　May I come in? (*lit.*, "I'm going to disturb you.")

VOCABULARY

ちょっと　まってください	please wait a minute
ちょっと	a little bit
よく　いらっしゃいました	welcome
おじゃまします	may I come in? (said when entering someone's home)

II. Mr. Smith is at an antique shop in Tokyo.

スミス:　　　　これは　いくらですか。
みせの　ひと: 8,000えんです。
スミス:　　　　ちょっと　たかいですね。
みせの　ひと: これは　6,500えんです。
スミス:　　　　じゃ、それを　ください。

Smith:　　　　How much is this?
salesperson:　It's 8,000 yen.
Smith:　　　　It's a little bit expensive, isn't it?
salesperson:　This is 6,500 yen.
Smith:　　　　Well then, I'll have that one.

Active Communication

Start a conversation with someone by talking about the weather. Say whether it is a nice day, a cold day, or a hot day. Refer to Exercise XI-A as necessary.

GIVING COMPLIMENTS

TARGET DIALOGUE

TRACK 48

Mr. Takahashi and Mr. Smith are talking about the flower vase that Mr. Takahashi received from Ms. Hoffman.

スミス：きれいな　かびんですね。

たかはし：ええ、たんじょうびに　ともだちの　ホフマンさんに

もらいました。

スミス：いい　いろですね。

たかはし：ええ、わたしの　すきな　いろです。

■ たかはしさんは　たんじょうびに　ホフマンさんに　かびんを
もらいました。

     Smith: That's a pretty vase, isn't it?
  Takahashi: Yes, I received it from my friend Ms. Hoffman for my birthday.
     Smith: That's a nice color, isn't it?
  Takahashi: Yes, it's my favorite color.

■ Mr. Takahashi received a vase for his birthday from Ms. Hoffman.

VOCABULARY

かびん	vase
もらいました	received
もらいます	receive
いろ	color
すきな	favorite (－な adj.)

NOTES

1. ともだちの　ホフマンさん
   This の is not possessive but appositive: "my friend Ms. Hoffman."

PRACTICE

WORD POWER

I. Verbs:

1. あげます   2. もらいます

II. Flower vocabulary:

1. ばら   2. カーネーション   3. チューリップ   4. はなたば

VOCABULARY			
あげます	give	チューリップ	tulip
もらいます	receive	はなたば	bouquet
ばら	rose		
カーネーション	carnation		

III. Gifts:

1. イヤリング　　　5. ブラウス　　　　　　8. ぼうし
2. ネックレス　　　6. えいがの　きっぷ　　9. ネクタイ
3. ゆびわ　　　　　7. れきしの　ほん　　　10. コート
4. スカーフ　　　　　　　　　　　　　　　11. きょうとの　おみやげ

KEY SENTENCES

1. スミスさんは　チャンさんに　はなを　あげました。
2. チャンさんは　スミスさんに　はなを　もらいました。

1. Mr. Smith gave Ms. Chan some flowers.
2. Ms. Chan received some flowers from Mr. Smith.

EXERCISES

I. **Practice conjugating verbs.** Repeat the verbs below and memorize their forms—present and past, affirmative and negative.

	PRESENT FORM		PAST FORM	
	aff.	*neg.*	*aff.*	*neg.*
give	あげます	あげません	あげました	あげませんでした
receive	もらいます	もらいません	もらいました	もらいませんでした

VOCABULARY					
イヤリング	earring	ブラウス	blouse	ネクタイ	necktie
ネックレス	necklace	きっぷ	ticket	コート	coat
ゆびわ	ring	れきし	history	おみやげ	gift, souvenir
スカーフ	scarf	ぼうし	hat, cap		

II. *State what someone will give to, or receive from, another.* Make up sentences following the pattern of the example. Substitute the underlined words with the alternatives given.

ex. スミスさんは　チャンさんに　<u>はな</u>を　あげます。
　　チャンさんは　スミスさんに　<u>はな</u>を　もらいます。

1. .... （きれいな　はな）

2. .... （えいがの　きっぷ）

3. .... （れきしの　ほん）

III. Make up dialogues following the patterns of the examples and based on the information in the illustration.

A. *Ask and answer whom someone gave something to.*

ex. A: スミスさんは　だれに　<u>えいがの　きっぷ</u>を　あげましたか。
　　B: <u>チャンさん</u>に　あげました。

1. A: ....

　　B: ....

2. A: ....

　　B: ....

B. *Ask and answer whom someone received something from.*

ex. A: <u>チャンさん</u>は　だれに　<u>えいがの　きっぷ</u>を　もらいましたか。
　　B: <u>スミスさん</u>に　もらいました。

1. A: ....

　　B: ....

2. A: ....

   B: ....

C. *Ask and answer what someone gave to another.*

   ex. A: スミスさんは　チャンさんに　なにを　あげましたか。
      B: えいがの　きっぷを　あげました。

   1. A: ....

      B: ....

   2. A: ....

      B: ....

 IV. Make up sentences or dialogues following the patterns of the examples and based on the information in the illustration.

A. *State who gave what to whom, and who received what from whom, on a specific day.*

   ex. 1. すずきさんは　クリスマスに　チャンさんに　でんしじしょを
      あげました。
      チャンさんは　クリスマスに　すずきさんに　でんしじしょを
      もらいました。

   1. ....

   2. ....

B. *Ask and answer what someone gave to another on a specific day.*

ex. 1. A: すずきさんは　クリスマスに　チャンさんに　なにを　あげましたか。
B: でんしじしょを　あげました。

1. A: ....

   B: ....

2. A: ....

   B: ....

C. *Ask and answer whom someone gave something to on a specific day.*

ex. 1. A: すずきさんは　クリスマスに　だれに　でんしじしょを　あげましたか。
B: チャンさんに　あげました。

1. A: ....

   B: ....

2. A: ....

   B: ....

D. *Ask and answer when someone gave something to another.*

ex. 1. A: すずきさんは　いつ　チャンさんに　でんしじしょを　あげましたか。
B: クリスマスに　あげました。

1. A: ....

   B: ....

2. A: ....

   B: ....

E. *Ask and answer what someone received on a specific day.*

ex. 2. A: すずきさんは　バレンタインデーに　チャンさんに　なにを
もらいましたか。
B: フランスの　チョコレートを　もらいました。

3. A: ....

   B: ....

4. A: ....

   B: ....

F. *Ask and answer whom someone received something from on a specific day.*

ex. 2. A: すずきさんは　バレンタインデーに　だれに　フランスの
チョコレートを　もらいましたか。
B: チャンさんに　もらいました。

3. A: ....

   B: ....

4. A: ....

    B: ....

G. *Ask and answer when someone received something from another.*

   ex. 2. A: すずきさんは　いつ　チャンさんに　フランスの　チョコレートを
          もらいましたか。
       B: バレンタインデーに　もらいました。

   3. A: ....

      B: ....

   4. A: ....

      B: ....

V. Make up dialogues following the patterns of the examples. Substitute the underlined parts with the alternatives given.

A. *Ask someone whether he or she will give a birthday present to another.*

  ex. チャン: かとうさん、あしたは　<u>スミスさんの</u>　たんじょうびですね。
         <u>スミスさん</u>に　プレゼントを　あげますか。
    かとう: ええ、<u>ネクタイ</u>を　あげます。
    チャン: そうですか。

   1. チャン: .... (グリーンさん)

     かとう: .... (れきしの　ほん)

     チャン: ....

   2. チャン: .... (おくさん)

     かとう: .... (あたらしい　かばん)

     チャン: ....

B. *Talk about presents to be given on special occasions.*

   ex. スミス: かとうさん、<u>ははの　ひ</u>に　<u>おかあさん</u>に　なにを　あげますか。
     かとう: <u>あかい　カーネーション</u>を　あげます。
     スミス: そうですか。

   1. スミス: .... (ちちの　ひ、おとうさん)

     かとう: .... (デジカメ)

     スミス: ....

VOCABULARY

プレゼント	present
ははの　ひ	Mother's Day
ちちの　ひ	Father's Day

2. スミス: .... (けっこんきねんび、おくさん)

　　かとう: .... (ばらの　はなたば)

　　スミス: ....

C. *Talk about an article of clothing someone is wearing.*

ex. Ms. Chan has a new necklace.

すずき: きれいな　ネックレスですね。
チャン: ええ、たんじょうびに　ともだちに　もらいました。
すずき: よく　にあいますね。
チャン: ありがとうございます。

1. すずき: .... (いい　とけい)

　　チャン: .... (クリスマス)

　　すずき: ....

　　チャン: ....

2. すずき: .... (きれいな　スカーフ)

　　チャン: .... (たんじょうび)

　　すずき: ....

　　チャン: ....

VI. Listen to the CD and answer the question based on the information you hear.

....

SHORT DIALOGUES

I. Mr. Smith is visiting Mr. Takahashi's house today. He glances at his watch.

スミス: 　じゃ、そろそろ　しつれいします。
　　　　　きょうは　どうも　ありがとうございました。
たかはし: どういたしまして。

Smith: 　　Well, I'll have to be leaving soon.
　　　　　Thank you for (inviting me) today.
Takahashi: You're welcome.

VOCABULARY

そろそろ　しつれいします	it's time to be going; I'd better get going
そろそろ	in just a short while
どうも　ありがとうございました	thank you very much (used to thank someone who has done you a favor or shown you kindness)

けっこんきねんび	wedding anniversary	よく	well
けっこん	marriage	にあいます	suit, look good on
きねんび	anniversary		

II. Mrs. Matsui, who lives next door to the Greens, has received a bunch of peaches from a friend, so she brings some to Mrs. Green.

まつい: ともだちに ももを たくさん もらいました。これ、どうぞ。
グリーン: どうも ありがとうございます。

Matsui: I received a lot of peaches from a friend. Please take some.
Green: Thank you very much.

VOCABULARY

もも   peach

Active Communication

Notice an item of clothing or an accessory that someone else is wearing and compliment him or her on it. Refer to Exercise V-C as necessary.

EXPRESSING GRATITUDE

TARGET DIALOGUE

TRACK
52

Mr. Smith, who visited Mr. Takahashi's house yesterday, phones Mr. Takahashi. Before getting to the point of the call, Mr. Smith thanks Mr. Takahashi for his hospitality.

スミス：もしもし、たかはしさんの　おたくですか。

たかはし：はい、そうです。

スミス：スミスです。

たかはし：あ、スミスさん。

スミス：きのうは　どうも　ありがとうございました。とても
　　　　たのしかったです。

たかはし：いいえ、どう いたしまして。わたしたちも　たのしかった
　　　　です。どうぞ　また　きてください。

スミス：どうも　ありがとうございます。

■スミスさんは　たかはしさんの　うちに　でんわを　しました。

    Smith: Hello, is this the Takahashi residence?
Takahashi: Yes, it is.
    Smith: This is Smith.
Takahashi: Oh, Mr. Smith.
    Smith: Thank you very much for yesterday. It was a lot of fun.
Takahashi: Oh, you're welcome. We had a lot of fun, too. Please come again.
    Smith: Thank you very much.

■ Mr. Smith phoned Mr. Takahashi's home.

VOCABULARY

おたく	(another person's) house
たのしかったです	was fun
たのしいです	be fun
わたしたち	we
また	again
きてください	please come

NOTES

1. たかはしさんの　おたく
   When speaking politely about your listener's house, use おたく instead of うち.

PRACTICE

WORD POWER

I. ーい adjectives:

1. たのしいです　　2. つまらないです　　3. わるいです

II. Events:

1. おまつり　　2. コンサート　　3. バーゲンセール　　4. ショー

KEY SENTENCES

1. きのうは　さむかったです。
2. きのうの　おまつりは　にぎやかでした。

1. It was cold yesterday.
2. Yesterday's festival was lively.

VOCABULARY	たのしいです	fun, enjoyable	コンサート	concert
	つまらないです	boring, tedious	バーゲンセール	clearance sale
	わるいです	bad	ショー	show
	おまつり	festival		

EXERCISES

I. Repeat the adjectives below and memorize their forms—present and past, affirmative and negative.

A. *Practice conjugating* ー い *adjectives.*

	PRESENT FORM		PAST FORM	
	aff.	*neg.*	*aff.*	*neg.*
cold	さむいです	さむくないです	さむかったです	さむくなかったです
hot	あついです	あつくないです	あつかったです	あつくなかったです
fun	たのしいです	たのしくないです	たのしかったです	たのしくなかったです
good	いいです	よくないです	よかったです	よくなかったです
bad	わるいです	わるくないです	わるかったです	わるくなかったです
interesting	おもしろいです	おもしろくないです	おもしろかったです	おもしろくなかったです
tasty	おいしいです	おいしくないです	おいしかったです	おいしくなかったです
boring	つまらないです	つまらなくないです	つまらなかったです	つまらなくなかったです

B. *Practice conjugating* ー な *adjectives.*

	PRESENT FORM		PAST FORM	
	aff.	*neg.*	*aff.*	*neg.*
pretty	きれいです	きれいではありません	きれいでした	きれいではありませんでした
quiet	しずかです	しずかではありません	しずかでした	しずかではありませんでした
lively	にぎやかです	にぎやかではありません	にぎやかでした	にぎやかではありませんでした

II. Make up sentences following the patterns of the examples. Substitute the underlined parts with the alternatives given, using the same grammatical forms as in the examples.

A. *Give one's opinion about a movie.*

ex. きのうの　えいがは　<u>おもしろかったです</u>。

1. .... （いいです）

2. .... （たのしいです）

B. *Give one's opinion about a party.*

ex. きのうの　パーティーは　<u>たのしくなかったです</u>。

1. .... （おもしろいです）

2. .... （いいです）

C. *Give one's opinion about a show.*

ex. きのうの　ショーは　<u>きれいでした</u>。

.... （にぎやかです）

D. *Give one's opinion about a festival.*

ex. きのうの　おまつりは　<u>にぎやかではありませんでした</u>。

.... （きれいです）

III. Make up sentences following the patterns of the examples and based on the information in the illustrations. Use the words in parentheses as a guide.

A. *Ask someone's opinion about an experience.*

ex. なかむら: きのうの　えいがは　おもしろかったですか。
　　チャン:　はい、<u>おもしろかったです</u>。
　　スミス:　いいえ、<u>おもしろくなかったです</u>。

1. なかむら: .... （パーティーの　りょうり、おいしいです）

　　チャン: ....

　　スミス: ....

2. なかむら: .... （おまつり、にぎやかです）

　　チャン: ....

　　スミス: ....

B. *Ask and give one's opinion about an experience.*

ex. かとう: きのうの　パーティーは　どうでしたか。
チャン: とても　たのしかったです。
スミス: あまり　たのしくなかったです。

1. かとう: .... (コンサート)

チャン: .... (いいです)

スミス: .... (いいです)

2. かとう: .... (バーゲンセール)

チャン: .... (やすいです)

スミス: .... (やすいです)

 IV. Make up dialogues following the patterns of the examples. Substitute the underlined parts with the alternatives given, using the same grammatical forms as in the examples.

A. *Use appropriate expressions when giving or receiving gifts.*

ex. チャン: しゅうまつに　きょうとに　いきました。これ、きょうとの　お
みやげです。どうぞ。
すずき: ありがとうございます。きょうとは　どうでしたか。
チャン: とても　きれいでした。

1. チャン: .... (さっぽろ)

すずき: .... (さっぽろ)

チャン: .... (さむいです)

2. チャン: .... (はこねの　おんせん)

すずき: .... (おんせん)

チャン: .... (たのしいです)

| VOCABULARY | どうでしたか | how was . . . ? |
| | どう | how |

B. *Thank someone for a gift one received.*

 ex. Ms. Chan received a box of chocolates from Ms. Nakamura on her birthday.

  チャン: なかむらさん、<u>チョコレート</u>を ありがとうございました。
      とても <u>おいしかったです</u>。
  なかむら: そうですか。よかったです。

 1. チャン: ....
                (コンサートの きっぷ、たのしいです)

  なかむら: ....

 2. チャン: ....
                (かぶきの ほん、おもしろいです)

  なかむら: ....

C. *Make a telephone call.*

 ex. すずき: もしもし、<u>なかむらさん</u>の おたくですか。
  なかむらさんの かぞく: はい、そうです。
  すずき: すずきです。<u>まゆみさん</u>は いらっしゃいますか。
  なかむらさんの かぞく: はい。ちょっと おまちください。

 1. すずき: .... (ささきさん)

  ささきさんの かぞく:..

  すずき: .... (おくさん)

  ささきさんの かぞく:..

 2. すずき: .... (かとうさん)

  かとうさんの かぞく:..

  すずき: .... (ごしゅじん)

  かとうさんの かぞく:..

V. Listen to the CD and fill in the blanks based on the information you hear.

  チャンさんは ....に おまつりを みました。おまつりは

  とても ....

VOCABULARY

| よかったです | that's good | いらっしゃいます | be (honorific word for います) |
| まゆみ | Mayumi (female first name) | ちょっと おまちください | please wait a minute (politer way of saying ちょっと まってください) |

SHORT DIALOGUE

TRACK 55

The morning after receiving some peaches from Mrs. Matsui, Mrs. Green happens to run into Mrs. Matsui. She thanks her for the peaches.

グリーン： おはようございます。

まつい： おはようございます。

グリーン： きのうは　ももを　ありがとうございました。とても　おいしかっ
たです。

まつい： そうですか。よかったです。

Green: Good morning.

Matsui: Good morning.

Green: Thank you for the peaches you gave us yesterday. They were very tasty.

Matsui: Were they? That's good.

Active Communication

Ask people for their impressions of places, movies, or other things or events. Refer to Exercise III.

GOING TO A FESTIVAL

The Japanese calendar is lined with seasonal festivals and events. Seasonal festivals such as cherry blossom viewing in spring and firework displays in the heat of summer are held to appreciate nature at its best. Festivals to celebrate a good harvest are held mainly in autumn, whereas those meant to invoke one are held in spring. At these fêtes, people carry around portable shrines, or *o-mikoshi*, and the men often wear *happi* coats designating neighborhood associations. Many festivals attract large crowds, and famous ones such as the Sapporo Snow Festival or the Gion Festival in Kyoto are always packed with people.

Inviting Someone to Do Something and Making Suggestions

| verb－ませんか |

| verb－ましょう |

ex. いっしょに　あさくさに　いきませんか。
"Won't you go to Asakusa with (me)?/What do you say to going to Asakusa together?
ええ／はい、いきましょう。"Yes, let's go."

The verb－ませんか pattern is used to invite someone to do something. Appropriate replies are as follows.
1. Acceptance:
　　a. ええ／はい、verb－ましょう。"Yes, let's [verb]."
　　b. ええ／はい、ぜひ。"Yes, I'd love to."
2. Refusal: ざんねんですが、つごうが　わるいです。
　　　　　　"I'm sorry, but it wouldn't be convenient (for me)."

The verb －ましょう pattern is generally translatable as "let's."

| verb－ましょうか |

ex. どこで　あいましょうか。"Where should we meet?"

The verb－ましょうか pattern is used to invite someone to decide a time, place, etc. for something.

Offering to Do Something

| verb－ましょうか |

ex. にもつを　もちましょうか。"Shall I carry your luggage?"

The verb－ましょうか pattern is also used when offering to do something for someone. Appropriate replies are as follows.
1. Acceptance: ええ／はい、おねがいします。"Yes, please."
2. Refusal: いいえ、けっこうです。"No, thank you."

INVITATIONS

TARGET DIALOGUE

Mr. Kato invites Mr. Smith to a festival in Asakusa.

かとう：スミスさん、こんしゅうの　どようびに　あさくさで　おま
　　　　つりが　あります。　いっしょに　いきませんか。

スミス：いいですね。　いきましょう。なんで　いきましょうか。

かとう：ちかてつで　いきませんか。

スミス：そう　しましょう。どこで　あいましょうか。

かとう：あさくさえきの　かいさつぐちで　あいませんか。

スミス：はい。なんじに　あいましょうか。

かとう：１０じは　どうですか。

スミス：１０じですね。じゃ、どようびに。

■こんしゅうの　どようびに　あさくさで　おまつりが　あります
　から、スミスさんは　かとうさんと　あさくさに　いきます。

　　Kato: Mr. Smith, there is a festival in Asakusa this Saturday. Won't you go with me?
Smith: That would be nice. Let's go. How should we go?
　Kato: Would you like to go by subway?
Smith: Let's do that. Where should we meet?
　Kato: Would you like to meet at the ticket gate at Asakusa Station?
Smith: All right. What time should we meet?
　Kato: How about 10:00?
Smith: 10:00, then. Well, I'll see you on Saturday.

■On Saturday there is a festival in Asakusa, so Mr. Smith is going to Asakusa with Mr. Kato.

VOCABULARY

あります	there is/are going to be (see Note 1 below)
いっしょに	together
いきませんか	won't you go (with me)?
いきましょう	let's go
いきましょうか	shall we go?
あさくさえき	Asakusa Station
かいさつぐち	ticket gate
どうですか	how is . . . ?
から	because (particle; see Note 3 below)

NOTES

1. あさくさで　おまつりが　あります。
   あります can also be used in the sense of "take place" or "happen." The place where the event happens is followed by the particle で.

2. じゃ、どようびに。
   どようびに is short for どようびに　あいましょう, "let's meet on Saturday." Japanese people often refer to the next meeting rather than saying good-bye.
   　ex. じゃ、また　あした。"Well then, (see you) again tomorrow."

3. こんしゅうの　どようびに　あさくさで　おまつりが　ありますから、スミスさん
   は　かとうさんと　あさくさに　いきます。
   This complex sentence consists of two clauses. The first clause, ending with the particle から, expresses a reason for what is stated in the second clause.

PRACTICE

WORD POWER

I. Events:

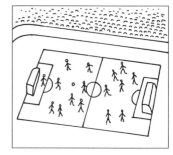

1. はなびたいかい

2. ゆきまつり

3. サッカーの　しあい

VOCABULARY

はなびたいかい	fireworks display	ゆきまつり	snow festival	サッカー	soccer
はなび	fireworks	ゆき	snow	しあい	game, match
たいかい	large gathering				

142

II. Parts of a station:

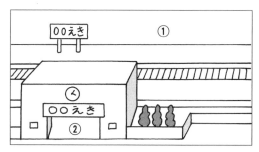 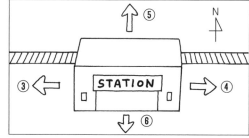

1. ホーム
2. いりぐち

3. にしぐち
4. ひがしぐち
5. きたぐち
6. みなみぐち

III. Variations on the －ます form:

	go	see	do	meet
V－ます	いきます	みます	します	あいます
V－ましょう	いきましょう	みましょう	しましょう	あいましょう
V－ましょうか	いきましょうか	みましょうか	しましょうか	あいましょうか
V－ませんか	いきませんか	みませんか	しませんか	あいませんか

KEY SENTENCES

1. しゅうまつに いっしょに えいがを みませんか。
2. えいがを みましょう。
3. なにを たべましょうか。
4. どようびに あさくさで おまつりが あります。
5. ２かいに レストランが ありますから、レストランで しょくじを しませんか。

1. Would you like to see a movie with me over the weekend?
2. Let's see a movie.
3. What should we eat?
4. There's a festival in Asakusa on Saturday.
5. There's a restaurant on the second floor, so won't you have a meal with me there?

VOCABULARY

ホーム platform
いりぐち entrance
にしぐち west exit
ひがしぐち east exit

きたぐち north exit
みなみぐち south exit

143

EXERCISES

I. *Invite someone to do something.* Make up sentences as in the example.

ex. ひるごはんを　たべます → ひるごはんを　たべませんか。

1. コーヒーを　のみます　　→ ....

2. ゴルフを　します　　　　→ ....

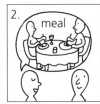

II. Make up dialogues following the patterns of the examples and based on the information in the illustrations.

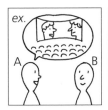  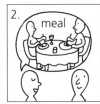 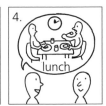

A. *Invite someone to do something and accept one's invitation.*

ex. A: しゅうまつに　いっしょに　<u>えいがを　みませんか</u>。
　　B: ええ、<u>みましょう</u>。

1. A: ....

　 B: ....

2. A: ....

　 B: ....

3. A: ....

　 B: ....

4. A: ....

　 B: ....

B. *Invite someone to do something and refuse one's invitation.*

ex. A: しゅうまつに　いっしょに　<u>えいがを　みませんか</u>。
　　B: ざんねんですが、つごうが　わるいです。

1. A: ....

　 B: ....

VOCABULARY		
	すもう	sumo wrestling
	ざんねんですが、つごうが　わるいです	I'm sorry, but it wouldn't be convenient (for me)

2. A: ....

    B: ....

3. A: ....

    B: ....

4. A: ....

    B: ....

III. Make up dialogues following the patterns of the examples. Substitute the underlined parts with the alternatives given, using the same grammatical forms as in the examples.

A. *Decide what to do.*

  ex. A: なにを　<u>たべましょうか</u>。
     B: <u>てんぷらを　たべませんか</u>。
     A: ええ、そう　しましょう。

  1. A: .... (のみます)

     B: .... (ワイン、のみます)

     A: ....

  2. A: .... (かいます)

     B: .... (かびん、かいます)

     A: ....

B. *Decide when to do something.*

  ex. A: いつ　<u>あいましょうか</u>。
     B: <u>あしたの　３じは</u>　どうですか。
     A: ええ、そう　しましょう。

  1. A: .... (プレゼントを　かいます)

     B: .... (どようび)

     A: ....

  2. A: .... (ゴルフを　します)

     B: .... (らいげつ)

     A: ....

C. *Decide where to do something.*

    ex. A: どこで　<u>あいましょうか</u>。
       B: <u>えきの　まえに　こうばんが　ありますから</u>、<u>こうばんの　まえで</u>
         <u>あいませんか</u>。
       A: ええ、そう　しましょう。

    1. A: ....(たべます)

        B: ....
          （ＡＢＣビルに　いい　レストランが　たくさん　あります、ＡＢＣビルで　たべます）

        A: ....

    2. A: .... (はなしを　します)

        B: ....
          （この　ちかくに　こうえんが　あります、こうえんで　はなしを　します）

        A: ....

IV. Make up sentences following the patterns of the examples and based on the information in the
    illustrations.

ex. Saturday	1. next month	2. tomorrow	3. Tuesday
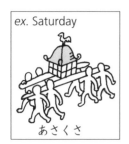			
あさくさ	さっぽろ		よこはま

A. *State when and where an event will take place.*

    ex. どようびに　あさくさで　おまつりが　あります。

    1. ....

    2. ....

    3. ....

B. *Invite someone to an event and accept one's invitation.*

ex. A: どようびに あさくさで おまつりが あります。いっしょに いきま
せんか。
B: いいですね。いきましょう。

1. A: ....

   B: ....

2. A: ....

   B: ....

3. A: ....

   B: ....

V. *Invite someone to an event and decide on a meeting place.* Make up dialogues following the pattern of the example. Substitute the underlined parts with the alternatives given.

ex. スミス: あさって おだいばで はなびたいかいが あります。いっし
ょに いきませんか。
なかむら: いいですね。いきましょう。
スミス: どこで あいましょうか。
なかむら: しんばしえきの きたぐちで あいませんか。
スミス: ええ、そう しましょう。

1. スミス: .... (たいしかん、パーティー)

   なかむら: ....

   スミス: ....

   なかむら: .... (しんじゅくえきの にしぐち)

   スミス: ....

2. スミス: .... (とうきょうホール、コンサート)

   なかむら: ....

   スミス: ....

   なかむら: .... (とうきょうえきの みなみぐち)

   スミス: ....

VOCABULARY			
いいですね	that sounds good	しんじゅくえき	Shinjuku Station
しんばし えき	Shimbashi Station	しんじゅく	Shinjuku (district in Tokyo)
しんばし	Shimbashi (district in Tokyo)	とうきょうホール	Tokyo Hall (fictitious building name)
		ホール	(concert) hall

VI. **Invite someone out to eat.** Make up a dialogue based on the information in the illustrations.

1. すずき: ....

2. チャン: ....

3. すずき: ....

4. チャン: ....

5. すずき: ....

6. すずき: ....

7. チャン: ....

8. すずき: ....

9. すずき: じゃ、どようびに。

10. チャン: じゃ、また。

VII. Listen to the CD and fill in the blanks based on the information you hear.

スミスさんは .... で .... に にっこうに いきます。

SHORT DIALOGUES

I. なかむら: らいしゅう スミスさんと テニスを します。チャンさんも
いっしょに しませんか。
チャン: ありがとうございます。ぜひ。

Nakamura: I'm going to be playing tennis with Mr. Smith next week. Won't you join us, Ms. Chan?
Chan: Thank you, I'd love to.

VOCABULARY

ぜひ   by all means, certainly

II. たかはし: スミスさん、こんしゅうの にちようびに うちで パーティーを
します。きませんか。
スミス: ありがとうございます。ぜひ。

Takahashi: Mr. Smith, I'm having a party at my house this Sunday. Won't you come?
Smith: Thank you. I certainly will.

VOCABULARY

パーティーを します   have a party

NOTES

1. （にちようびに うちに）きませんか。
When inviting someone to your own home, use the phrase きませんか. Appropriate replies are ええ／
はい、ありがとうございます ("yes, thank you") or, to decline the offer, ざんねんですが、つごうが
わるいです ("I'm sorry, I'm afraid it wouldn't be convenient [for me]").

Active Communication

Invite a friend to an event.

149

TARGET DIALOGUE

TRACK
60

Mr. Smith meets Mr. Suzuki, who is wearing a *happi* coat, and calls out to him.

かとう：あ、スミスさん、あそこに　すずきさんが　いますよ。

スミス：ほんとうですね。すずきさん。

すずき：あ、スミスさん。スミスさんも　いっしょに　おみこしを
　　　　　かつぎませんか。

スミス：でも、はっぴが　ありません。

すずき：わたしのを　かしましょうか。

スミス：いいんですか。

すずき：ええ、わたしは　２まい　ありますから。

スミス：ありがとうございます。じゃ、おねがいします。

■スミスさんは　あさくさで　すずきさんに　あいました。いっしょに
　おみこしを　かつぎます。

　Kato: Oh, Mr. Smith, there's Mr. Suzuki over there.
　Smith: You're right. Mr. Suzuki!
Suzuki: Oh, Mr. Smith. Would you like to carry the *o-mikoshi* with us?
　Smith: But I don't have a *happi* coat.
Suzuki: Shall I lend you mine?
　Smith: Is it all right with you?
Suzuki: Yes, I have two.
　Smith: Thank you. I'll ask you to do that, then.

■ Mr. Smith has met Mr. Suzuki in Asakusa. They will carry the *o-mikoshi* together.

VOCABULARY

ほんとう	true
おみこし	portable shrine (carried during festivals)
かつぎます	carry (on one's shoulders)
でも	but
はっぴ	*happi* coat
わたしの	mine
かしましょうか	shall I lend you?
かします	lend

いいんですか　　　　　is it all right? (expressing reserve)
あります　　　　　　　have (see Note 1 below)

NOTES

1. （わたしは）はっぴが　ありません。
   あります can also be used in the sense of "have" or "own."

PRACTICE

WORD POWER

I. Verbs:

1. かします

2. つけます

3. けします

4. もちます

5. あけます

6. しめます

7. （しゃしんを）とります

VOCABULARY			
かします	lend	あけます	open
つけます	turn on	しめます	close, shut
けします	turn off	（しゃしんを）とります	take (a photograph)
もちます	carry, hold	しゃしん	photograph

151

II. Words that can be used with あります ("to have"):

1. じかん   2. くるま   3. やすみ   4.にほんごの
                                                          じゅぎょう

KEY SENTENCES

1. ちずを　かきましょうか。
2. スミスさんは　えいがの　きっぷが　２まい　あります。

1. Shall I draw a map?
2. Mr. Smith has two movie tickets.

EXERCISES

I. *Offer to do something.* Make up sentences as in the example.

ex. しゃしんを　とります → しゃしんを　とりましょうか。

1. ちずを　かきます   → ....

2. この　ほんを　かします → ....

VOCABULARY   じかん   time
              じゅぎょう   class
              ちず   map

II. ***Offer to do something and accept or reject one's offer.*** Make up dialogues following the pattern of the example and based on the information in the illustrations.

ex. スミス：　にもつを　もちましょうか。
　　なかむら：ええ、おねがいします。
　　すずき：　いいえ、けっこうです。

1. スミス：　...

　　なかむら：...

2. スミス：　...

　　すずき：　...

3. スミス：　...

　　なかむら：...

4. スミス：　...

　　すずき：　...

VOCABULARY		
	にもつ	luggage, baggage
	ドア	door
	まど	window
	エアコン	air conditioner

153

III. **State what one has.** Make up sentences following the pattern of the example. Substitute the underlined word with the words suggested by the illustration.

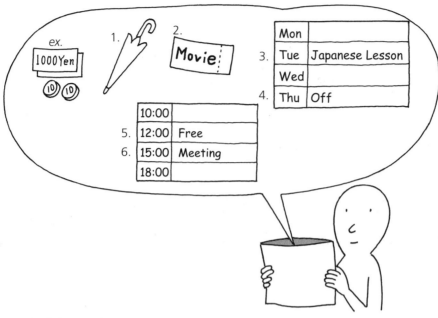

ex. わたしは　<u>おかね</u>が　あります。

1. ....

2. ....

3. ....

4. ....

5. ....

6. ....

IV. Make up dialogues following the patterns of the examples. Substitute the underlined parts with the alternatives given, using the same grammatical forms as in the examples.

A. **Offer to lend someone something, giving a reason for doing so, and accept one's offer.**

ex. A: (わたしは)　<u>かさ</u>が　<u>2ほん</u>　ありますから、かしましょうか。
    B: はい、おねがいします。

1. A: .... (ペン、2ほん)

   B: ....

2. A: .... (はっぴ、2まい)

   B: ....

B. *Invite someone to do something, giving a reason for doing so, and accept one's invitation.*

ex. A:(わたしは) <u>くるまが　あります</u>から、いっしょに　<u>にっこうに　いきま</u>
<u>せんか</u>。
B: ええ、ぜひ。

1. A: ....
(おもしろい　DVD、みます)

　 B: ....

2. A: ....
(えいがの　きっぷ、いきます)

　 B: ....

V. Make up dialogues following the patterns of the examples. Substitute the underlined parts with the alternatives given, using the same grammatical forms as in the examples.

A. *Refuse an invitation by stating one's situation.*

ex. すずき: えいがの　きっぷが　２まい　あります。チャンさん、こんばん
いっしょに　いきませんか。
チャン: すみません、こんばん　<u>じかんが　ありません</u>。
すずき: そうですか。じゃ、また　こんど。

1. すずき: ....

　 チャン: ....
(かいぎが　あります)

　 すずき: ....

2. すずき: ....

　 チャン: ....
(にほんごの　じゅぎょうが　あります)

　 すずき: ....

B. *Invite someone to do something.*

ex. スミス: すずきさん、らいしゅう　いっしょに　<u>ゴルフを</u>　しませんか。
すずき: でも、<u>クラブ</u>が　ありません。
スミス: わたしのを　かしましょうか。
すずき: ありがとうございます。おねがいします。

1. スミス: .... (スキー)

　 すずき: .... (どうぐ)

　 スミス: ....

　 すずき: ....

VOCABULARY	こんばん	this evening
	また　こんど	next time
	クラブ	golf club
	どうぐ	tool, equipment

2. スミス: .... (テニス)

すずき: .... (ラケット)

スミス: ....

すずき: ....

 VI. *Offer to help someone.* Make up a dialogue based on the information in the illustrations.

1. すずき: ....

2. スミス: ....

3. すずき: ....

4. スミス: ....

VII. Listen to the CD and answer the question based on the information you hear.

TRACK 62

....

VOCABULARY

ラケット　　　　　　racket
コピーを　します　　make a photocopy

SHORT DIALOGUES

I. At the festival site, Mr. Smith accidentally steps on someone's foot.

おんなの　ひと: あ、いたい。
スミス:　　　　あ、すみません。だいじょうぶですか。
おんなの　ひと: ええ、だいじょうぶです。
スミス:　　　　どうも　すみませんでした。

woman: Oh, ouch!
Smith:　Oh, I'm sorry. Are you all right?
woman: Yes, I'm fine.
Smith:　I'm really sorry.

VOCABULARY

いたい	painful, ouch!
だいじょうぶですか	are you all right?
すみませんでした	I'm sorry (for what I did a while ago)

II. Mr. Kato calls out to Mr. Smith, who appears to be ill.

かとう: だいじょうぶですか。
スミス: ちょっと　きぶんが　わるいんです。
かとう: あそこに　ベンチが　ありますから、ちょっと　やすみましょう。
スミス: はい。

Kato:　　Are you all right?
Smith:　I'm feeling a bit out of sorts.
Kato:　　There's a bench over there, so let's take a little break.
Smith:　All right.

VOCABULARY

きぶんが　わるいんです	I feel out of sorts; I don't feel well
ベンチ	bench
やすみます	rest, relax, take time off

Active Communication

You have two tickets for an event. Invite someone to that event.

Ⅰ Fill in the blank(s) in each sentence with the appropriate particle. Where a particle is not needed, write in an *X*.

1. チャンさんは　たかはしさん(　　　　　)はなを　もらいました。
2. わたしは　たんじょうびに　ははに　スカーフ(　　　　　)あげました。
3. どようびに　あさくさで　おまつり(　　　　　)あります。
4. わたしはくるま(　　　　　)あります。
5. わたしはえいがの　きっぷ(　　　　　)2まい(　　　　　)あります。

Ⅱ Complete each question by filling in the blank with the appropriate word.

1. とうきょうレストランは(　　　　　)レストランですか。
   きれいな　レストランです。
2. スミスさんは(　　　　　)に　えいがの　きっぷを　もらいましたか。
   ともだちに　もらいました。
3. きのうの　コンサートは(　　　　　)でしたか。
   とても　よかったです。
4. にちようびに(　　　　　)で　バーゲンセールが　ありますか。
   とうきょうデパートで　あります。

Ⅲ Change the word in parentheses to the form that is appropriate in the context of the sentence..

1. とうきょうホテルは(　　　　　　　　)ホテルです。(きれいです)
2. これは(　　　　　　　　)ケーキです。(おいしいです)
3. あのレストランは　あまり(　　　　　　　　)。(しずかです)
4. きのうの　パーティーは　とても(　　　　　　　　)。(にぎやかです)
5. きのうの　えいがは　あまり(　　　　　　　　)。(おもしろいです)

Ⅳ Change the words in parentheses to the forms that are appropriate in the context of the dialogue.

1. A: しゅうまつに　いっしょに　えいがを(　　　　　　　　)。(みます)
   B: ええ、みましょう。
   A: どこで(　　　　　　　　)。(あいます)
   B: とうきょうえきは　どうですか。
2. A: エアコンを　(　　　　　　　　)。(つけます)
   B: いいえ、けっこうです。
   A: では、まどを　(　　　　　　　　)。(あけます)
   B: はい、おねがいします。

UNIT

8

ON BUSINESS OUTSIDE TOKYO

Looking at Japan from a satellite, one would be surprised to see how mountainous the country is. In fact, about 73 percent of the land is mountain terrain. Another notable point is that because the country stretches more than 3,000 kilometers from northeast to southwest, its climate varies considerably according to latitude; and this in turn has given rise to differences in ways of life and a variety of local dialects. The city of Sapporo on the island of Hokkaido in northern Japan (see photo above) is both a tourist and a business destination. Other such cities include Osaka, Niigata, Nagoya, and Fukuoka. (See map on front end paper.)

UNIT 8 GRAMMAR

The ー て Form

■ Japanese verbs have several forms

Japanese verbs have several conjugated forms. All the verbs presented so far have been in, or derived from, the ー ます form. Now we'll look at a new form, the ー て form.

■ How to form the ー て form

Japanese verbs are divided into three classes according to their conjugations: Regular I, Regular II and Irregular. The ー て forms of Regular II and Irregular verbs always end with ー て: the ー ます comes off and ー て is added to the stem. The ー て forms of Regular I verbs vary, as shown in the following chart.

REGULAR I			REGULAR II		
buy	かいます	かって	eat	たべます	たべて
wait	まちます	まって	open	あけます	あけて
return, go home	かえります	かえって	see	みます	みて
listen	ききます	きいて	IRREGULAR		
write	かきます	かいて	come	きます	きて
read	よみます	よんで	do	します	して
drink	のみます	のんで			
turn off	けします	けして			

NOTE: A more detailed explanation of the grouping of Japanese verbs is given in Unit 9 Grammar, p. 178.

■ How the ー て form is used

The ー て form occurs in the middle of a sentence

ex. グレイさんは　さっぽろししゃに　いって、さとうさんに　あいます。
　　"Mr. Grey will go to the Sapporo branch office and meet Mr. Sato."

or is combined with ください to form a polite imperative.

ex. カタログを　おくってください。"Please send a catalog."

When one action is followed by another, the first clause is terminated by a verb in the ー て form. In this type of sentence, the subject of the first and second clause must be the same. The ー て form can be used to link up to three clauses, in which case the verbs of the first two end in the ー て form. The ー て form cannot be used if the moods and tenses of the clauses it combines are not the same. For example, the following two sentences cannot be connected using the ー て form:

1. Statement: わたしは　きっぷが　2まい　あります。"I have two tickets."
2. Suggestion: あした　いっしょに　えいがを　みませんか。
　　　　　　　　"What do you say to seeing a movie together tomorrow?"

Furthermore, if the first clause contains a motion verb like いきます, きます, or かえります, the verb in the second clause must express an action that occurs in the location to which the subject went in the first clause. For example, きのう　ぎんざに　いって、ひるごはんを　たべました ("Yesterday I went to Ginza and ate lunch [there]") is correct, but きのう　ぎんざに　いって、しぶやで　ひるごはんを　たべました ("Yesterday I went to Ginza and ate lunch in Shibuya") is incorrect, since the act of eating took place in Shibuya, not Ginza.

TALKING ABOUT PLANS

 TARGET DIALOGUE

Ms. Chan is talking with Ms. Sasaki about her sudden business trip.

チャン：ささきさん、ちょっと　よろしいですか。

ささき：はい。

チャン：あした　ほっかいどうで　はんばいかいぎが　ありますから、
　　　　　さっぽろに　いきます。

ささき：かいぎは　なんじからですか。

チャン：ごぜん　１０じから　ごご　３じまでです。かいぎの　あと
　　　　　で　さっぽろししゃに　いって、さとうさんに　あいます。
　　　　　あさって　はこだての　チョコレートこうじょうを　みて、
　　　　　１じの　ひこうきで　とうきょうに　かえります。

ささき：わかりました。では、きを　つけて。

■チャンさんは　あした　さっぽろに　いきます。あさって　チョコ
　レートこうじょうを　みて、とうきょうに　かえります。

Chan: Ms. Sasaki, do you have a moment?
Sasaki: Yes, please (tell me what you want to talk about).
Chan: There's a sales meeting in Hokkaido tomorrow, so I'm going to Sapporo.
Sasaki: What time does the meeting start?
Chan: It's from 10:00 a.m. to 3:00 p.m. After the meeting, I'll go to the Sapporo branch office and meet Mr. Sato. The day after tomorrow, I'll see the chocolate factory in Hakodate and fly back to Tokyo on a 1:00 (p.m.) flight.
Sasaki: I see. Well then, take care.

■ Ms. Chan is going to Sapporo tomorrow. The day after tomorrow she will see a chocolate factory and return to Tokyo.

VOCABULARY

ちょっと　よろしいですか	do you have a moment?
よろしい	good, all right (polite form of いい; used in interrogative sentences)
ほっかいどう	Hokkaido (the northernmost of the main islands of Japan)
はんばい	sales, marketing
〜の　あとで	after
さとう	Sato (Surname)
はこだて	Hakodate (city in southern Hokkaido)
こうじょう	factory, manufacturing plant
きを　つけて	take care

NOTES

1. ちょっと　よろしいですか。
   This expression is used to get the attention of someone who is in the midst of something.

PRACTICE

WORD POWER

The ーて form:

1.
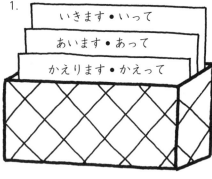

いきます・いって
あいます・あって
かえります・かえって

2.
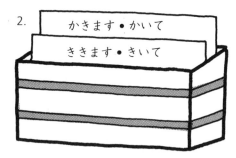

かきます・かいて
ききます・きいて

3.
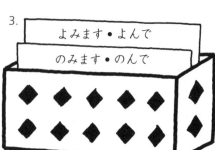

よみます・よんで
のみます・のんで

4.
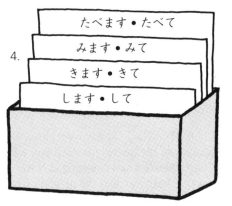

たべます・たべて
みます・みて
きます・きて
します・して

KEY SENTENCES

1. スミスさんは　きのう　ほんやに　いって、じしょを　かいました。
2. スミスさんは　かいぎの　まえに　コピーを　します。
3. スミスさんは　きのう　パーティーの　あとで　タクシーで　うちに　かえりました。

1. Mr. Smith went to a bookstore yesterday and bought a dictionary.
2. Mr. Smith will make copies before the meeting.
3. Mr. Smith went home by taxi after yesterday's party.

VOCABULARY 　　　～の　まえに　　　　　　before

EXERCISES

 I. *Practice conjugating verbs.* Repeat the verbs below and memorize their ーて forms.

	ーます FORM	ーて FORM		ーます FORM	ーて FORM
buy	かいます	かって	turn off	けします	けして
meet	あいます	あって	eat	たべます	たべて
return, go home	かえります	かえって	open	あけます	あけて
go	いきます	*いって	close	しめます	しめて
write	かきます	かいて	turn on	つけます	つけて
listen (to), ask	ききます	きいて	see	みます	みて
drink	のみます	のんで	come	きます	きて
read	よみます	よんで	do	します	して

*irregular inflection

 II. *Practice the* ーて *form.* Change the following verbs to their -て forms.

ex. たべます → たべて

1. きます　　　→ ....　　6. よみます　→ ....

2. のみます　→ ....　　7. みます　　→ ....

3. かきます　→ ....　　8. ききます　→ ....

4. あいます　→ ....　　9. します　　→ ....

5. かえります → ....　　10. いきます　→ ....

 III. *Express a sequence of actions.* Combine the sentences below as in the example.

ex. メールを　かきます。おくります。
　→ メールを　かいて、おくります。

1. でんきを　つけます。ドアを　しめます。

　→ ....

2. でんわばんごうを　ききます。でんわを　します。

　→ ....

3. うちで　ほんを　よみます。レポートを　かきます。

　→ ....

VOCABULARY	でんき	(electric) light
	レポート	report

163

IV. *Ask and answer what one will do. In answering, express a sequence of actions.* Make up dialogues following the pattern of the example. Substitute the underlined parts with the appropriate forms of the alternatives given.

ex. A: あした　なにを　しますか。
B: <u>ほんやに　いって、じしょを　かいます。</u>

1. A: ....

 B: ....
（ぎんざで　かいものを　します、えいがを　みます）

2. A: ....

 B: ....
（レストランで　ひるごはんを　たべます、びじゅつかんに　いきます）

V. *Express a sequence of actions.* Combine the sentences below as in the example.

ex. うちに　きませんか。ひるごはんを　たべませんか。
→ うちに　きて、ひるごはんを　たべませんか。

1. スミスさんに　あいました。いっしょに　テニスを　しました。

 → ....

2. ドアを　あけましょうか。でんきを　つけましょうか。

 → ....

VI. *Ask and answer what one did. In answering, express a sequence of actions.* Make up dialogues following the pattern of the example. Substitute the underlined parts with the appropriate forms of the alternatives given.

ex. A: きのう　なにを　しましたか。
B: <u>デパートで　ケーキを　かって、ともだちの　うちに　いきました。</u>

1. A: ....

 B: ....
（ろっぽんぎに　いきます、しょくじを　します）

2. A: ....

 B: ....
（ともだちに　あいます、いっしょに　すもうを　みます）

VOCABULARY　びじゅつかん　　art museum

VII. ***State what someone will do before or after a given event.*** Make up sentences following the patterns of the examples. Use the information in the illustration as a guide and substitute the underlined parts in each example with the alternatives given.

やまもとさん

ex. 1. ごご　７じから　<u>かいぎが</u>　あります。<u>かいぎの</u>　まえに　<u>しょくじを</u>
<u>します</u>。

1. ....

　　　　　　　　　　　　　　　　　　　　（かいぎ、コピーを　します）

2. ....

　　　　　　　　　　　　　　　　　　　　（パーティー、ワインを　かいます）

ex. 2. ごご　７じ　から　<u>パーティーが</u>　あります。<u>パーティーの</u>　あとで
<u>タクシーで　うちに　かえります</u>。

3. ....

　　　　　　　　　　　　　　　　　　　　（かいぎ、レポートを　かきます）

4. ....

　　　　　　　　　　　　　　　　　　　　（かいぎ、やまもとさんに　あいます）

VIII. *Ask and answer what one did after work. In answering, express a sequence of actions* Make up dialogues following the pattern of the example and based on the information in the illustrations.

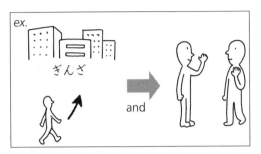

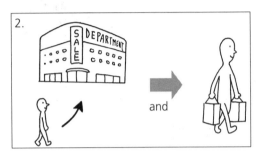

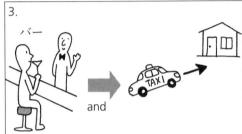

ex. A: きのう　しごとの　あとで　なにを　しましたか。
    B: ぎんざに　いって、ともだちに　あいました。

1. A: ....

   B: ....

2. A: ....

   B: ....

3. A: ....

   B: ....

IX. **Describe a schedule.** Look at the schedule of Mr. Smith's business trip and make up sentences following the pattern of the example.

ex.	Thursday	Osaka	Meeting	→ Call Mr. Green
1.	Friday	Kobe	Golf	→ Go to a friend's house
2.	Saturday	Kyoto	Have a meal with Mr. Yamamoto	→ See old temples and gardens

ex. スミスさんは　もくようびに　おおさかに　いって、かいぎを　します。
かいぎの　あとで　グリーンさんに　でんわを　します。

1. ....

2. ....

X. **Talk about a plan.** Make up dialogues on the pattern of the example. Substitute the underlined parts with the alternatives given.

ex. ささき: チャンさん、かいぎの　あとで　どこに　いきますか。
チャン: <u>はこだて</u>に　いって、<u>チョコレートこうじょうを　みます</u>。
ささき: そうですか。

1. ささき: ....

チャン: ....
（おたる、すしを　たべます）

ささき: ....

2. ささき: ....

チャン: ....
（デパート、ほっかいどうの　おみやげを　かいます）

ささき: ....

XI. Listen to the CD and choose the correct answer to the question asked.

TRACK 66

a) 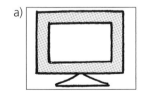　　b) 　　c)

VOCABULARY

こうべ	Kobe (city near Osaka)
かいぎを　します	hold a meeting
おたる	Otaru (city in Hokkaido)

SHORT DIALOGUES

I. Mrs. Green is planning a party. She calls up Mrs. Matsui to invite her.

グリーン: にほんじんの　ともだちに　きょうとの　ゆうめいな　おさけを
　　　　　もらいました。にちようびに　ともだちを　よんで、パーティーを
　　　　　します。まついさんも　きませんか。
まつい：　ありがとうございます。ぜひ。

Green:　　I've received some famous sake from Kyoto from a Japanese friend. On Sunday I'm
　　　　　getting some friends together to have a party. Won't you come, Mrs. Matsui?
Matsui:　Thank you. I'll be there.

VOCABULARY

よんで　　　　　（ーて form of よびます）
よびます　　　　call, invite

II. Ms. Nakamura asks Ms. Chan if she plans to attend Mrs. Green's party.

なかむら：あしたの　パーティーに　いきますか。
チャン：　いいえ、いきません。
なかむら：どうしてですか。
チャン：　ホンコンから　ははが　きますから。

Nakamura: Will you go to the party tomorrow?
Chan:　　No, I will not.
Nakamura: Why (not)?
Chan:　　Because my mother is visiting (*lit.*, "will come") from Hong Kong.

VOCABULARY

どうして　　　　why
に　　　　　　　（particle indicating a purpose）

Active Communication

Tell someone what you did yesterday. Then talk about your plans for the coming weekend.

MAKING A REQUEST

 TARGET DIALOGUE

TRACK 68

Ms. Chan has come to Sapporo to attend a sales meeting.

チャン：もしもし、チャンですが、おはようございます。

すずき：あ、チャンさん、おはようございます。すずきです。

チャン：いま　さっぽろに　います。すみませんが、メールであたら
　　　　しい　しょうひんの　カタログを　すぐ　おくってくださ
　　　　い。かいぎで　つかいますから。

すずき：はい、わかりました。

チャン：それから、サンプルの　しゃしんも　おくってください。

すずき：はい、すぐ　おくります。

チャン：じゃ、おねがいします。

■チャンさんは　さっぽろから　ほんしゃの　すずきさんに　でんわを
　しました。すずきさんは　チャンさんに　メールで　あたらしい
　しょうひんの　カタログと　サンプルの　しゃしんを　おくります。

　Chan: Hello, this is Chan. Good morning.
Suzuki: Oh, Ms. Chan. Good morning. This is Suzuki.
　Chan: I'm in Sapporo. I'm sorry to bother you, but could you please send me the new product
　　　　catalog by e-mail right away, because I'm going to use it during the meeting.
Suzuki: Yes, all right.
　Chan: Also, please send photographs of the samples.
Suzuki: Yes, I'll send them right away.
　Chan: Thank you. Bye now.

■ Ms. Chan made a phone call from Sapporo to Mr. Suzuki at the main office. Mr. Suzuki sends
　Ms. Chan the new product catalog and sample photographs by e-mail.

VOCABULARY

が	(particle; see Note 1 below)
しょうひん	product, merchandise
カタログ	catalog
すぐ	soon, right away
おくってください	please send
つかいます	use

それから	also, in addition
サンプル	sample
ほんしゃ	main/central/head office

NOTES

1. チャンですが...

   This が is a conjunction that joins two clauses. It expresses a kind of courteous hesitation and indicates that the phrase before it is merely a preliminary to the principal matter.

2. メールで

   This で indicates a means of telecommunication or post.

   ex. メールで　しりょうを　おくります。"I'll send the materials by e-mail."
   　　 たくはいびんで　にもつを　おくります。"I'll send the luggage by courier."

PRACTICE

WORD POWER

I. Verbs:

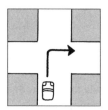

1. まがります

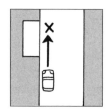

2. とめます

3. いいます

4. おしえます

5. もってきます

6. とどけます

7. まちます

VOCABULARY				
	まがります	turn	もってきます	bring
	とめます	stop, park	とどけます	deliver
	いいます	say	まちます	wait
170	おしえます	teach, show, tell		

II. Positions and directions:

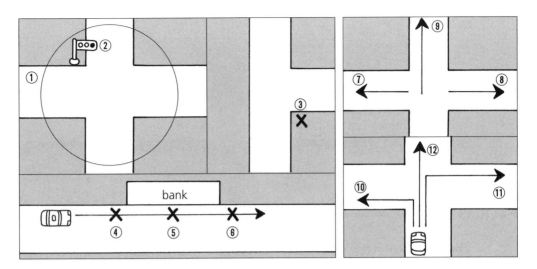

1. こうさてん
2. しんごう
3. かど
4. ぎんこうの　てまえ
5. ぎんこうの　まえ
6. ぎんこうの　さき

7. ひだり
8. みぎ
9. まっすぐ
10. こうさてんを　ひだりに　まがります
11. こうさてんを　みぎに　まがります
12. まっすぐ　いきます

III. Means of communication or delivery:

1. ファックス
2. こうくうびん
3. ふなびん
4. たくはいびん

VOCABULARY							
こうさてん	intersection	まえ	before	まっすぐ	straight ahead	こうくうびん	airmail
しんごう	traffic signal	さき	ahead	を	(particle indicating a point of passage)	ふなびん	surface mail
かど	corner	ひだり	left			たくはいびん	courier service
てまえ	just before	みぎ	right	ファックス	fax		

KEY SENTENCES

1. もう　いちど　いってください。
2. この　にもつを　たくはいびんで　おくってください。
3. つぎの　しんごうを　みぎに　まがってください。

1. Please say it again.
2. Please send this luggage by courier.
3. Turn right at the next traffic signal.

EXERCISES

 I. **Practice conjugating verbs.** Repeat the verbs below and memorize their －ます and －て forms.

	－ます FORM	－て FORM
say	いいます	いって
wait	まちます	まって
turn	まがります	まがって
take	とります	とって
lend	かします	かして
show	みせます	みせて
stop	とめます	とめて
tell	おしえます	おしえて
deliver	とどけます	とどけて
bring	もってきます	もってきて

 II. **Make a request.** Make up sentences as in the example.

ex. なまえを　かきます　→ なまえを　かいてください。

1. ちょっと　まちます　→ ....
2. しゃしんを　とります　→ ....
3. もう　いちど　いいます → ....
4. ペンを　かします　　→ ....
5. ピザを　とどけます　→ ....

III. Make up dialogues following the patterns of the examples. Substitute the underlined parts with the alternatives given, changing their forms as necessary.

A. *Make and accept a request.*

ex. A: すみません。あの　レストランの　なまえを　おしえてください。
B: はい。

1. A: .... (メールアドレス、かきます)

    B: ....

2. A: .... (メニュー、みせます)

    B: ....

3. A: .... (かいぎの　しりょう、もってきます)

    B: ....

B. *Make and accept a request to send something by a certain means.*

ex. A: スミスさんに　メールで　しりょうを　おくってください。
B: はい、わかりました。

1. A: ....
   　　　　　　　　　　(のぞみデパート、ファックス、しりょう)

    B: ....

2. A: ....
   　　　　　　　(ロンドンししゃの　ジョンソンさん、こうくうびん、カタログ)

    B: ....

3. A: ....
   　　　　　　　(よこはまししゃの　ひと、ゆうびん、このにもつ)

    B: ....

IV. *Give directions to a taxi driver.* Make up sentences following the patterns of the examples. Substitute the underlined parts with the alternatives given.

A. ex. つぎの　しんごうを　みぎに　まがってください。

1. .... (つぎの　こうさてん、ひだり)

2. .... (ふたつめの　かど、みぎ)

B. ex. ぎんこうの　まえで　とめてください。

1. .... (びょういんの　てまえ)

2. .... (ゆうびんきょくの　さき)

VOCABULARY			
メニュー	menu	ふたつめ	second
しりょう	data, information, material, documents, literature	～め	(suffix that attaches to a number and turns it into an ordinal number)
ゆうびん	mail, post		

173

V. **Give directions to a taxi driver.** Tell the driver to follow the route indicated by the arrows and to stop at the point indicated by the *X*.

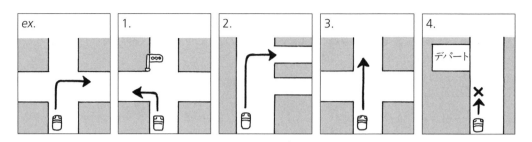

ex. つぎの　こうさてんを　みぎに　まがってください。

1. ....

2. ....

3. ....

4. ....

VI. Make up dialogues following the patterns of the examples. Substitute the underlined parts with the alternatives given.

A. **Request that a purchase be delivered.**

ex. スミス:　　すみません。うちに　この　<u>テレビ</u>を　とどけてください。
みせの　ひと: はい。
スミス:　　<u>あしたの　ごご</u>　とどけてください。
みせの　ひと: はい、わかりました。では、おなまえと　ごじゅうしょを
おねがいします。

1. スミス:　..　(パソコン)

みせの　ひと: ....

スミス:　..　(きんようびの　2じまでに)

みせの　ひと: ....

2. スミス:　..　(ソファー)

みせの　ひと: ....

スミス:　..　(にちようびに)

みせの　ひと: ....

VOCABULARY　ごじゅうしょ　　(another person's) address
　　　までに　　by (the time)

174

B. *Give directions to a taxi driver.*

ex. チャン:　　　とうきょうタワーの　ちかくまで　おねがいします。
うんてんしゅ: はい。
チャン:　　　(*after a while*) つぎの　しんごうを　ひだりに　まがってください。
うんてんしゅ: はい。
チャン:　　　あの　しろい　ビルの　まえで　とめてください。
うんてんしゅ: はい、わかりました。
うんてんしゅ: (*after a while*) ４，０００えんです。
チャン:　　　はい。
うんてんしゅ: ありがとうございました。
チャン:　　　どうも。

1. チャン: .... (ろっぽんぎこうさてん)

うんてんしゅ: ....

チャン: .... (みぎ)

うんてんしゅ: ....

チャン: .... (コンビニの　てまえ)

うんてんしゅ: ....

チャン: ....

うんてんしゅ: ....

チャン: ....

2. チャン: .... (しぶやえき)

うんてんしゅ: ....

チャン: .... (ひだり)

うんてんしゅ: ....

チャン: .... (マンションの　まえ)

うんてんしゅ: ....

うんてんしゅ: ....

チャン: ....

うんてんしゅ: ....

チャン: ....

VOCABULARY			
とうきょうタワー	Tokyo Tower	ろっぽんぎこうさてん	Roppongi Crossing
まで	to, as far as (particle)	しぶやえき	Shibuya Station
しろい	white	マンション	apartment (in a high-rise building), condominium
どうも	thanks (colloquial shortening of どうも ありがとう)		

175

VII. Listen to the CD and fill in the blanks based on the information you hear.

チャンさんは .... に .... で　かいぎの
しりょうを　おくります。

SHORT DIALOGUES

I. Ms. Chan phones room service because her room is cold.

ホテルの　ひと: はい、ルームサービスです。
チャン:　　　　すみません、２０１の　チャンですが、もうふを　もってき
　　　　　　　てください。
ホテルの　ひと: はい、わかりました。

hotel employee: Yes, this is room service.
Chan:　　　　This is Ms. Chan in room 201. Please bring me a blanket.
hotel employee: Yes, will do.

VOCABULARY

ルームサービス	room service
もうふ	blanket

II. Ms. Chan is checking out of the hotel.

チャン:　　　　　　すみません。
フロントの　ひと: はい、なんでしょうか。
チャン:　　　　　　この　にもつを　５じまで　あずかってください。
フロントの　ひと: はい、わかりました。

Chan:　　　　Excuse me.
front desk clerk: Yes, how may I help you?
Chan　　　　Please take care of this luggage for me till 5:00 (p.m.).
front desk clerk: Yes, will do.

VOCABULARY

なんでしょうか	how may I help you? (softer way of saying なんですか)
あずかってください	please take care of
あずかります	take care of, be in charge of

Active Communication

If you're in Japan, try giving a taxi driver instructions in Japanese. Or, alternatively, next time you purchase a large item, ask to have it delivered to your home.

SEEING A MUSEUM

From Western art to ukiyoe, and from cutting-edge technology to ghosts and goblins, Japan is abundant in museums of all sorts. Among the many museums in the Tokyo area are the Edo-Tokyo Museum, which showcases architecture and culture from an older Japan; the Ghibli Museum, which was designed and is under the supervision of the anime genius Hayao Miyazaki; and the National Museum of Emerging Science and Innovation, where visitors can play with robots or take a ride in a spaceship module. Pictured here is the Tokyo National Museum, which houses paintings, sculptures, and other pieces from all regions of Asia.

UNIT ■
9 GRAMMAR

The ーない Form

■ Classifications of Japanese verbs

As discussed briefly in Unit 8 Grammar (p. 160), Japanese verbs are divided into three classes based on their conjugations: Regular I, Regular II, and Irregular. The stems of Regular I verbs (the part just before the ーます ending) end with **-i**, and they change as the verbs are conjugated. The stems of Regular II verbs, on the other hand, end with either **-e** or **-i** but remain the same even as the verbs are conjugated. There are only two Irregular verbs: します and きます. For more on verb conjugation, see Appendix E, pp. 244–46.

■ How to form the ーない form

For Regular I verbs, the sound before ーます changes as shown in the chart below, and ーない is added to obtain the ーない form. For Regular II verbs, the rule is simpler: ーます comes off and ーない is added. The Irregular verbs have irregular conjugations.

REGULAR I					
buy	か**い**ます	か**わ**ない	write	か**き**ます	か**か**ない
return, go home	か**え**ります	か**え**らない	go	い**き**ます	い**か**ない
wait	ま**ち**ます	ま**た**ない	read	よ**み**ます	よ**ま**ない
play	あそ**び**ます	あそ**ば**ない	turn off	け**し**ます	け**さ**ない
REGULAR II					
eat	た**べ**ます	た**べ**ない	see	**み**ます	**み**ない
show	**みせ**ます	**みせ**ない	be	**い**ます	**い**ない
IRREGULAR					
come	**き**ます	**こ**ない	do	**し**ます	**し**ない

■ How the ーない form is used

ex. ここに　くるまを　とめないでください。 "Please do not park your car here."

A negative verb used in mid-sentence usually takes the ーない form rather than the ーません form it has at the end of a sentence. For now, however, just remember the following use of the ーない form: verb ーないでください ("please do not . . .").

GOING TO AN ART MUSEUM

TARGET DIALOGUE

TRACK 72

Ms. Nakamura recently heard that the Sakura Art Museum is open till 8 p.m. on Fridays.

なかむら：チャンさん、あした　しごとの　あとで　さくらびじゅつ
　　　　　かんに　いきませんか。

　チャン：いいですね。いきましょう。

なかむら：なんじに　かいしゃを　でましょうか。

　チャン：ここから　さくらびじゅつかんまで　どのぐらい　かかり
　　　　　ますか。

なかむら：４０ぷんぐらい　かかります。

　チャン：じゃ、６じに　かいしゃを　でませんか。

なかむら：ええ。じゃ、あした　６じに。

■ なかむらさんと　チャンさんは　あした　しごとの　あとで　さく
　らびじゅつかんに　いきます。６じに　かいしゃを　でます。かい
　しゃから　さくらびじゅつかんまで　４０ぷんぐらい　かかります。

Nakamura: Ms. Chan, how about going to the Sakura Art Museum tomorrow after work?
　　Chan: That would be nice. Let's go.
Nakamura: At what time should we leave the office?
　　Chan: How long does it take to get from here to the Sakura Art Museum?
Nakamura: It takes about forty minutes.
　　Chan: Well, how about leaving the office at 6:00?
Nakamura: OK. Tomorrow at 6:00, then.

■ Ms. Nakamura and Ms. Chan are going to the Sakura Art Museum tomorrow after work.
They will leave the office at 6:00. It takes about forty minutes to get from the company to the
Sakura Art Museum.

VOCABULARY

さくらびじゅつかん	Sakura Art Museum (fictitious museum name)
を	(particle; see Note 1 below)
でましょうか	shall we leave?
でます	leave
どのぐらい	how long
かかります	take (time)

NOTES

1. なんじに　かいしゃを　でましょうか。

The particle を here indicates a point of departure.

 ex. ６じに　かいしゃを　でます。"I'll leave the office at 6:00."

  しんじゅくえきで　でんしゃを　おります。"I'll get off the train at Shinjuku Station."

The particle に, on the other hand, indicates a point of arrival or a location toward which an action such as going, coming, entering, or boarding is directed.

 ex. ７じに　びじゅつかんに　つきます。"I'll arrive at the art museum at 7:00."

  とうきょうえきで　でんしゃに　のります。"I'll board the train at Tokyo Station."

PRACTICE

WORD POWER

I. Verbs:

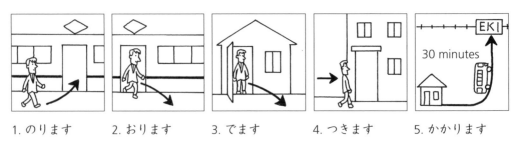

1. のります 2. おります 3. でます 4. つきます 5. かかります

II. Periods:

	MINUTES		HOURS	DAYS
5	ごふん（かん）	1	いちじかん	いちにち
10	じゅっぷん（かん）	2	にじかん	ふつか（かん）
15	じゅうごふん（かん）	3	さんじかん	みっか（かん）
20	にじゅっぷん（かん）	4	よじかん	よっか（かん）
25	にじゅうごふん（かん）	5	ごじかん	いつか（かん）
30	さんじゅっぷん（かん）	6	ろくじかん	むいか（かん）

NOTE: さんじかんはん, three and a half hours (see also Appendix J, pp. 249–50)

VOCABULARY	のります	get on (a vehicle), take	かかります	take (time)
	おります	get off (a vehicle)	～ふん／ぷん（かん）	minute(s)
	でます	go out, leave	～じかん	hour(s)
	つきます	arrive	～か／にち（かん）	day(s) (counter)

	WEEKS	MONTHS	YEARS
1	いっしゅうかん	いっかげつ（かん）	いちねん（かん）
2	にしゅうかん	にかげつ（かん）	にねん（かん）
3	さんしゅうかん	さんかげつ（かん）	さんねん（かん）
4	よんしゅうかん	よんかげつ（かん）	よねん（かん）
5	ごしゅうかん	ごかげつ（かん）	ごねん（かん）
6	ろくしゅうかん	ろっかげつ（かん）	ろくねん（かん）

NOTE: いちねんはん, one and a half years (see also Appendix J, pp. 249–50)

KEY SENTENCES

1. スミスさんは　とうきょうえきで　でんしゃに　のります。
2. スミスさんは　しんじゅくえきで　でんしゃを　おります。
3. ひこうきは　9じに　とうきょうを　でて、10じはんに　さっぽろに　つきます。
4. とうきょうから　にっこうまで　でんしゃで　1じかんはん　かかります。

1. Mr. Smith will get on the train at Tokyo Station.
2. Mr. Smith will get off the train at Shinjuku Station.
3. The plane leaves Tokyo at 9:00 and arrives in Sapporo at 10:30.
4. It takes an hour and a half to go by train from Tokyo to Nikko.

EXERCISES

I. *Practice conjugating verbs.* Repeat the verbs below and memorize their －て forms.

	－ます FORM	－て FORM
get on, take	のります	のって
get off	おります	おりて
go out, leave	でます	でて
arrive	つきます	ついて
take (time)	かかります	かかって
walk	あるきます	あるいて

VOCABULARY

～しゅうかん	week(s)
～かげつ	month(s) (counter)
～ねん（かん）	year(s)
あるきます	walk

181

II. Make up dialogues following the patterns of the examples. Substitute the underlined parts with the alternatives given.

A. *State where someone will get on and off a means of public transportation.*

ex. スミスさんは　とうきょうえきで　<u>でんしゃ</u>に　のります。しんじゅくえきで　<u>でんしゃ</u>を　おります。

1. .... （ちかてつ）

2. .... （タクシー）

3. .... （バス）

B. *State a person's departure and arrival time.*

ex. たかはしさんは　<u>7じ</u>に　<u>うち</u>を　でました。<u>8じ</u>に　<u>かいしゃ</u>に　つきました。

1. .... （10じに　ホテル、11じに　くうこう）

2. .... （あさ　とうきょう、1じごろ　きょうと）

III. Make up dialogues following the patterns of the examples. Substitute the underlined words with the words suggested by the illustrations.

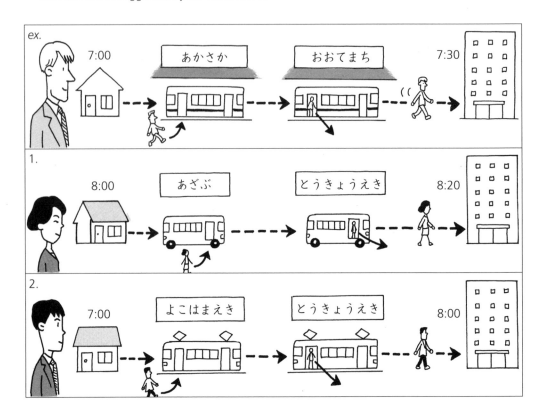

VOCABULARY

どうやって	how, in what way
あかさか	Akasaka (district in Tokyo)
おおてまち	Otemachi (district in Tokyo)
182　あざぶ	Azabu (district in Tokyo)

A. *Ask and give the route by which one commutes to work.*

ex. たかはし: スミスさんは　どうやって　かいしゃに　いきますか。
　　スミス: <u>あかさかで</u>　<u>ちかてつに</u>　のって、<u>おおてまち</u>で　おります。
　　　　　　<u>おおてまち</u>から　かいしゃまで　あるきます。

1. たかはし: チャンさんは ....

　　チャン: ....

2. たかはし: すずきさんは ....

　　すずき: ....

B. *Ask and answer what time one leaves home every day and what time one arrives at the office.*

ex. たかはし: まいにち　なんじに　うちを　でますか。
　　スミス: <u>7じに</u>　でます。
　　たかはし: なんじに　かいしゃに　つきますか。
　　スミス: <u>7じはんに</u>　つきます。

1. たかはし: ....

　　チャン: ....

　　たかはし: ....

　　チャン: ....

2. たかはし: ....

　　すずき: ....

　　たかはし: ....

　　すずき: ....

IV. *State how long one's commute to work is.* Make up sentences following the pattern of the example. Substitute the underlined words with the alternatives given.

ex. うちから　かいしゃまで　<u>ちかてつで</u>　<u>40ぷん</u>　かかります。

1. .... (でんしゃ、1じかん)

2. .... (バス、45ふん)

V. *Ask and answer how long it takes to get somewhere.* Make up dialogues following the pattern of the example. Substitute the underlined words with the words suggested by the illustrations.

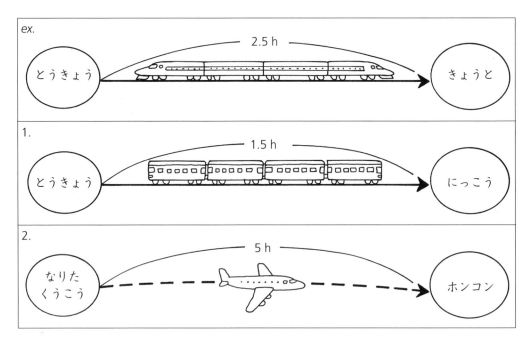

ex. スミス：　とうきょうから　きょうとまで　どのぐらい　かかりますか。
　　なかむら：<u>しんかんせん</u>で　<u>２じかんはん</u>　かかります。

1.　スミス：　...

　　なかむら：...

2.　なかむら：...

　　チャン：　...

VI. *Ask and answer how long one stayed in a certain place.* Make up dialogues following the pattern of the example. Substitute the underlined words with the alternatives given.

ex. スミス：　たかはしさんは　どのぐらい　<u>ニューヨーク</u>に　いましたか。
　　たかはし：<u>４か</u>　いました。

1.　スミス：　..　（ホンコン）

　　たかはし：..　（２しゅうかん）

2.　スミス：　..　（さっぽろ）

　　たかはし：..　（５かげつ）

3.　スミス：　..　（サンフランシスコ）

　　たかはし：..　（３ねん）

VII. Make up dialogues following the patterns of the examples. Substitute the underlined words with the alternatives given.

A. *Talk about a summer vacation plan.*

ex. すずき:　なつやすみに　どこに　いきますか。
　　なかむら:　<u>パリに</u>　いって、<u>びじゅつかん</u>を　みます。
　　すずき:　そうですか。どのぐらい　<u>パリ</u>に　いますか。
　　なかむら:　<u>1しゅうかん</u>　います。
　　すずき:　いいですね。

1.　すずき:　...
　　なかむら:　..　（ニューヨーク、ミュージカル）
　　すずき:　...　（ニューヨーク）
　　なかむら:　...　（6か）
　　すずき:　...

2.　すずき:　...
　　なかむら:　..　（きょうと、おてら）
　　すずき:　...　（きょうと）
　　なかむら:　...　（5か）
　　すずき:　...

B. *Invite someone to an event and tell him or her what the departure time will be.*

ex. かとう:　あした　11じから　<u>とうきょうホテル</u>で　おかしの　フェアが
　　　　あります。チャンさんも　いっしょに　いきませんか。
　　チャン:　はい。なんじに　かいしゃを　でますか。
　　かとう:　<u>とうきょうホテル</u>まで　<u>1じかん</u>ぐらい　かかりますから、<u>10じ</u>に
　　　　でます。
　　チャン:　わかりました。

1.　かとう:　...　（おだいば）
　　チャン:　...
　　かとう:　...　（おだいば、30ぷん、10じはん）
　　チャン:　...

2.　かとう:　...　（よこはま）
　　チャン:　...
　　かとう:　...　（よこはま、1じかんはん、9じはん）
　　チャン:　...

VOCABULARY	パリ	Paris
	ミュージカル	musical
	フェア	fair

VIII. **Talk about a flight itinerary.** Complete the following dialogue using the information in the illustrations as a guide.

1. チャン: ....

2. りょこうがいしゃの　ひと: ....

3. チャン: ....

4. りょこうがいしゃの　ひと: ....

5. チャン: ....

IX. Listen to the CD and fill in the blanks based on the information you hear.

TRACK
74

かいしゃから　のぞみデパートまで .... で .... ぐらい
かかります。

ホノルル　　　　　Honolulu
りょこうがいしゃ　travel agency

SHORT DIALOGUE

Mr. Green wants to go to Kamakura.

グリーン: すみません、この　でんしゃは　かまくらに　いきますか。
えきいん: いいえ、いきません。よこすかせんに　のってください。
グリーン: よこ—... なんですか。
えきいん: よこすかせんです。ちか　１かいの　１ばんせんですよ。
グリーン: ありがとうございます。

Green:	Excuse me. Does this train go to Kamakura?
station employee:	No, it doesn't. Please take the Yokosuka Line.
Green:	Yoko— . . . what is that?
station employee:	The Yokosuka Line. It's platform no. 1 on the first underground floor.
Green:	Thank you.

VOCABULARY

えきいん	Station employee
よこすかせん	Yokosuka Line
～せん	(train) line
１ばんせん	platform number one
～ばんせん	platform number

NOTES

1. よこ—...なんですか。
When you only hear one part of a word and want to ask someone to repeat it, say なんですか after the part of the word that you understood.

Active Communication

If you're in Japan, ask a station employee the route and time required to get to a place you want to go to.

AT AN ART MUSEUM

TARGET DIALOGUE

Ms. Chan and Ms. Nakamura are looking at woodblock prints at the Sakura Art Museum. The two of them ask a museum employee some questions.

なかむら：きれいな　うきよえですね。

チャン：ほんとうに　きれいですね。

なかむら：すみません。うきよえの

しゃしんを　とっても　いいですか。

びじゅつかんの　ひと：はい。

なかむら：あ、ここに　えいごの　パンフレットが　あり

ますよ。

チャン：そうですね。すみません。この　パンフレットを

もらってもいいですか。

びじゅつかんの　ひと：はい、どうぞ。

■チャンさんは　さくらびじゅつかんで　えいごの　パンフレットを
もらいました。

Ukiyoe

Nakamura: These are lovely ukiyoe prints, aren't they?
Chan: They really are lovely, aren't they?
Nakamura: Excuse me. Is it all right to take pictures of the ukiyoe prints?
museum employee: Yes.
Nakamura: Oh, here's an English-language pamphlet.
Chan: You're right. Excuse me, is it all right to take this pamphlet?
museum employee: Sure, go ahead.

■ Ms. Chan received an English-language pamphlet.

VOCABULARY

うきよえ	ukiyoe (woodblock print)
とっても　いいですか	may I take (a photograph)?
パンフレット	pamphlet, brochure

NOTES

1. しゃしんを　とっても　いいですか。
Asking permission to do something is done using the following sentence construction: verb ーて form ＋も　いいですか。To grant permission, say はい、どうぞ ("yes, please [do]"), and to refuse permission, say すみませんが、ちょっと . . . ("I'm sorry, but that would be a little [difficult] . . .").

PRACTICE

WORD POWER

I. Verbs:

1. つかいます　　　2.（たばこを）すいます 3. はいります

II. Things available at the information counter of a museum:

1. えはがき　　2. イヤホーンガイド　　3. パンフレット　　4. カタログ

VOCABULARY					
つかいます	use	えはがき	(picture) postcard	パンフレット	pamphlet
たばこを　すいます	smoke (a cigarette)	イヤホーンガイド	recorded guide	カタログ	catalog
たばこ	cigarette	イヤホーン	earphones, headphones		
はいります	enter	ガイド	guide		189

KEY SENTENCES

1. この　えの　しゃしんを　とっても　いいですか。
2. この　ペンを　つかっても　いいですか。

1. Is it all right to take a photograph of this picture?
2. Is it all right to use this pen?

EXERCISES

 I. *Practice conjugating verbs.* Repeat the verbs below and memorize their ーて forms.

	ーます FORM	ーて FORM
use	つかいます	つかって
smoke	すいます	すって
enter	はいります	はいって
rest	やすみます	やすんで

 II. *Ask permission to do something.* Change the sentences below as in the example.

ex. この　カタログを　もらいます。
　　→ この　カタログを　もらっても　いいですか。

1. まどを　あけます。

　→

2. この　イヤホーンガイドを　つかいます。

　→

3. この　えの　しゃしんを　とります。

　→

4. ここで　たばこを　すいます。

　→ ....

5. あした　やすみます。

　→ ....

III. ***Ask and grant permission to do something.*** Make up dialogues following the pattern of the example and based on the information in the illustrations.

ex. すずき: この　しりょうの　コピーを　しても　いいですか。
かとう: はい、どうぞ。

1. すずき: ....

   かとう: ....

2. すずき: ....

   かとう: ....

3. すずき: ....

   かとう: ....

VOCABULARY　　おきゃくさん　　　customer, client (polite form of きゃく)

IV. *Ask and refuse permission to do something.* Make up dialogues following the pattern of the example and based on the information in the illustrations.

ex. スミス:　　　　　　ここで　おかしを　たべても　いいですか。
　おてらの　ひと: すみませんが、ちょっと...。

1.　スミス:　　　　　...

　　おてらの　ひと:...

2.　スミス:　　　　　...

　　おてらの　ひと:...

3.　スミス:　　　　　...

　　おてらの　ひと:...

 V. *Get and give assistance at a store.* Make up dialogues following the pattern of the example. Substitute the underlined words with the words in parentheses.

ex. スミス:　　　　　すみません、この　<u>テレビ</u>の　<u>カタログ</u>が　ありますか。
　みせの　ひと: はい、これです。
　スミス:　　　　　もらっても　いいですか。
　みせの　ひと: はい、どうぞ。

1.　スミス:　　　　　.. (りょかん、パンフレット)

　　みせの　ひと:...

　　スミス:　　　　　...

　　みせの　ひと:...

2. スミス: .... （レストラン、カード）

みせの　ひと: ....

スミス: ....

みせの　ひと: ....

 VI. ***Ask for permission to borrow a pen.*** Look at the illustrations and make up a dialogue that reflects what is happening.

1. みせの　ひと: ....

2. スミス: ....

3. スミス: ....

4. みせの　ひと: ....

5. スミス: ....

 VII. Listen to the CD and fill in the blanks based on the information you hear.

スミスさんは .... から .... を　つかいます。

SHORT DIALOGUES

I. Mr. Green has gone to the hospital to visit a sick friend. He first goes to the reception desk in the visiting area.

うけつけ: ごじゅうしょと　おなまえを　かいてください。
グリーン: ローマじで　かいても　いいですか。
うけつけ: はい。

receptionist: Please write your address and your name.
Green:　　　 May I write in Roman letters?
receptionist: Yes.

VOCABULARY

ローマじ　　　　　　romanized Japanese

II. Mr. Green is visiting a friend.

グリーン: ここに　にもつを　おいても　いいですか。
ともだち: はい、どうぞ。
グリーン: (after chatting for a while) すみません。おてあらいを　つかっても
　　　　　 いいですか。
ともだち: はい、どうぞ。

Green:　　 May I put my luggage here?
friend:　　 Yes, please do.
Green:　　 Excuse me. May I use your bathroom?
friend:　　 Yes, go right ahead.

VOCABULARY

おいて　　　　　　(－て form of おきます)
おきます　　　put

Active Communication

If you're in Japan, go to various stores or public institutions and ask permission to do something—to take a photograph, for example.

BEING WARNED OR ADVISED

TARGET DIALOGUE

Ms. Chan and Ms. Nakamura are looking at a picture of Mt. Fuji in the art museum.

チャン：この　ふじさんの　えは　とても　きれいですね。

なかむら：そうですね。

チャン：なかむらさん、この　えの　まえで　わたしの
しゃしんを　とってください。

なかむら：はい、わかりました。とりますよ。(takes a flash
picture)

びじゅつかんの　ひと：すみません、ここで　フラッシュを　つかわな
いでください。

なかむら：すみません、わかりました。

■ なかむらさんは　ふじさんの　えの　まえで　チャンさんの　しゃ
しんを　とりました。

        Chan: This picture of Mt. Fuji is really lovely, isn't it?
Nakamura: Yes, it is.
        Chan: Ms. Nakamura, please take a photograph of me in front of this picture.
Nakamura: Okay, right. Are you ready?
museum employee: Excuse me. Please don't use a flash here.
Nakamura: I'm sorry, I understand.

■ Ms. Nakamura took a photograph of Ms. Chan in front of a picture of Mt. Fuji.

VOCABULARY

ふじさん	Mt. Fuji
とりますよ	(said when you are about to take someone's photo)
フラッシュ	flash
つかわないでください	please don't use

NOTES

1. ここで　フラッシュを　つかわないでください。

The "please do not . . ." construction is formed as follows: verb －ない + で + ください. This expression is often used by managers or officials when asking someone to refrain from doing something, although it can also be used by restaurant customers when requesting that a specific ingredient not be used.

   ex. さとうを　いれないでください。 "Please don't put any sugar in it."

To make this rather strong expression sound softer, give the reason why you would like the other person to refrain from doing what they are about to do.

　　ex. ここに　くるまを　とめないでください。でぐちですから。

　　　"Please do not park your car here. (This) is an exit."

PRACTICE

WORD POWER

I. The −ない form:

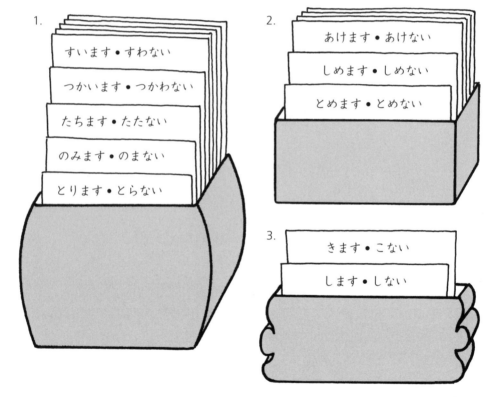

1.

すいます・すわない

つかいます・つかわない

たちます・たたない

のみます・のまない

とります・とらない

2.

あけます・あけない

しめます・しめない

とめます・とめない

3.

きます・こない

します・しない

II. Restrictions:

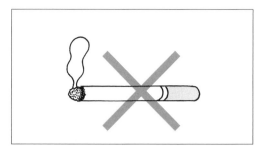

1. きんえん

2. ちゅうしゃきんし

KEY SENTENCES

1. ここは　いりぐちですから、くるまを　とめないでください。
2. すしに　わさびを　いれないでください。

1. This is the entrance, so please don't park your car here.
2. Please don't put any wasabi in the sushi.

EXERCISES

I. **Practice conjugating verbs.** Repeat the verbs below and memorize their －ない forms.

REGULAR I		REGULAR II		IRREGULAR	
－ます FORM	－ない FORM	－ます FORM	－ない FORM	－ます FORM	－ない FORM
あいます	あわない	みせます	みせない	きます	こない
かきます	かかない	いれます	いれない	します	しない
けします	けさない	たべます	たべない		
たちます	たたない	あけます	あけない		
のみます	のまない	しめます	しめない		
かえります	かえらない	みます	みない		

VOCABULARY				
きんえん	no smoking, nonsmoking		いれます	put in, add
ちゅうしゃきんし	no parking			
わさび	wasabi, Japanese (green) horseradish			

197

II. **Practice the** －ない **form.** Change the following verbs to their －ない forms.

ex. あいます → あわない

1. あけます → ....

2. しめます → ....

3. とります → ....

4. かいます → ....

5. よみます → ....

6. ききます → ....

III. **Forbid someone to do something.** Look at the illustrations and make up sentences as in the example.

ex. まどを　あけます　→ まどを　あけないでください。

1. しゃしんを　とります → ....

2. ドアを　しめます　　 → ....

3. でんきを　けします　 → ....

4. くるまを　とめます　 → ....

IV. **Forbid someone to do something and give a reason.** Make up sentences following the pattern of the example. Substitute the underlined part with the alternatives given.

ex. ここは　いりぐちですから、くるまを　とめないでください。

1. .... (でぐちです)

2. .... (みせの　まえです)

3. .... (ちゅうしゃきんしです)

V. Make up dialogues following the patterns of the examples. Substitute the underlined part(s) with the alternatives given.

A. *Ask someone to refrain from smoking.*

ex. チャン:　　　　すみません、<u>この　でんしゃは　きんえんですから</u>、たばこを　すわないでください。
おとこの　ひと: はい、わかりました。すみません。

1. チャン:　　　　... (この　レストランは　きんえんです)

   おとこの　ひと: ....

2. チャン:　　　　... (あかちゃんが　います)

   おとこの　ひと: ....

B. *Order something at a restaurant and request that a specific ingredient not be used.*

ex. チャン:　　　　すみません、<u>ハンバーガー</u>を　おねがいします。
みせの　ひと: はい。
チャン:　　　　すみませんが、<u>ケチャップ</u>を　いれないでください。
みせの　ひと: はい、わかりました。

1. チャン:　　　　... (すし)

   みせの　ひと: ....

   チャン:　　　　... (わさび)

   みせの　ひと: ....

2. チャン:　　　　... (サンドイッチ)

   みせの　ひと: ....

   チャン:　　　　... (マヨネーズ)

   みせの　ひと: ....

3. チャン:　　　　... (アイスコーヒー)

   みせの　ひと: ....

   チャン:　　　　... (さとう)

   みせの　ひと: ....

 VI. Listen to the CD and fill in the blanks based on the information you hear.

ごごから .... で .... が　あります。

VOCABULARY			
あかちゃん	baby	マヨネーズ	mayonnaise
ハンバーガー	hamburger	アイスコーヒー	iced coffee
ケチャップ	ketchup	さとう	sugar

SHORT DIALOGUES

I. Mr. Smith got drunk at the Sasakis' house and spilled red wine on their clean carpet. The next day, he apologizes at the office.

スミス: ささきさん、きのうは　すみませんでした。
ささき: いいえ、どうぞ　きに　しないでください。

Smith:　Ms. Sasaki, I'm so sorry about yesterday.
Sasaki:　No, please don't let it bother you.

VOCABULARY

きに　しないでください　　　don't worry about it; don't let it bother you
　きに　します　　　　　　　worry (about), be bothered (by)

II. Mr. Smith goes to the clinic with a stomachache.

いしゃ: きょうは　おさけを　のまないでください。
スミス: はい、わかりました。

Doctor: Don't drink any alcohol today.
Smith:　Ok, I understand.

VOCABULARY

いしゃ　　　　　　　　　　　(medical) doctor

Active Communication

What would you say in these situations?

1. A stranger is trying to park in front of your house.

2. The person next to you lights up a cigarette in a nonsmoking car on the shinkansen.

Quiz 4 (Units 8–9)

I Fill in the blank(s) in each sentence with the appropriate particle. Where a particle is not needed, write in an *X*.

1. スミスさんは かいぎの まえ（　　　　）しりょうを よみました。
2. ふたつめの かど（　　　　）ひだり（　　　　）まがってください。
3. デパートの さき（　　　　）とめてください。
4. たかはしさんは しぶや（　　　　）でんしゃ（　　　　）おりて、バス（　　　　）のります。
5. しぶや（　　　　）あさくさ（　　　　）ちかてつ（　　　　）４０ぷん かかります。
6. たかはしさんは ホンコン（　　　　）１しゅうかん（　　　　）いました。
7. しんかんせんは ８じ（　　　　）とうきょうえき（　　　　）でて、１０じ（　　　　）きょうとえき（　　　　）つきます。
8. ここ（　　　　）ちゅうしゃきんしです（　　　　）、くるま（　　　　）とめないで ください。

II Complete each question by filling in the blank with the appropriate word.

1. しゅうまつに（　　　　）を しましたか。
   ぎんざにいって、かいものを しました。
2. （　　　　）おおさかししゃに でんわを しましたか。
   かいぎの まえに しました。
3. （　　　　）かいしゃに いきますか。
   しぶやで ちかてつに のって、ぎんざで おります。ぎんざから かいしゃ まで １０ぷん あるきます。
4. とうきょうから おおさかまで ひこうきで（　　　　）かかりますか。
   １じかんぐらい かかります。

III Complete the table by writing in the appropriate forms of the verbs.

	ーます FORM	ーて FORM	ーない FORM
ex.	つかいます	つかって	つかわない
1.	かきます	かいて	
2.		けして	けさない
3.	のみます		のまない
4.	とります	とって	
5.	しめます		しめない
6.		あけて	あけない
7.	みます		みない
8.	きます	きて	
9.		して	しない

IV Complete the sentences by filling in the blank(s) with the appropriate form of the word(s) given at the end.

1. スミスさんは　きのう　しごとの　あとで　ともだちと　えいがを(　　　)、
   ばんごはんを　たべました。(みます)

2. スミスさんは　きのう　はなを(　　　)、うちに　かえりました。(かいます)

3. おいしい　すしやを(　　　　　　　　)ください。(おしえます)

4. つぎの　こうさてんを　みぎに(　　　)、まっすぐ(　　　)ください。(ま
   がります、いきます)

5. この　カタログを(　　　)も　いいですか。(もらいます)

6. ここは　でぐちですから、くるまを(　　　　　　　)ください。(とめます)

AT THE OFFICE

Walking into a traditional Japanese company, one will notice the absence of high partitions and cubicles: most Japanese offices are open, with desks facing one another so that employees can readily communicate. This arrangement is efficient because it saves on space; and in a country where land prices can be astronomical, such efficiency is important. Another feature of such offices is the conspicuous hierarchy: in one desk with a view of all others sits the office manager, and in front of him the division chief, then the section chief, and so on down to the bottom. Recently, however, Japanese companies have been modifying the traditional layout to make their offices more functional for the people who work in them, or more aesthetically pleasing to visitors.

10 GRAMMAR

Present Progressive and Habitual Actions

person は verb ー て います

> *ex.* グレイさんは　いま　かいぎしつで　レポートを　よんでいます。
> "Mr. Grey is reading a report in the meeting room now."
> グレイさんは　まいしゅう　どようびに　テニスを　しています。
> "Mr. Grey plays tennis every Saturday."

A verb in the ー て form followed by います expresses a present-progressive action ("is doing"), as in the first example above, or, when accompanied by an adverb like まいしゅう ("every week") or まいにち ("every day"), a habitual action, as in the second example.

Current States

person は verb ー て います

> *ex.* グレイさんは　よこはまに　すんでいます。"Mr. Grey lives in Yokohama."
> グレイさんは　ぎんこうに　つとめています。"Mr. Grey is employed at a bank."
> あのみせで　テレビを　うっています。"At that store, (they) sell TVs."
> グレイさんは　よしださんの　じゅうしょを　しっています。
> "Mr. Grey knows Mr. Yoshida's address."

The ー ています form can also express a current state when the verb is one of those used in the examples above—すみます, つとめます, うります, or しります.
NOTE: The verb しります ("know"), from which しっています derives, is usually used in the ー て form followed by います. But the form this verb takes when used in response to the question しっていますか ("do you know?") varies, and in this way it is unlike other verbs.

> *ex.* A*a*: はい、　しっています。"Yes, (I) know."
> A*n*: いいえ、　しりません。"No, (I) don't know."

BUSY AT THE MOMENT

TARGET DIALOGUE

Mr. Smith is looking for Ms. Chan. He enters the sales department office and asks Mr. Suzuki where she is.

スミス：すみません。チャンさんは　いますか。

すずき：いいえ。いま　3がいの　かいぎしつに　います。

スミス：そうですか。

すずき：いま、のぞみデパートの　たかはしさんに　あたらしい
　　　　しょうひんの　せつめいを　しています。

スミス：そうですか。わかりました。どうも。

■スミスさんは　えいぎょうぶに　いきましたが、チャンさんは
　いませんでした。

Smith: Excuse me. Is Ms. Chan here?
Suzuki: No, she's in the conference room on the third floor.
Smith: Is that so?
Suzuki: Yes, she's explaining new products to Mr. Takahashi of Nozomi Department Store.
Smith: Is that so? I see. Thanks.

■ Mr. Smith went to the sales department office (to look for Ms. Chan), but Ms. Chan was not there.

VOCABULARY

せつめいを　しています	is/are explaining
せつめいを　します	explain
えいぎょうぶ	sales department (office)
が	but (see Note 1 below)

NOTES

1. スミスさんは　えいぎょうぶに　いきましたが、チャンさんは　いませんでした。
   This が is a kind of conjunction that joins two clauses. It can be translated as "but."

PRACTICE

WORD POWER

I. Verbs:

1. はなしを　します　　2. せつめいを　します　　3. そうじを　します　　4. つくります

II. Parts of a building:

1. ロビー　　　2. エレベーター　　　3. エスカレーター　　　4. かいだん

VOCABULARY			
はなしを　します	talk	ロビー	lobby
せつめいを　します	explain	エレベーター	elevator
そうじを　します	clean	エスカレーター	escalator
つくります	make	かいだん	stairs

KEY SENTENCES

1. スミスさんは　いま　しんぶんを　よんでいます。
2. もう　かいぎの　レポートを　かきましたか。
3. スミスさんは　たかはしさんの　うちに　いきましたが、たかはしさん　は　うちに　いませんでした。

1. Mr. Smith is reading a newspaper now.
2. Have you already written the report about the meeting?
3. Mr. Smith went to Mr. Takahashi's house, but Mr. Takahashi was not at home.

EXERCISES

I. *Practice conjugating verbs.* Repeat the verbs below and memorize their ーています forms, affirmative and negative.

	ーます FORM	ーています FORM	
		aff.	*neg.*
talk	はなしを　します	はなしを　しています	はなしを　していません
explain	せつめいを　します	せつめいを　しています	せつめいを　していません
clean	そうじを　します	そうじを　しています	そうじを　していません
make	つくります	つくっています	つくっていません

II. *State what someone is doing now.* Change the following sentences as in the example.

ex. スミスさんは　しんぶんを　よみます。
→ スミスさんは　しんぶんを　よんでいます。

1. スミスさんは　そうじを　します。

   → ....

2. スミスさんは　てがみを　かきます。

   → ....

3. スミスさんは　コピーを　します。

   → ....

4. スミスさんは　たかはしさんと　はなしを　します。

   → ....

5. スミスさんは　りょうりを　つくります。

   → ....

III. Make up dialogues following the patterns of the examples and based on the situations depicted in the illustrations.

A. *Ask and answer what one is doing now.*

ex. 1. A: グリーンさんは　いま　なにを　していますか。
B: でんわを　しています。

1. A: ....

B: ....

2. A: ....

B: ....

3. A: ....

B: ....

4. A: ....

B: ....

5. A: ....

B: ....

6. A: ....

B: ....

B. *Answer what one is doing now in response to a question.*

 ex. 2. A: かとうさんは　いま　レポートを　かいていますか。
    B: いいえ、かいぎしつで　せつめいを　しています。

 7. A: ささきさんは　いま　かいぎを　していますか。

   B: ....

 8. A: なかむらさんは　いま　でんわを　していますか。

   B: ....

 9. A: チャンさんは　いま　ささきさんと　はなしを　していますか。

   B: ....

IV. *Ask and answer whether one has completed an action.* Make up dialogues following the pattern of the example. Substitute the underlined words with the alternatives given. Be sure to use the same grammatical form as in the example.

 ex. A: もう　<u>ひるごはん</u>を　<u>たべました</u>か。
   B: はい、<u>たべました</u>。

 1. A: .... (りょこうの　しゃしん、みます)
   B: .... (みます)

 2. A: .... (かいぎの　レポート、かきます)
   B: .... (かきます)

V. *Connect two clauses.* Link each pair of sentences as in the example.

 ex. わたしは　たかはしさんの　うちに　いきました。たかはしさんは　うち
   に　いませんでした。
   →　わたしは　たかはしさんの　うちに　いきましたが、たかはしさんは
    うちに　いませんでした。

 1. わたしは　えいぎょうぶの　チャンさんに　でんわを　しました。チャンさんは
   いませんでした。

   →　...

 2. わたしは　きのう　デパートに　いきました。デパートは　やすみでした。

   →　...

VI. Make up dialogues following the patterns of the examples. Substitute the underlined parts with the alternatives given. Be sure to use the same grammatical forms as in the examples.

A. *Explain that one is in the midst of something.*

    ex. かとう: もう　<u>コピー</u>を　<u>しました</u>か。
        すずき: すみません、いま　<u>しています</u>から、ちょっと　まってください。
        かとう: はい。

   1.　かとう: .... (メール、よみます)

      すずき: .... (よみます)

      かとう: ....

   2.　かとう: ....

                                                    (かいぎの　しりょう、つくります)

      すずき: .... (つくります)

      かとう: ....

B. *Respond to a cell phone call by suggesting it is inconvenient or inappropriate to talk at the moment.*

    ex. Mr. Smith gets a call on his cell phone from his friend Mr. Yamada. Since he is in a meeting, he answers quietly.

        やまだ: もしもし、スミスさんですか。
        スミス: はい。
        やまだ: やまだです。
        スミス: やまださん、すみませんが、いま　<u>かいぎを　しています</u>。
        やまだ: じゃ、また　あとで　でんわを　します。
        スミス: おねがいします。

   1.　やまだ: ....

      スミス: ....

      やまだ: ....

      スミス: ....

                                      (おきゃくさんと　はなしを　します)

      やまだ: ....

      スミス: ....

VOCABULARY　　また　あとで　　　see you later; talk to you later

2. やまだ: ....

　スミス: ....

　やまだ: ....

　スミス : ....

（にほんごの　がっこうで　べんきょうを　します）

　やまだ: ....

　スミス: ....

VII. Listen to the CD and choose the correct answer to the question asked.

a)  b)  c)

SHORT DIALOGUES

I. Ms. Sasaki is waiting for Ms. Chan's report on her business trip to Hokkaido.

さP さき: チャンさん、レポートは　もう　かきましたか。
チャン: すみません、まだです。もうすこし　まってください。

Sasaki:　Ms. Chan, have you already written the report?
Chan:　I'm sorry. Not yet. Please wait a bit more.

VOCABULARY

まだ	not yet
もうすこし	a little more

II. Mr. Suzuki is looking for an empty room.

すずき:　すみません。３がいの　かいぎしつを　つかっても　いいですか。
なかむら:ええ。いま　だれも　つかっていませんから、どうぞ。

Suzuki:　Excuse me. Is it all right to use the conference room on the third floor?
Nakamura: Yes, since no one is using it now. Go right ahead.

NOTES

1. レポートは...
Although レポート ("report") is the object, Ms. Sasaki is singling it out as a topic for discussion, so は replaces the object marker を.

2. レポートは　もう　かきましたか。

It should be noted that the verb ending ーました, when used with もう ("already"), expresses completion in addition to indicating the past tense.

Active
Communication

Imagine that you are in a meeting or involved in some activity that you can't break away from, and a call comes in on your cell phone. Explain in Japanese to the person on the other end of the line why it is inconvenient for you to talk at the moment.

RESPONDING TO AN INQUIRY

 TARGET DIALOGUE

A customer from Nagoya has phoned to inquire about ABC Foods' new products.

チャン：はい、ＡＢＣフーズでございます。

きゃく：すみません、ＡＢＣフーズの　あたらしい　チョコレートは
　　　　どこで　うっていますか。

チャン：「ショコラショコラ」ですか。

きゃく：ええ、そうです。

チャン：とうきょうの　スーパーと　コンビニで　うっています。

きゃく：わたしは　なごやに　すんでいます。なごやでも　うってい
　　　　ますか。

チャン：いいえ、なごやでは　うっていません。もうしわけございま
　　　　せん。

きゃく：そうですか。わかりました。

チャン：たいへん　もうしわけございません。

■ＡＢＣフーズの　「ショコラショコラ」は　とうきょうの　スーパー
　と　コンビニで　うっています。

　　Chan: Yes, this is ABC Foods.
customer: Excuse me, about ABC Foods' new chocolates—where do you sell them?
　　Chan: Do you mean "Chocolat-Chocolat"?
customer: Yes, that's right.
　　Chan: We sell them at supermarkets and convenience stores in Tokyo.
customer: I live in Nagoya. Do you sell them in Nagoya?
　　Chan: No, we do not sell them in Nagoya. I'm sorry to have to tell you this.
customer: Is that so? I see.
　　Chan: I'm really very sorry.

■ As for Chocolat-Chocolat, ABC Foods sells it in supermarkets and convenience stores in Tokyo.

VOCABULARY

うっています	sell
うります	sell
ショコラショコラ	Chocolat-Chocolat (fictitious product name)
なごや	Nagoya (city in central Japan)

すんでいます	live
すみます	live
もうしわけございません	I'm sorry to have to tell you this (politer way of saying すみません)
たいへん	very much, extremely (politer way of saying とても)

NOTES

1. ＡＢＣフーズの　あたらしい　チョコレートは　どこで　うっていますか。
   Although チョコレート is the object, here it is being singled out as the topic and therefore takes the particle は instead of を.

2. わたしは　なごやに　すんでいます。
   The particle に is used to indicate the place where one lives or is employed.
   ex. やまださんは　ぎんこうに　つとめています。 "Ms. Yamada is employed at a bank."

3. なごやでも　うっていますか。
   いいえ、なごやでは　うっていません。
   Note the positions of the particles で and も here. In Ms. Chan's reply, she uses the topic marker は after で to show that "Nagoya" is the topic: "As for Nagoya, (Chocolat-Chocolat) is not sold there." Note that while one particle may normally follow another, as do も and は after で in the sentences above, も and は never follow the particles が or を but simply take their place. Similarly, も and は are never used together; one or the other is used.

PRACTICE

WORD POWER

I. Verbs:

information

1. すんでいます	2. つとめています	3. しっています	4. うっています

II. Family:

	RELATED TO THE SPEAKER	RELATED TO OTHERS
child	こども	おこさん
son	むすこ	むすこさん
daughter	むすめ	おじょうさん／むすめさん
older brother	あに	おにいさん
older sister	あね	おねえさん
younger brother	おとうと	おとうとさん
younger sister	いもうと	いもうとさん

KEY SENTENCES

1. たかはしさんは　よこはまに　すんでいます。
2. スミスさんは　ＡＢＣフーズに　つとめています。
3. スミスさんは　いとうさんを　しっています。
4. コンビニで　コンサートの　きっぷを　うっています。

1. Mr. Takahashi lives in Yokohama.
2. Mr. Smith is employed by ABC Foods.
3. Mr. Smith knows Ms. Ito.
4. They sell concert tickets at convenience stores.

EXERCISES

I. **_Practice conjugating verbs._** Repeat the verbs below and memorize their －ています forms, affirmative and negative.

	－ます FORM	－ています FORM	
		aff.	*neg.*
live	すみます	すんでいます	すんでいません
be employed	つとめます	つとめています	つとめてません
know	*	しっています	しりません**
sell	うります	うっています	うっていません

* しります—the affirmative present tense—is hardly ever used.

** The negative －ています form is しっていません, but this form is not used.

II. *State where someone lives.* Make up sentences following the pattern of the example. Substitute the underlined words with the words in parentheses.

ex. <u>やまもとさん</u>は <u>きょうと</u>に すんでいます。

1. .... (グリーンさん、しぶや)

2. .... (なかむらさん、しんじゅく)

III. *Ask and answer where someone lives.* Make up dialogues following the pattern of the example. Substitute the underlined words with the words in parentheses.

ex. A: <u>たかはしさん</u>は どこに すんでいますか。
   B: <u>よこはま</u>に すんでいます。

1. A: .... (やまださん)

   B: .... (しぶや)

2. A: .... (ホワイトさん)

   B: .... (ろっぽんぎ)

IV. *State where someone is employed.* Make up sentences following the pattern of the example. Substitute the underlined words with the words in parentheses.

ex. <u>たかはしさん</u>は <u>デパート</u>に つとめています。

1. .... (やまださん、ぎんこう)

2. .... (スミスさん、ＡＢＣフーズ)

V. *Ask and answer where someone is employed.* Make up dialogues following the pattern of the example. Substitute the underlined words with the words in parentheses.

ex. やまだ: <u>ブラウンさん</u>は どこに つとめていますか。
   スミス: <u>ロンドンぎんこう</u>に つとめて います。

1. やまだ: .... (ホワイトさん)

   スミス: .... (ＪＢＰジャパン)

2. やまだ: .... (すずきさんの おにいさん)

   スミス: .... (りょこうがいしゃ)

VOCABULARY ＪＢＰジャパン JBP Japan (fictitious company name)

216

VI. *State where someone lives and is employed.* Use the information in the table to make up sentences as in the example.

	PERSON	RESIDENCE	EMPLOYER
ex.	あんどうさん	しながわ	ＪＢＰジャパン
1.	グリーンさん	しぶや	ＡＢＣフーズ
2.	なかむらさんの　いもうとさん	さっぽろ	ぎんこう
3.	チャンさんの　おねえさん	ホンコン	デパート

ex. あんどうさんは　しながわに　すんでいます。
そして、ＪＢＰジャパンに　つとめています。

1. ....
....

2. ....

3. ....
....

VII. Make up dialogues following the patterns of the examples. Substitute the underlined words with the alternatives given.

A. *Confirm whether one knows someone or something.*

ex. A: <u>ささきさん</u>を　しっていますか。
B: はい、しっています。

1. A: .... （ブラウンさん）

   B: はい、..

2. A: .... （たかはしさんの　じゅうしょ）

   B: はい、..

B. *Deny that one knows someone or something.*

ex. A: <u>ホワイトさん</u>を　しっていますか。
B: いいえ、しりません。

1. A: .... （チャンさんの　メールアドレス）

   B: いいえ、..

2. A: .... （すずきさんの　でんわばんごう）

   B: いいえ、..

VOCABULARY
あんどう　Ando (surname)
しながわ　Shinagawa (district in Tokyo)
そして　and (NOTE: Unlike と, which connects words, そして connects sentences.)

VIII. ***Ask and answer whether one knows a particular address or fax number.*** Use the information in the table to make up a dialogue as in the example.

	Restaurant Tokyo's fax	Restaurant Tokyo's address	Sapporo branch office's fax
Suzuki	ex. yes	1. yes	2. no

ex. スミス: レストランとうきょうの　ファックスの　ばんごうを　しっていますか。
　　すずき: はい、しっています。

1. スミス: ....

　　すずき: ....

2. スミス: ....

　　すずき: ....

IX. ***Ask where a product is sold.*** Make up dialogues following the pattern of the example. Substitute the underlined parts with the alternatives given.

ex. A: <u>コンサートの　きっぷ</u>は　どこで　うっていますか。
　　B: <u>コンビニ</u>で　うっています。

1. A: .... (デジカメ)

　　B: .... (のぞみデパート)

2. A: .... (くすり)

　　B: .... (あの　みせ)

X. Make up dialogues following the patterns of the examples. Substitute the underlined parts with the alternatives given.

A. ***Talk about a new product.***

ex. ホフマン: <u>ＡＢＣフーズの　あたらしい　おかし</u>を　しっていますか。
　　まつい: 　ええ、しっています。
　　ホフマン: どこで　うっていますか。
　　まつい: 　<u>ぎんざの　デパート</u>で　うっています。

1. ホフマン: ....
　　　　　　　　　　　　　　　　　　　　　(ふじコンピューターの　あたらしい　ゲーム)

　　まつい: 　...

　　ホフマン: ....

　　まつい: 　...
　　　　　　　　　　　　　　　　　　　　　　　　　　(しんじゅくの　でんきや)

VOCABULARY

レストランとうきょう	Restaurant Tokyo (fictitious restaurant name)
ふじコンピューター	Fuji Computers (fictitious company name)
でんきや	electronics store

2. ホフマン: .... (メープルシロップ)

 まつい: ....

 ホフマン: ....

 まつい: .... (スーパー)

B. *Talk about a particular person.*

ex. Mr. Smith meets various people for the first time at a party.

スミス:　あんどうさん、おしごとは　なんですか。
あんどう: <u>エンジニア</u>です。ＪＢＰジャパンに　つとめています。
スミス:　そうですか。じゃ、<u>よこはまししゃの　いとうさん</u>を　しって
　　　　　いますか。
あんどう: ええ、しっています。

1. スミス: ....

 こじま: .... (ひしょ)

 スミス: ....
                 (おおさかししゃの　やましたさん)

 こじま: ....

2. スミス: ....

 こばやし: .... (べんごし)

 スミス: ....
                 (ホンコンししゃの　ワンさん)

 こばやし: ....

C. *Talk about a particular person's telephone number or e-mail address.*

ex. スミス:　ＪＢＰジャパンの　<u>いとうさん</u>を　しっていますか。
なかむら: はい、しっています。
スミス:　じゃ、<u>いとうさんの　でんわばんごう</u>を　しっていますか。
なかむら: いいえ、しりません。

1. スミス: .... (ワンさん)

 なかむら: ....

 スミス: ....
               (ワンさんの　メールアドレス)

 なかむら: ....

VOCABULARY			
メープルシロップ	maple syrup	ホンコンししゃ	Hong Kong (branch) office
こじま	Kojima (surname)	ワン	Wang (surname)
やました	Yamashita (surname)		
こばやし	Kobayashi (surname)		

2. スミス: .... (あんどうさん)

　　 なかむら: ....

　　 スミス: ....

　　　　　　　　　　　　　　　　　　　(あんどうさんの　けいたいの　ばんごう)

　　 なかむら: ....

XI. Listen to the CD and answer the question based on the information you hear.

....

SHORT DIALOGUE

Mr. Smith wants to make a reservation at the sushi restaurant Sushimasa, but he doesn't know the phone number.

スミス:　すみません。すしまさの　でんわばんごうを　しっていますか。
なかむら:さあ、わかりません。すずきさんに　きいてください。

Smith:　　　Excuse me. Do you know the phone number for Sushimasa?
Nakamura: Actually, I don't. Please ask Mr. Suzuki.

VOCABULARY

すしまさ	Sushimasa (fictitious sushi bar)
さあ、わかりません	I don't know (NOTE: The さあ here expresses the speaker's hesitation about immediately answering, "I don't know.")
さあ	let me see

Active Communication

1. Next time you meet a Japanese person for the first time, tell him or her where you live and where you are employed. Then ask that person where he or she lives and is employed.

2. If you're in Japan, ask where something you are looking for is sold.

SOCIALIZING

The Japanese have an international reputation of being hardworking people, the men devoted to their work and the women to their families. But while they may be diligent, they are also social, and there are many kinds of celebrations—most season-inspired—that they participate in. From cherry blossom viewing in the spring, when friends and colleagues get together to appreciate the beauty of the ephemeral cherry blossoms, to excursions in autumn to see the changing of the colors of the leaves, to year-end and new-year parties, the Japanese have get-togethers whenever the seasons beckon them. In addition to these annual events, though, they also enjoy Western-style gatherings: drinking parties, barbecues, and even home parties.

Preference and Desire

> person は noun が　すきです
> 〃　　　　 じょうずです
> 〃　　　　 わかります

> *ex.* グレイさんは　ビールが　すきです。"Mr. Grey likes beer."
> グレイさんは　テニスが　じょうずです。"Mr. Grey is good at tennis."
> グレイさんは　ちゅうごくごが　わかります。"Mr. Grey understands/knows Chinese."

■ The particle が used with すきです, じょうずです, いたいです, and わかります

が is used before the adjectives すきです ("like"; *lit.*, "be likable"), じょうずです ("be skilled"), and いたいです ("be painful"), and also before the verb わかります ("understand"), to show what one likes or is skilled at, what part of one's body hurts, or what one understands.
NOTE: With いたいです, the topic of the sentence is always the speaker, and the subject is a body part.

> わたしは verb －たいです

■ Expressing desire: verb －たいです

Constructions expressing desire ("I want to . . .") can be made from the －ます form by dropping －ます and adding －たい as follows:
> いきます　→　いきたい
> たべます　→　たべたい

NOTE: －たい is inflected like an －い adjective.
> *ex.* いきたいです。"(I) want to go."
> いきたくないです。"(I) don't want to go."
> いきたかったです。"(I) wanted to go."
> いきたくなかったです。"(I) didn't want to go."

■ －たい expresses the speaker's desire, not a third person's

> *ex.* タクシーで　いきたいです。"(I) want to go by taxi."

The particle か may be added to －たいです to form a question ("do you want to . . .?"), although this type of question is often considered impolite, especially when directed at a social superior. To ask if someone wants to do something, it is safest to use the －ます form followed by か, as in タクシーでいきますか ("Do you [want to] go by taxi?").
NOTE: The particle が is sometimes used instead of を.
> *ex.* ワインを／が　のみたいです。"(I) want to drink wine."

BEING INTRODUCED TO SOMEONE

TARGET DIALOGUE

The Greens are having a formal party at their house. During the party, Mr. Green introduces Mr. Smith to his friend Mr. Ogawa.

グリーン：スミスさん、こちらは　おがわさんです。

おがわ：はじめまして、おがわです。よろしく　おねがいします。

スミス：ＡＢＣフーズの　スミスです。よろしく　おねがいします。

グリーン：おがわさん、わたしは　スミスさんと　まいしゅう　どようびに　テニスを　しています。スミスさんは　テニスが　とても　じょうずです。

おがわ：そうですか。わたしも　テニスが　すきです。

スミス：じゃ、こんしゅうの　どようびに　おがわさんも　いっしょに　テニスを　しませんか。

おがわ：ありがとうございます。ぜひ。

■ グリーンさんは　まいしゅう　どようびに　スミスさんと　テニスを　しています。こんしゅうの　どようびは　おがわさんも　いっしょに　テニスを　します。

  Green: Mr. Smith, this is Mr. Ogawa.
 Ogawa: How do you do. I'm Ogawa. Pleased to meet you.
  Smith: I'm Smith from ABC Foods. Pleased to meet you.
  Green: Mr. Ogawa, I play tennis with Mr. Smith every Saturday. He's very good at tennis.
 Ogawa: Is that so? I like tennis, too.
  Smith: Well, would you like to play tennis with us this Saturday, too?
 Ogawa: Thank you. I'll definitely be there.

■ Mr. Green plays tennis with Mr. Smith every Saturday. This Saturday, Mr. Ogawa will play tennis with them.

VOCABULARY

テニス	tennis
じょうずです	be skilled, be good at (ーな adj.)

NOTES

1. スミスさんは　テニスが　とても　じょうずです。

The adjective じょうずです ("be skilled") is applied to another person. Japanese never use this word in reference to themselves or members of their families. Therefore, one does not usually ask ... が じょうずですか ("are you good at ... ?").

PRACTICE

WORD POWER

I.

1. じょうずです 　　　2. すきです 　　　3. わかります

II. Sports:

1. スキー 　　　2. サッカー 　　　3. やきゅう 　　　4. すいえい

KEY SENTENCES

1. スミスさんは　テニスが　じょうずです。
2. たかはしさんは　くだものが　すきです。
3. スミスさんは　にほんごが　わかります。

1. Mr. Smith is good at tennis.
2. Mr. Takahashi likes fruit.
3. Mr. Smith understands Japanese.

VOCABULARY

じょうずです	be skilled (ーな adj.)	サッカー	soccer (see also p. 142)
すきです	like (ーな adj.)	やきゅう	baseball
わかります	understand	すいえい	swimming
スキー	skiing	くだもの	fruit

EXERCISES

I. **Practice conjugating verbs and adjectives.** Repeat the words below and memorize their forms—present and past, affirmative and negative.

		PRESENT FORM		PAST FORM	
		aff.	*neg.*	*aff.*	*neg.*
ーな ADJ.	be skilled	じょうずです	じょうずではありません	じょうずでした	じょうずではありませんでした
	like, love	すきです	すきではありません	すきでした	すきではありませんでした
VERB	understand	わかります	わかりません	わかりました	わかりませんでした

II. Make up sentences following the patterns of the examples. Substitute the underlined words with the words in parentheses.

A. **State what someone is skilled at.**

ex. なかむらさんは　ゴルフが　じょうずです。

1. .... (テニス)

2. .... (スキー)

3. .... (えいご)

B. **State what someone likes.**

ex. なかむらさんは　くだものが　すきです。

1. .... (すきやき)

2. .... (りょこう)

3. .... (サッカー)

C. **State what someone understands.**

ex. スミスさんは　にほんごが　わかります。

1. .... (フランスご)

2. .... (かんじ)

VOCABULARY　かんじ　　　kanji, Chinese character(s)

225

III. Make up sentences or dialogues following the patterns of the examples and based on the information in the chart below.

VOCABULARY

ウイスキー	whiskey	ドイツご	German (language)
ダンス	dancing		
ちゅうごくご	Chinese (language)		
かんこくご	Korean (language)		

A. *State the things someone likes, is skilled at, and understands.*

　　ex. かとうさんは　おさけが　すきです。ゴルフが　じょうずです。えいごが
　　　　わかります。

　　　　1. ....

　　　　2. ....

　　　　3. ....

B. *State the things someone dislikes, is unskilled at, and does not understand.*

　　ex. かとうさんは　コーヒーが　すきではありません。テニスが　じょうずで
　　　　はありません。フランスごが　わかりません。

　　　　1. ....

　　　　2. ....

　　　　3. ....

C. *Ask and answer whether someone likes or understands something.*

　　ex. たかはし: かとうさんは　おさけが　すきですか。
　　　　かとう:　　はい、すきです。
　　　　たかはし: かとうさんは　フランスごが　わかりますか。
　　　　かとう:　　いいえ、わかりません。

　　　　1. たかはし: スミスさんは　ビールが　すきですか。

　　　　　　スミス: ....

　　　　　　たかはし: スミスさんは　にほんごが　わかりますか。

　　　　　　スミス: ....

　　　　2. たかはし: チャンさんは　コーヒーが　すきですか。

　　　　　　チャン: ....

　　　　　　たかはし: チャンさんは　かんこくごが　わかりますか。

　　　　　　チャン: ....

　　　　3. たかはし: ささきさんは　ウイスキーが　すきですか。

　　　　　　ささき: ....

　　　　　　たかはし: ささきさんは　ちゅうごくごが　わかりますか。

　　　　　　ささき: ....

D. *Ask and answer whether someone is skilled at something.*

ex. たかはし: かとうさんは　ゴルフが　じょうずですか。
なかむら: はい、じょうずです。

1. たかはし:スミスさんは　ダンスが　じょうずですか。

なかむら: ....

2. たかはし:チャンさんは　ダンスが　じょうずですか。

なかむら: ....

3. たかはし:ささきさんは　ゴルフが　じょうずですか。

なかむら: ....

IV. *Ask for and provide detailed information about one's likes.* Make up dialogues following the pattern of the example. Substitute the underlined words with the words in parentheses.

ex. チャン: すずきさんは　スポーツが　すきですか。
すずき: はい、すきです。
チャン: どんな　スポーツが　すきですか。
すずき: サッカーが　すきです。

1. チャン: .... (くだもの)

すずき: ....

チャン: .... (くだもの)

すずき: .... (りんご)

2. チャン: .... (イタリアりょうり)

すずき: ....

チャン: .... (イタリアりょうり)

すずき: .... (ピザ)

3. チャン: .... (おんがく)

すずき: ....

チャン: .... (おんがく)

すずき: .... (ジャズ)

| VOCABULARY | イタリアりょうり | Italian food, Italian cuisine |
| | ジャズ | jazz |

V. *Introduce a friend and give information about his or her likes.* Complete the dialogues below following the pattern of the example and based on the information in the illustrations.

ex. たかはし: チャンさん、こちらは カーペンターさんです。
カーペンター: はじめまして。カーペンターです。よろしく おねがいします。
たかはし: カーペンターさんは りょうりが じょうずです。フランスの ワインが すきです。

1. たかはし: チャンさん、こちらは おちあいさんです。

おちあい: はじめまして。おちあいです。よろしく おねがいします。

たかはし: ....

2. たかはし: チャンさん、こちらは こじまさんです。

こじま: はじめまして。こじまです。よろしく おねがいします。

たかはし: ....

3. たかはし: チャンさん、こちらは あんどうさんです。

あんどう: はじめまして。あんどうです。よろしく おねがいします。

たかはし: ....

VOCABULARY		
ピアノ	piano	
うみ	ocean, sea	
カーペンター	Carpenter (surname)	
おちあい	Ochiai (surname)	

VI. Make up dialogues following the patterns of the examples. Substitute the underlined words with the words in parentheses.

A. ***Talk about a mutual interest.***

ex. グリーン：どようびに　<u>はこね</u>に　いって、<u>ゴルフ</u>を　します。
　　かとう：　いいですね。グリーンさんは　<u>ゴルフ</u>が　すきですか。
　　グリーン：ええ、すきです。かとうさんは?
　　かとう：　わたしも　すきです。
　　グリーン：じゃ、こんど　いっしょに　いきませんか。
　　かとう：　ありがとうございます。ぜひ。

1. グリーン：...
　　　　　　　　　　　　　　（とうきょうスタジアム、やきゅう、みます）

　　かとう：...　（やきゅう）

　　グリーン：...

　　かとう：...

　　グリーン：...

　　かとう：...

2. グリーン：...
　　　　　　　　　　　　　　（ぎんざ、フランスりょうり、たべます）

　　かとう：...　（フランスりょうり）

　　グリーン：...

　　かとう：...

　　グリーン：...

　　かとう：...

B. ***Describe someone in detail.***

ex. すずき：ささきさん、あちらは　どなたですか。
　　ささき：ＪＢＰジャパンの　<u>おちあいさん</u>です。おちあいさんは　<u>ちゅうごく</u>に　すんでいましたから、<u>ちゅうごくご</u>が　とても　じょうずです。
　　すずき：そうですか。わたしは　らいしゅうから　<u>ちゅうごくご</u>を　ならいます。
　　ささき：じゃ、しょうかいしましょうか。
　　すずき：ええ、おねがいします。

1. すずき：...

　　ささき：...
　　　　　　　　　　　（カーペンターさん、フランス、フランスご）

VOCABULARY	とうきょうスタジアム	Tokyo Stadium (fictitious building name)		しょうかいします	introduce
	フランスりょうり	French food			
	あちら	that person over there			
230	ならいます	learn, take lessons in			

すずき: .... (フランスご)

ささき: ....

すずき: ....

2. すずき: ....

ささき: ....
(こじまさん、かんこく、かんこくご)

すずき: .... (かんこくご)

ささき: ....

すずき: ....

VII. Listen to the CD and fill in the blank based on the information you hear.

チャンさんは .... が じょうずです。

SHORT DIALOGUE

Ms. Nakamura is interested in Mr. Ogawa.

なかむら:グリーンさん、あちらは どなたですか。
グリーン:あ、おがわさんです。ときどき いっしょに けんどうの
　　　　　れんしゅうを します。
なかむら:そうですか。すてきな ひとですね。
グリーン:しょうかいしましょうか。
なかむら:ええ、おねがいします。

Nakamura: Mr. Green, who is that?
Green:　　Oh, that's Mr. Ogawa. We sometimes practice kendo together.
Nakamura: Is that so? He's a fine person, isn't he?
Green:　　Shall I introduce you to him?
Nakamura: Yes, please do.

VOCABULARY

けんどう	kendo (a martial art in which the contestants fight with bamboo swords)
れんしゅうを します	practice
すてきな	fine, wonderful, lovely (－な adj.)

Active Communication

Imagine you are at a party. Introduce your friends or colleagues to one another and give details about their interests and skills.

AT A PARTY

TARGET DIALOGUE

Mrs. Green is serving food to Mr. Smith and Mr. Ogawa. Mr. Smith and Mr. Ogawa are eating Japanese food that Mrs. Green made.

スミス：おいしいですね。

おがわ：ほんとうに　おいしいですね。グリーンさんは　りょうりが

じょうずですね。

グリーン：ありがとうございます。まいしゅう　すいようびに　ぎんざの

クッキングスクールで　にほんりょうりを　ならっています。

スミス：わたしも　にほんりょうりを　ならいたいです。その

クッキングスクールは　どこに　ありますか。

グリーン：のぞみデパートの　となりに　あります。

■ グリーンさんは　まいしゅう　すいようびに　ぎんざの　クッキング
スクールで　にほんりょうりを　ならっています。

Smith: This is delicious, isn't it?
Ogawa: It really is delicious, isn't it? You are a good cook, Mrs. Green.
Green: Thank you. I take lessons in Japanese cuisine at a cooking school in GInza every Wednesday.
Smith: I'd like to learn Japanese cuisine, too. Where is that cooking school?
Green: It's next door to Nozomi Department Store.

■ Mrs. Green takes lessons in Japanese cuisine at a cooking school in GInza every Wednesday.

VOCABULARY

クッキングスクール	cooking school
にほんりょうり	Japanese food
ならいたいです	want to learn
その	(see Note 1 below)

NOTES

1. その　クッキングスクール
その here is in reference to what came up just before in the conversation.

PRACTICE

WORD POWER

I. Hobbies:

1. じゅうどう   2. いけばな   3. おちゃ

II. Parts of the body:

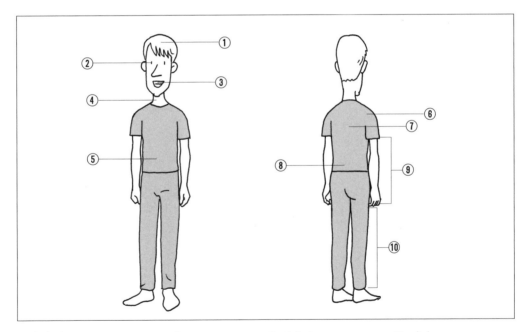

1. あたま	4. のど	7. せなか	10. あし
2. め	5. おなか	8. こし	
3. は	6. かた	9. て	

VOCABULARY							
じゅうどう	judo	め	eye	かた	shoulder	あし	leg, foot
いけばな	ikebana, flower arranging	は	tooth	せなか	back		
おちゃ	tea ceremony	のど	throat	こし	lower back		
あたま	head	おなか	belly, stomach	て	hand, arm		233

KEY SENTENCES

1. わたしは　おんせんに　いきたいです。
2. わたしは　あたまが　いたいです。

1. I want to go to a spa.
2. I have a headache.

EXERCISES

I. *Practice conjugating verbs.* Repeat the -たい forms of the following verbs until you memorize them.

	PRESENT FORM		PAST FORM	
	aff.	*neg.*	*aff.*	*neg.*
want to learn	ならいたいです	ならいたくないです	ならいたかったです	ならいたくなかったです
want to go	いきたいです	いきたくないです	いきたかったです	いきたくなかったです

II. *State what you want to do.* Change the sentences below as in the examples.

ex. わたしは　おんせんに　いきます。
　 → わたしは　おんせんに　いきたいです。
　 わたしは　おんせんに　いきません。
　 → わたしは　おんせんに　いきたくないです。

1. わたしは　テレビを　みます。

　 → ....

2. わたしは　たかはしさんに　あいません。

　 → ....

3. わたしは　ふるい　かぐを　かいます。

　 → ....

4. わたしは　じゅうどうを　ならいません。

　 → ....

VOCABULARY	いきたいです	want to go
	いたいです	be painful, hurt
	かぐ	furniture

III. Make up dialogues following the patterns of the examples. Substitute the underlined parts with the alternatives given, being careful to use the correct grammatical form.

A. *Ask and answer where one wants to live.*

ex. A: しょうらい　どんなところに　すみたいですか。
　　B: <u>うみの　ちかくに</u>　すみたいです。

1. A: ....
　　B: .... (あたたかい　ところ)

2. A: ....
　　B: .... (しずかな　まち)

3. A: ....
　　B: .... (おきなわ)

B. *Ask for information.*

ex. A: <u>にほんごを　ならいたいです</u>。いい　<u>がっこう</u>を　しっていますか。
　　B: すみません、しりません。

1. A: ....
　　　　　　　　　　　　　　　　　　　　　　　　　(おんせんに　いきます、ところ)
　　B: ....

2. A: ....
　　　　　　　　　　　　　　　　　　　　　　　　　(いけばなを　ならいます、クラス)
　　B: ....

3. A: ....
　　　　　　　　　　　　　　　　　　　　　　　　　(ふるい　かぐを　かいます、みせ)
　　B: ....

IV. *State which part of your body hurts.* Make up sentences following the pattern of the example. Substitute the underlined word with the words in parentheses.

ex. わたしは　<u>あたま</u>が　いたいです。

1. .... (は)

2. .... (おなか)

V. ***Tell a doctor one's symptoms.*** Make up dialogues following the pattern of the example and based on the information in the illustration.

ex. いしゃ: どうしましたか。
チャン: <u>きぶんが　わるいです。</u>

1. いしゃ: ....

   チャン: ....

2. いしゃ: ....

   チャン: ....

3. いしゃ: ....

   チャン: ....

VI. ***State what you do every week, and assuming the role of your listener, express envy and your own desire.*** Make up dialogues following the pattern of the example. Substitute the underlined parts with the alternatives given. Be sure to use the same grammatical forms as in the example.

ex. A: わたしは　まいしゅう　<u>にほんごを　ならっています。</u>
B: いいですね。わたしも　<u>ならいたいです。</u>

1. A: .... (ジョギングを　します)

   B: .... (します)

2. A: .... (おちゃを　ならいます)

   B: .... (ならいます)

VOCABULARY	どうしましたか	what's the matter with you?
	ねつ	fever
	３８ど	38 degrees (Celsius)
236	～ど	degree

VII. Make up dialogues following the patterns of the examples. Substitute the underlined parts with the alternatives given. Be sure to use the same grammatical forms as in the examples.

A. *Give information.*

ex. たかはし: にちようびに　おんせんに　いきました。
スミス:　　いいですね。わたしも　いきたいです。
たかはし: いい　おんせんを　おしえましょうか。
スミス:　　ええ、おねがいします。

1. たかはし: .... (テニスを　します)

   スミス: .... (します)

   たかはし: .... (テニスクラブ)

   スミス: ....

2. たかはし: ....
   　　　　　　(かまくらに　いって、にほんの　ふるい　かぐを　かいます)

   スミス: .... (かいます)

   たかはし: .... (みせ)

   スミス: ....

B. *Explain why one did not go to a farewell party for a colleague.*

ex. かとう: きのう　ホワイトさんの　そうべつかいに　いきましたか。
スミス: いいえ、いきたかったですが、あたまが　いたかったですから、
　　　　いきませんでした。
かとう: そうですか。ざんねんでしたね。

1. かとう: ....

   スミス: .... (はが　いたかったです)

   かとう: ....

2. かとう: ....

   スミス: .... (ねつが　ありました)

   かとう: ....

VIII. Listen to the CD and choose the correct answer based on the information you hear.

What kind of place does Mr. Smith want to live in?

a) しずかな　まち　　b) おおきい　まち　　c) ちいさい　まち

VOCABULARY　　そうべつかい　　　　farewell party

SHORT DIALOGUE

The party has come to an end.

おがわ:　なかむらさん、くるまで　きましたか。
なかむら:いいえ、でんしゃで　きました。
おがわ:　おそいですから、わたしの　くるまで　かえりませんか。
なかむら:ありがとうございます。
おがわ:　スミスさんも　いっしょに　いかがですか。
スミス:　ありがとうございます。おねがいします。

Ogawa:　　Ms. Nakamura, did you come by car?
Nakamura: No, I came by train.
Ogawa:　　It's late, so wouldn't you like to go home in my car?
Nakamura: Thank you.
Ogawa:　　Mr. Smith, how about going home with us?
Smith:　　Thank you. I'd like that.

VOCABULARY

おそいです　　　　be late

Active Communication

1. Get information about schools and teachers, or about a subject you want to take lessons in.

2. Get information about things you want to buy and places you want to visit.

I Fill in the blank in each sentence with the appropriate particle. Where a particle is not needed, write in an *X*.

1. スミスさんは　ゴルフ（　　　　）じょうずです。
2. たかはしさんの　おとうさんは　ぎんこう（　　　　）つとめています。
3. コンサートの　きっぷは　どこ（　　　　）うっていますか。
4. どう　しましたか。
   あたま（　　　　）いたいです。
5. スミスさんの　おかあさんは　サンフランシスコ（　　　　）すんでいます。

II Choose the word that is appropriate in the context of the sentence.

1. スミスさんは　いま　なにを　していますか。
   かいぎしつで　たかはしさんと　はなしを（します／しています）。
2. たかはしさんの　でんわばんごうを（しります／しっています）か。
   いいえ、（しりません／しっていません）。
3. わたしは　きのう　パーティーに（いきたいです／いきたかったです）が、いそがしかったですから、いきませんでした。

III Look at the illustrations and complete the dialogue by filling in the blanks with the appropriate forms of the three words given in brackets. (You may use the same word more than once.)

[します、じょうずです、すきです]

たかはし: スミスさんは　テニスが（1.　　　　　　　）か。
スミス:　　ええ、でも　あまり（2.　　　　　　　　　）。
たかはし: あした　ともだちと　テニスを（3.　　　　　）。スミスさんも
　　　　　いっしょに（4.　　　　　　）か。
スミス:　　ええ、ぜひ。

239

APPENDIXES

A. Particles

Particles	Examples	Unit	Lesson
は	1. わたしは　スミスです。	1	1
	2. スミスさんは　あした　きょうとに　いきます。	3	6
	3. なごやでは　うっていません。	10	23
	4. こんしゅうの　どようびは　おがわさんも　いっしょに　テニスを　します。	11	24
	5. "ショコラショコラ"は　とうきょうの　スーパーと　コンビニで　うっています。	10	23
の	1. のぞみデパートの　たなかです。	I	1
	2. わたしの　めいしです。	I	2
	3. わたしのです。	I	2
	4. にほんの　くるまです。	2	5
	5. きょうとの　ししゃに　いきました。	3	6
	6. テーブルの　うえに　はなと　しんぶんが　あります。	4	8
	7. らいしゅうの　きんようびに　にほんに　きます。	3	7
	8. かいぎの　あとで　さっぽろししゃに　いきます。	8	17
	9. つぎの　しんごうを　みぎに　まがってください。	8	18
	10. ともだちの　ホフマンさんに　もらいました。	6	13
	11. わたしの　すきな　いろです。	6	13
か	1. スミスさんは　アメリカじんですか。	I	1
	2. べんごしですか、エンジニアですか。	I	1
	3. どなたですか。	1	2
	4. そうですか。	2	3
から	1. 10じからです。	2	3
	2. 10じから　8じまでです。	2	3
	3. ホンコンから　きました。	3	6
	4. とうきょうから　にっこうまで　でんしゃで　1じかんはん　かかります。	9	19
	5. 2かいに　レストランが　ありますから、レストランで　しょくじを　しませんか。	7	15
まで	1. 8じまでです。	2	3
	2. 10じから　8じまでです。	2	3
	3. かいしゃまで　あるきます。	9	19
	4. とうきょうから　にっこうまで　でんしゃで　1じかんはん　かかります。	9	19
を	1. それを　ください。	2	4
	2. かぶきを　みます。	5	10
	3. べんきょうを　します。	5	10
	4. つぎの　しんごうを　みぎに　まがってください。	8	18
	5. スミスさんは　しんじゅくえきで　でんしゃを　おります。	9	19
も	1. あれも　3000えんです。	2	4
	2. "ショコラショコラ"は　なごやでも　うっていますか。	10	23
	3. サンプルの　しゃしんも　おくってください。	8	18
	4. テーブルの　うえに　なにも　ありません。	4	8
で	1. ひとりで　きますか。	3	6
	2. タクシーで　きました。	3	7
	3. スミスさんは　きのう　レストランで　ばんごはんを　たべました。	5	10
	4. どようびに　あさくさで　おまつりが　あります。	7	15

	5. スミスさんは　きのう　パーティーの　あとで　タクシーで　かえりました。	8	17
	6. カタログを　すぐ　メールで　おくってください。	8	18
と	1. チャンさんは　きのう　ともだちと　レストランに　いきました。	3	6
	2. テーブルの　うえに　しんぶんと　はなが　あります。	4	8
が	1. どの　でんしゃが　いきますか。	3	6
	2. 1かいに　ぎんこうが　あります。	4	8
	3. スミスさんは　えいぎょうぶに　いきましたが、チャンさんは　いませんでした。	10	22
	4. もしもし、チャンですが、おはようございます。	8	18
に	1. スミスさんは　あした　ぎんこうに／へ　いきます。	3	6
	2. ひこうきは　10じはんに　さっぽろに　つきます。	9	19
	3. 3がつ　26にちに　イギリスから　きました。	3	7
	4. うけつけに　おんなの　ひとが　います。	4	8
	5. スミスさんは　あした　ともだちに　あいます。	5	11
	6. スミスさんは　ともだちに　でんわを　します。	5	11
	7. チャンさんは　スミスさんに　はなを　もらいました。	6	13
	8. スミスさんは　ＡＢＣフーズに　つとめています。	10	23
	9. たなかさんは　よこはまに　すんでいます。	10	23
や	1. かばんの　なかに　かぎや　ほんが　あります。	4	8
ね	1. かいぎは　3じから　ですね。	3	6
よ	1. にほんの　スパですよ。	4	8
…は…が		7	16
	1. スミスさんは　えいがの　きっぷが　2まい　あります。	7	16
	2. たなかさんは　くだものが　すきです。	11	24
	3. わたしは　あたまが　いたいです。	11	25
	4. わたしは　ワインを／が　のみたいです。	11	25

B. Interrogatives

Interrogatives	Examples	Unit	Lesson
どなた	こちらは　どなたですか。	1	1
だれの	これは　だれの　かさですか。	1	2
だれと	スミスさんは　だれと　のぞみデパートに　いきますか。	3	6
だれが	うけつけに　だれが　いますか。	4	8
だれに	スミスさんは　だれに　てがみを　かきますか。	5	11
	だれに　あいましたか。	5	11*
	だれに　えいがの　きっぷを　もらいましたか。	6	13
なん	これは　なんですか。	1	2
なんばん	たなかさんの　でんわばんごうは　なんばんですか。	1	2
なんにん	ぎんこうの　まえに　おとこの　ひとが　なんにん　いますか。	4	9
なんじ	いま　なんじですか。	2	3
なんようび	おまつりは　なんようびですか。	3	7

*This type of sentence does not appear in the lesson's exercises.

なんにち	おまつりは　<u>なんにち</u>ですか。	3	7
なんがつ	おまつりは　<u>なんがつ</u>　ですか。	3	7
なんで	スミスさんは　<u>なんで</u>　おおさかに　いきますか。	3	7
なにが	1かいに　<u>なにが</u>　ありますか。	4	8
なにを	しゅうまつに　<u>なにを</u>　しますか。	5	10
いつ	たんじょうびは　<u>いつ</u>　ですか。	3	7
	たなかさんは　<u>いつ</u>　おおさかししゃに　いきますか。	3	6
いかが	おかしは　<u>いかが</u>　ですか。	5	11
いくら	それは　<u>いくら</u>　ですか。	2	4
いくつ	テーブルの　うえに　りんごが　<u>いくつ</u>　ありますか。	4	9
どこ	こうばんは　<u>どこ</u>ですか。	4	9
どこの	これは　<u>どこの</u>　パソコンですか。	2	5
どこに	スミスさんは　あした　<u>どこに</u>　いきますか。	3	6
	スミスさんは　<u>どこに</u>　いますか。	4	9
	ちゅうしゃじょうは　<u>どこに</u>　ありますかか。	4	9
	スミスさんは　<u>どこに</u>　てがみを　かきますか。	5	11
	スミスさんは　<u>どこに</u>　すんでいますか。	10	23
どこで	かとうさんは　<u>どこで</u>　ゴルフを　しましたか。	5	10
どの	<u>どの</u>　バスが　いきますか。	3	6
どれ	あの　Tシャツは　いくらですか。<u>どれ</u>ですか。	2	5
どんな	にっこうは　<u>どんな</u>　ところですか。	6	12
	<u>どんな</u>　スポーツが　すきですか。	11	24
どう	きのうの　パーティーは　<u>どう</u>でしたか。	6	14
	<u>どう</u>しましたか。	11	25
どうして	<u>どうして</u>ですか。	8	17
どのぐらい	たなかさんは　<u>どのぐらい</u>　ニューヨークに　いましたか。	9	19
	<u>どのぐらい</u>　かかりますか。	9	19
どうやって	スミスさんは　<u>どうやって</u>　かいしゃに　いきますか。	9	19

C. Sentence Patterns

Sentence Patterns	Examples	Unit	Lesson
...は　...です	1. (わたしは) スミスです。	1	1
	2. これは　はやしさんの　かさです。	1	2
	3. しごとは　9じから　5じまでです。	2	3
	4. たなかさんの　うちは　あたらしいです。	6	12
	5. これは　おもしろい　ほんです。	6	12
...は...が...です	1. たなかさんは　くだものが　すきです。	11	24
	2. わたしは　あたまが　いたいです。	11	25

―たいです	1. わたしは おんせんに いきたいです。	11	25
...に...があります	1. 1かいに ぎんこうが あります。	4	8
／います	2. うけつけに おんなの ひとが います。	4	8
...は...にあります	1. タクシーのりばは えきの ちかくに あります。	4	9
／います	2. スミスさんは 2かいに います。	4	9
...をください	1. その りんごを ふたつ ください。	2	5
...に／へ―ます	1. スミスさんは あした ぎんこうに／へ いきます。	3	6
...で...を―ます	1. スミスさんは きのう レストランで ばんごはんを たべました。	5	10
...に...を―ます	1. チャンさんは よく おかあさんに てがみを かきます。	5	11
	2. チャンさんは スミスさんに はなを もらいました。	6	13
...は...が―ます	1. スミスさんは えいがの きっぷが 2まい あります。	7	16
	2. スミスさんは にほんごが わかります。	11	24
...で...があります	1. どようびに あさくさで おまつりが あります。	7	15
...に―ます	1. スミスさんは とうきょうえきで でんしゃに のります。	9	19
...を―ます	1. スミスさんは しんじゅくえきで でんしゃを おります。	9	19
―ませんか	1. しゅうまつに いっしょに えいがを みませんか。	7	15
	2. にちようびに うちに きませんか。	7	15
―ましょうか	1. なにを たべましょうか。	7	15
	2. ちずを かきましょうか。	7	15
―て、―ます	1. スミスさんは きのう ほんやに いって、じしょを かいました。	8	17
―ています	1. スミスさんは いま しんぶんを よんでいます。	10	22
	2. たなかさんは よこはまに すんでいます。	10	23
	3. スミスさんは さとうさんを しっています。	10	23
―てください	1. もう いちど いってください。	8	18
―ても いいですか	1. この ペンを つかっても いいですか。	9	20
―ないでください	1. ここは いりぐち ですから、くるまを とめないでください。	9	21

D. Adjectives

Included in the following list of adjectives are some (in gray) which do not appear in the text.

―い adjectives

あかるい	bright	すずしい	cool
あたたかい	warm	すっぱい	sour
あたらしい	new, fresh	せまい	narrow
あつい	hot	たかい	expensive, high
あぶない	dangerous	ただしい	correct
あまい	sweet	たのしい	pleasant, enjoyable
いい	good, fine	ちいさい	small
いそがしい	busy	ちかい	near
いたい	painful	つまらない	boring

おいしい	delicious	つめたい	cold
おおい	many, much	とおい	far
おおきい	big	ながい	long
おそい	slow, late	はやい	fast, early
おもい	heavy	ひくい	low
おもしろい	interesting	ひろい	wide
からい	hot, spicy	ふるい	old
かるい	light	みじかい	short
きたない	dirty	むずかしい	difficult
くらい	dark	やさしい	easy
さむい	cold	やすい	inexpensive
しおからい	salty	わかい	young
すくない	few, a little	わるい	bad

−な adjectives

あんぜんな	safe	だいじな	important
いろいろな	various	だめな	no good
きらいな	detestable	ていねいな	polite
きれいな	clean, pretty	にぎやかな	lively
げんきな	well, healthy	ひまな	free
しずかな	quiet	ふしんせつな	unkind
しつれいな	rude	ふべんな	inconvenient
じょうずな	skillful	へたな	unskillful
しんせつな	kind	べんりな	convenient
すきな	favorite, likable	ゆうめいな	famous
すてきな	fine, wonderful, lovely		

Color Words

Below are words for colors. Those in gray are not introduced in this text.

あおい	blue, green	しろい	white
あかい	red	ちゃいろい、ちゃいろの*	brown
きいろい、きいろの*	yellow	みどりいろの*	green
くろい	black	むらさきの*	purple

*These words are nouns followed by the particle の.

| E. Verb Conjugation |

The conjugations of Japanese verbs fall into the following three categories:

Regular I: Five-vowel conjugation

Regular II: Single-vowel conjugation

Irregular: There are only two irregular verbs: きます and します. See Irregular Verbs, p. 246.

Regular I verbs are conjugated according to the Japanese vowel order: あ, い, う, え, お. Regular II verbs are based on the vowels **-i** and **-e** only. From the −ない form it can be seen whether a verb is Regular I or Regular II. If the vowel preceding −ない is **-a**, the verb is Regular I. If it is **-i** or **-e**, the verb is Regular II. The chart below shows the conjugations of the verbs かきます ("write") and たべます ("eat").

	REGULAR I	REGULAR II
−ない form	かかない	たべない
−ます form	かきます	たべます
dictionary form	かく	たべる
conditional form	かけば	たべれば
volitional form	かこう	たべよう

−て form	かいて	たべて
−た form	かいた	たべた

Of the seven forms above, this book introduces the −ない, −ます and −て forms; the dictionary, conditional, volitional and −た forms are discussed in Books II and III of this series.

Note that the dictionary form—so called because it is the form listed in dictionaries—can be used at the end of a sentence instead of the −ます form. Likewise, the −ない form can be used at the end of a sentence instead of −ません. However, these forms are less polite than −ます and −ません.

For reference, the following are the −ます, −て, −ない, dictionary and −た forms of typical Regular I, Regular II and Irregular verbs. Some of the verbs listed (in gray) are not introduced in this book.

REGULAR I VERBS					
−ます	−て	−ない	dictionary	−た	meaning
あいます	あって	あわない	あう	あった	meet
あずかります	あずかって	あずからない	あずかる	あずかった	take care of, look after
あります	あって	ない	ある	あった	be, exist, have
あるきます	あるいて	あるかない	あるく	あるいた	walk
いいます	いって	いわない	いう	いった	say
いきます	いって	いかない	いく	いった	go
いただきます	いただいて	いただかない	いただく	いただいた	accept
うります	うって	うらない	うる	うった	sell
おきます	おいて	おかない	おく	おいた	put, place
おくります	おくって	おくらない	おくる	おくった	send
おします	おして	おさない	おす	おした	push
おわります	おわって	おわらない	おわる	おわった	finish
かいます	かって	かわない	かう	かった	buy
かえります	かえって	かえらない	かえる	かえった	return, go home
かかります	かかって	かからない	かかる	かかった	(it) takes
かきます	かいて	かかない	かく	かいた	write
かします	かして	かさない	かす	かした	lend
かつぎます	かついで	かつがない	かつぐ	かついだ	carry (on one's shoulders)
がんばります	がんばって	がんばらない	がんばる	がんばった	do one's best
ききます	きいて	きかない	きく	きいた	listen (to), ask
けします	けして	けさない	けす	けした	turn off
こみます	こんで	こまない	こむ	こんだ	be crowded
しります*	しって	しらない	しる	しった	know
すいます	すって	すわない	すう	すった	smoke (cigarettes)
すみます	すんで	すまない	すむ	すんだ	live
たちます	たって	たたない	たつ	たった	stand up
ちがいます	ちがって	ちがわない	ちがう	ちがった	be wrong
つかいます	つかって	つかわない	つかう	つかった	use
つきます	ついて	つかない	つく	ついた	arrive
つくります	つくって	つくらない	つくる	つくった	make
とります	とって	とらない	とる	とった	take (a picture)
ならいます	ならって	ならわない	ならう	ならった	learn
にあいます	にあって	にあわない	にあう	にあった	suit, look good on
のみます	のんで	のまない	のむ	のんだ	drink
のります	のって	のらない	のる	のった	ride, get on
はいります	はいって	はいらない	はいる	はいった	enter
まがります	まがって	まがらない	まがる	まがった	turn
まちます	まって	またない	まつ	まった	wait

*This form is hardly ever used. Instead, しっています (the −て form) is used.

もちます	もって	もたない	もつ	もった	have, hold
もらいます	もらって	もらわない	もらう	もらった	receive
よびます	よんで	よばない	よぶ	よんだ	invite, call, summon
よみます	よんで	よまない	よむ	よんだ	read
わかります	わかって	わからない	わかる	わかった	understand

REGULAR II VERBS					
－ます	－て	－ない	dictionary	－た	meaning
あけます	あけて	あけない	あける	あけた	open
あげます	あげて	あげない	あげる	あげた	give
います	いて	いない	いる	いた	be
いれます	いれて	いれない	いれる	いれた	put in/into
おしえます	おしえて	おしえない	おしえる	おしえた	tell
おります	おりて	おりない	おりる	おりた	get off
しめます	しめて	しめない	しめる	しめた	close
たべます	たべて	たべない	たべる	たべた	eat
つけます	つけて	つけない	つける	つけた	turn on
(きを)つけます	つけて	つけない	つける	つけた	be careful
つとめます	つとめて	つとめない	つとめる	つとめた	work for
でます	でて	でない	でる	でた	leave
とどけます	とどけて	とどけない	とどける	とどけた	deliver
とめます	とめて	とめない	とめる	とめた	stop, park
みせます	みせて	みせない	みせる	みせた	show
みます	みて	みない	みる	みた	see

IRREGULAR VERBS					
－ます	－て	－ない	dictionary	－た	meaning
きます	きて	こない	くる	きた	come
もってきます	もってきて	もってこない	もってくる	もってきた	bring
します	して	しない	する	した	do
しつれいします	しつれいして	しつれいしない	しつれいする	しつれいした	be rude
しょうかいします	しょうかいして	しょうかいしない	しょうかいする	しょうかいした	introduce

The verb します ("do") follows various nouns, sometimes with and sometimes without the particle を, to express a variety of meanings. Below is a sampling of "noun を します" combinations. The words in gray are not introduced in this text.

うんてんを します	drive	せつめいを します	explain
かいぎを します	have a meeting	そうじを します	clean
かいものを します	shop	そうべつかいを します	give a farewell party
コピーを します	make a copy	テニスを します	play tennis
ゴルフを します	play golf	でんわを します	telephone
さんぽを します	go for a walk	ドライブを します	go for a drive
しごとを します	work	パーティーを します	give a party
しゅっちょうを します	go on a business trip	はなしを します	talk
ジョギングを します	jog	べんきょうを します	study
しょくじを します	have a meal	よやくを します	make a reservation
スキーを します	ski	りょこうを します	take a trip
スポーツを します	play sports	れんしゅうを します	practice

F. Ko-so-a-do Words

	こ−words	そ−words	あ−words	ど−words
direction	こちら here, this way	そちら there, that way	あちら over there	どちら where
people	こちら this person	そちら that person	あちら that person over there	どなた、だれ who
thing	これ this	それ that	あれ that over there	どれ which
place	ここ here	そこ there	あそこ over there	どこ where
demonstrative	この　カメラ this camera	その　カメラ that camera	あの　カメラ that camera over there	どの　カメラ which camera

G. Countries, Nationalities and Languages

	Country	Nationality	Language
Australia	オーストラリア	オーストラリアじん	えいご
Brazil	ブラジル	ブラジルじん	ポルトガルご
Canada	カナダ	カナダじん	えいご／フランスご
China	ちゅうごく	ちゅうごくじん	ちゅうごくご
Egypt	エジプト	エジプトじん	アラビアご
France	フランス	フランスじん	フランスご
Germany	ドイツ	ドイツじん	ドイツご
Indonesia	インドネシア	インドネシアじん	インドネシアご
Italy	イタリア	イタリアじん	イタリアご
Japan	にほん	にほんじん	にほんご
New Zealand	ニュージーランド	ニュージーランドじん	えいご
Russia	ロシア	ロシアじん	ロシアご
Spain	スペイン	スペインじん	スペインご
Switzerland	スイス	スイスじん	ドイツご／フランスご／イタリアご
Thailand	タイ	タイじん	タイご
United Kingdom	イギリス	イギリスじん	えいご
United States	アメリカ	アメリカじん	えいご

H. Counters

The abstract numbers (いち, に, さん) are given on p. 10 (0–10), p. 23 (10–30; 40, 50, . . .) and p. 30 (100, 200, . . .). (For an explanation of very large numbers, see Note 2, p. 29.) The ひとつ, ふたつ, みっつ system is explained on p. 38 and given in full on p. 39, along with examples of two counters, まい and ほん. Below are other counters used in this book.

Floors of a house or building: ～かい

いっかい	1st floor	ごかい	5th floor	きゅうかい	9th floor
にかい	2nd floor	ろっかい	6th floor	じゅっかい	10th floor
さんがい	3rd floor	ななかい	7th floor	じゅういっかい	11th floor
よんかい	4th floor	はちかい	8th floor	じゅうにかい	12th floor

なんかい／なんがい how many floors, which floor

Also: ちか　いっかい, (1st) basement floor (of several), ちか　にかい, 2nd basement floor, etc.

Liquid measure (cupful, glassful): 〜はい／ばい／ぱい

いっぱい	1 cupful	ごはい	5 cupfuls	きゅうはい	9 cupful
にはい	2 cupfuls	ろっぱい	6 cupfuls	じゅっぱい	10 cupfuls
さんばい	3 cupfuls	ななはい	7 cupfuls	じゅういっぱい	11 cupfuls
よんはい	4 cupfuls	はっぱい	8 cupfuls	じゅうにはい	12 cupfuls

なんばい　　how many cups/glasses

People: 〜にん

ひとり	1 person	ろくにん	6 people	きゅうにん	9 people
ふたり	2 people	しちにん	7 people	くにん	〃
さんにん	3 people	ななにん	〃	じゅうにん	10 people
よにん	4 people	はちにん	8 people	じゅういちにん	11 people
ごにん	5 people			じゅうににん	12 people

なんにん　　how many people

Times: 〜かい、〜ど

いっかい、いちど	once	ななかい、ななど		7 times
にかい、にど	twice	はちかい、はちど		8 times
さんかい、さんど	3 times	きゅうかい、きゅうど		9 times
よんかい、よんど	4 times	じゅっかい、じゅうど		10 times
ごかい、ごど	5 times	じゅういっかい、じゅういちど		11 times
ろっかい、ろくど	6 times	じゅうにかい、じゅうにど		12 times

なんかい　　　　how many times
なんど　　　　　how many times/degrees

NOTE: Generally speaking, かい and ど may be used interchangeably.

I. Extent, Frequency, Quantity

Extent

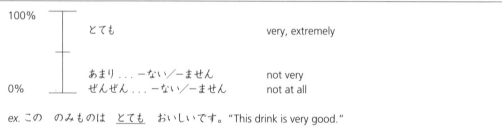

100%	とても	very, extremely
	あまり . . . −ない／−ません	not very
0%	ぜんぜん . . . −ない／−ません	not at all

ex. この　のみものは　<u>とても</u>　おいしいです。 "This drink is very good."
　　この　のみものは　<u>あまり</u>　おいし<u>くない</u>です。 "This drink is not very good."
　　この　のみものは　<u>ぜんぜん</u>　おいし<u>くない</u>です。 "This drink is not good at all."

Frequency

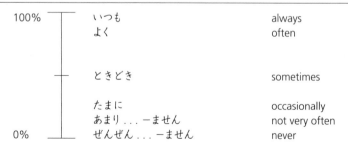

100%	いつも	always
	よく	often
	ときどき	sometimes
	たまに	occasionally
	あまり . . . −ません	not very often
0%	ぜんぜん . . . −ません	never

ex. ばんごはんの　あとで　<u>いつも</u>　テレビを　みます。 "(I) always watch TV after dinner."
　　ばんごはんの　あとで　<u>よく</u>　テレビを　みます。 "(I) often watch TV after dinner."
　　ばんごはんの　あとで　<u>ときどき</u>　テレビを　みます。 "(I) sometimes watch TV after dinner."
　　ばんごはんの　あとで　<u>たまに</u>　テレビを　みます。 "(I) occasionally watch TV after dinner."
　　ばんごはんの　あとで　<u>あまり</u>　テレビを　み<u>ません</u>。 "(I) don't often watch TV after dinner."
　　ばんごはんの　あとで　<u>ぜんぜん</u>　テレビを　み<u>ません</u>。 "(I) never watch TV after dinner."

Quantity

```
100% ┬
     │
     │        たくさん                      a lot, many
     ┼
     │
     │        すこし                        a few, a little
     │        あまり ... ーません            not much/many
  0% ┴        ぜんぜん ... ーません          none at all
```

ex. うちの　ちかくに　みせが　<u>たくさん</u>　あります。 "There are a lot of stores near my house."
　　うちの　ちかくに　みせが　<u>すこし</u>　あります。 "There are a few stores near my house."
　　うちの　ちかくに　みせが　<u>あまり</u>　あり<u>ません</u>。 "There aren't many stores near my house."
　　うちの　ちかくに　みせが　<u>ぜんぜん</u>　あり<u>ません</u>。 "There are no stores near my house."

J. Time Expressions

Every: まい〜

まいあさ	every morning	まいしゅう	every week
まいばん	every evening, every night	まいつき／まいげつ	every month
まいにち	every day	まいねん／まいとし	every year

Periods

Minutes: 〜ふん／ぷん

いっぷん (かん)	(for) 1 minute	はっぷん (かん)	(for) 8 minutes
にふん (かん)	(for) 2 minutes	はちふん (かん)	〃
さんぷん (かん)	(for) 3 minutes	きゅうふん (かん)	(for) 9 minutes
よんぷん (かん)	(for) 4 minutes	じゅっぷん (かん)	(for) 10 minutes
ごふん (かん)	(for) 5 minutes	じゅういっぷん (かん)	(for) 11 minutes
ろっぷん (かん)	(for) 6 minutes	じゅうにふん (かん)	(for) 12 minutes
ななふん (かん)	(for) 7 minutes		

なんぷん (かん)	how many minutes

Hours: 〜じかん

いちじかん	(for) 1 hour	ななじかん	(for) 7 hours
にじかん	(for) 2 hours	しちじかん	〃
さんじかん	(for) 3 hours	はちじかん	(for) 8 hours
よじかん	(for) 4 hours	くじかん	(for) 9 hours
ごじかん	(for) 5 hours	じゅうじかん	(for) 10 hours
ろくじかん	(for) 6 hours	じゅういちじかん	(for) 11 hours
		じゅうにじかん	(for) 12 hours

なんじかん	how many hours

Days: 〜にち (かん)

いちにち	(for) 1 day	なのか (かん)	(for) 7 days
ふつか (かん)	(for) 2 days	ようか (かん)	(for) 8 days
みっか (かん)	(for) 3 days	ここのか (かん)	(for) 9 days
よっか (かん)	(for) 4 days	とうか (かん)	(for) 10 days
いつか (かん)	(for) 5 days	じゅういちにち (かん)	(for) 11 days
むいか (かん)	(for) 6 days	じゅうににち (かん)	(for) 12 days

なんにち (かん)	how many days

Weeks: 〜しゅうかん

いっしゅうかん	(for) 1 week	ななしゅうかん	(for) 7 weeks
にしゅうかん	(for) 2 weeks	はっしゅうかん	(for) 8 weeks
さんしゅうかん	(for) 3 weeks	きゅうしゅうかん	(for) 9 weeks
よんしゅうかん	(for) 4 weeks	じゅっしゅうかん	(for) 10 weeks
ごしゅうかん	(for) 5 weeks	じゅういっしゅうかん	(for) 11 weeks
ろくしゅうかん	(for) 6 weeks	じゅうにしゅうかん	(for) 12 weeks

なんしゅうかん　　　　how many weeks

Months: 〜かげつ（かん）

いっかげつ（かん）	(for) 1 month	ななかげつ（かん）	(for) 7 months
にかげつ（かん）	(for) 2 months	はっかげつ（かん）	(for) 8 months
さんかげつ（かん）	(for) 3 months	きゅうかげつ（かん）	(for) 9 months
よんかげつ（かん）	(for) 4 months	じゅっかげつ（かん）	(for) 10 months
ごかげつ（かん）	(for) 5 months	じゅういっかげつ（かん）	(for) 11 months
ろっかげつ（かん）	(for) 6 months	じゅうにかげつ（かん）	(for) 12 months

なんかげつ（かん）　　how many months

Years: 〜ねん（かん）

いちねん（かん）	(for) 1 year	ななねん（かん）	(for) 7 years
にねん（かん）	(for) 2 years	しちねん（かん）	〃
さんねん（かん）	(for) 3 years	はちねん（かん）	(for) 8 years
よねん（かん）	(for) 4 years	きゅうねん（かん）	(for) 9 years
ごねん（かん）	(for) 5 years	じゅうねん（かん）	(for) 10 years
ろくねん（かん）	(for) 6 years	じゅういちねん（かん）	(for) 11 years
		じゅうにねん（かん）	(for) 12 years

なんねん（かん）　　　how many years

NOTE: Except for with じかん and しゅうかん, the suffix かん may be considered optional and need be added only when specificity is called for.

Relative Time

Day

おととい	day before yesterday
きのう	yesterday
きょう	today
あした	tomorrow
あさって	day after tomorrow

Month

せんせんげつ	month before last
せんげつ	last month
こんげつ	this month
らいげつ	next month
さらいげつ	month after next

Morning

おとといの　あさ	morning before last
きのうの　あさ	yesterday morning
けさ	this morning
あしたの　あさ	tomorrow morning
あさっての　あさ	morning of the day after tomorrow

Evening

おとといの　ばん／よる	evening/night before last
きのうの　ばん／よる	yesterday evening/night
こんばん	this evening
あしたの　ばん／よる	tomorrow evening/night
あさっての　ばん／よる	evening/night of the day after tomorrow

Week

せんせんしゅう	week before last
せんしゅう	last week
こんしゅう	this week
らいしゅう	next week
さらいしゅう	week after next

Year

おととし	year before last
きょねん	last year
ことし	this year
らいねん	next year
さらいねん	year after next

Seasons

はる	spring	あき	autumn
なつ	summer	ふゆ	winter

ANSWERS TO SELECTED EXERCISES AND QUIZZES

Lesson 1
V.　　べんごし

Lesson 2
II.　A.　1. A: これは　ほんですか。B: はい、ほんです。2. A: これは　かさですか。B: はい、かさです。3. A: これは　とけい　ですか。B: はい、とけいです。
　　B.　1. B: いいえ。かさではありません。2. B: いいえ。とけいではありません。3. B: いいえ。かぎではありません。
III.　　1. A: これは　なんですか。B: かぎです。2. A: これは　なんですか。B: とけいです。3. A: これは　なんですか。B: けいたいです。
IV.　　1. これは　なかむらさんの　かさです。2. これは　かとうさんの　とけいです。3. これは　ささきさんの　かぎです。
V.　A.　1. A: これは　スミスさんの　ほんですか。B: はい、スミスさんのです。2. A: これは　なかむらさんの　かぎですか。B: はい、なかむらさんのです。3. A: これは　チャンさんの　けいたいですか。B: はい、チャンさんのです。
　　B.　1. B: いいえ、ささきさんのではありません。2. B: いいえ、チャンさんのではありません。3. B: いいえ、スミスさんのではありません。
　　C.　1. A: これは　だれの　ほんですか。B: スミスさんのです。2. A: これは　だれの　かぎですか。B: なかむらさんのです。3. A: これは　だれの　けいたいですか。B: チャンさんのです。
VI.　A.　1. ささきさんの　でんわばんごうは　ゼロ　さんの　さん　に　きゅう　はちの　なな　なな　よん　はちです。2. たいしかんの　でんわばんごうは　ゼロ　さんの　さん　に　にごの　いち　いち　いち　ろくです。3. ぎんこうの　でんわばんごうは　ゼロ　さんの　ご　ろく　きゅう　ゼロの　さん　いち　いち　いちです。4. たかはしさんの　でんわばんごうは　ゼロ　さんの　さん　よん　ご　きゅうの　きゅう　ろく　に　ゼロです。
　　B.　1. A: ささきさんの　でんわばんごうは　なんばんですか。B: ゼロ　さんの　さん　に　きゅう　はちの　なな　なな　よん　はちです。2. A: たいしかんの　でんわばんごうは　なんばんですか。B: ゼロ　さんの　さん　に　にごの　いち　いち　いち　ろくです。3. A: ぎんこうの　でんわばんごうは　なんばんですか。B: ゼロ　さんの　ご　ろく　きゅう　ゼロの　さん　いち　いち　いちです。4. A: たかはしさんの　でんわばんごうは　なんばんですか。B: ゼロ　さんの　さん　よん　ご　きゅうの　きゅう　ろく　に　ゼロです。
VIII.　　ゼロ　さんの　さん　よん　ご　きゅうの　きゅう　ろく　ろく　ゼロ

Lesson 3
I.　　1. 4じ　2. 9じ　3. 7じ15ふん　4. 10じ20ぷん　5. 6じはん
II.　　1. A: いま　なんじですか。B: 4じです。2. A: いま　なんじですか。B: 9じです。3. A: いま　なんじですか。B: 7じ15ふんです。4. A: いま　なんじですか。B: 10じ20ぷんです。5. A: いま　なんじですか。B: 6じはんです。
VI.　　7じはん

Lesson 4
I.　　1. はちじゅうえん　2. ひゃくえん　3. ひゃく　にじゅうえん　4. さんびゃくえん　5. はっぴゃく　ろくじゅうえん　6. せん　にひゃくえん　7. さんぜんえん　8. よんせん　はっぴゃくえん　9. いちまん　ななせんえん　10. さんまん　きゅうせんえん
IV.　　1. A: それは　いくらですか。2. A: あれは　いくらですか。3. A: これは　いくらですか。4. A: それは　いくらですか。5. A: あれは　いくらですか。
IX.　　38,000

Lesson 5
II.　　1. A: その　くろい　カメラは　いくらですか。B: 20,000えんです。2. A: この　あおい　カメラは

いくらですか。B: １３，０００えんです。**3.** A: あの　おおきい　テレビは　いくらですか。B: ８０，０００
えんです。**4.** A: その　ちいさい　テレビは　いくらですか。B: ３０，０００えんです。

V.　　**1.** スミス: そのビールを　３ぼん　ください。**2.** スミス: そのおおきい　りんごを　よっつ　ください。**3.**
スミス: そのあおい　Ｔシャツを　２まい　ください。**4.** スミス: そのみかんを　２キロ　ください。

VII.　　**1.** b) **2.** a)

QUIZ 1 **UNITS 1–2**

I.　　**1.** は　**2.** の　**3.** か、か　**4.** の、の　**5.** から、まで　**6.** は、も　**7.** を、X　**8.** の、の

II.　　**1.** ドイツじん　**2.** なん　**3.** たかはしさん、だれ　**4.** なんばん　**5.** なんじ、なんじ　**6.** いくら　**7.** どこ

UNIT 3

Lesson 6

VIII.　　**1.** スミスさんは　らいしゅう　ささきさんと　おおさかししゃに　いきます。**2.** スミスさんは　あした　だ
れと　ホンコンに　いきますか。**3.** スミスさんは　あさって　うちに　かえります。**4.** スミスさんは　き
のう　ともだちと　ぎんざの　デパートに　いきました。**5.** スミスさんは　せんげつ　すずきさんと　どこ
に　いきましたか。

X.　　ともだち、デパート

Lesson 7

VII.　　**1.** スミスさんは　あさって　バスで　デパートに　いきます。**2.** スミスさんは　２０００ねんに　たかは
しさんと　しんかんせんで　きょうとに　いきました。**3.** スミスさんは　７がつ　１５にちに　ちかてつで
たいしかんに　いきます／いきました。**4.** スミスさんは　あした　あるいて　ともだちの　うちに　いき
ます。

VIII.　　**1.** スミスさんは　すいようびに　ひとりで　ひこうきで　おおさかししゃに　いきます。**2.** スミスさんは
きんようびの　１２じに　ひしょと　レストランに　いきます。４じに　ささきさんと　よこはまししゃに
いきます。６じに　アメリカたいしかんに　いきます。**3.** スミスさんは　にちようびの　ごぜん　９じに
ともだちと　こうえんに　いきます。ごご　７じに　すずきさんと　ともだちの　うちに　いきます。

X.　　**1.** b) **2.** c) [ひこうき]

UNIT 4

Lesson 8

VI.　　**1.** ３がいに　レストランが　あります。**2.** １かいに　おとこの　ひとが　います。**3.** ４かいに　なにが
ありますか。**4.** ちか　１かいに　だれが　いますか。**5.** いすの　うえに　かばんが　あります。**6.** テー
ブルの　うえに　はなと　ほんが　あります。**7.** ベッドの　ちかくに　たかはしさんが　います。**8.** れい
ぞうこの　なかに　なにが　ありますか。

VIII.　　**1.** ぎんこう　**2.** ゆうびんきょく　**3.** レストラン

Lesson 9

V.　　**1.** チャン: タクシーのりばは　どこに　ありますか。**2.** チャン: ぎんこうは　どこに　ありますか。**3.** チャン:
カートは　どこに　ありますか。**4.** チャン: くすりやは　どこに　ありますか。**5.** チャン: ほんやは　どこに
ありますか。**6.** チャン: おてあらいは　どこに　ありますか。

VII.　　スーパーの　となり

UNIT 5

Lesson 10

III.　　A.　**1.** スミスさんは　ほんを　よみます。**2.** スミスさんは　コーヒーを　のみます。**3.** スミスさんは　きってを
かいます。**4.** スミスさんは　テニスを　します。

　　B.　**1.** A: スミスさんは　なにを　よみますか。B: ほんを　よみます。**2.** A: スミスさんは　なにを　のみます
か。B: コーヒーを　のみます。**3.** A: スミスさんは　なにを　かいますか。B: きってを　かいます。**4.** A:
スミスさんは　なにを　しますか。B: テニスを　します。

V.　　A.　**1.** スミスさんは　としょかんで　ほんを　よみます。**2.** スミスさんは　かいしゃで　しごとを　します。
　　3. スミスさんは　ゆうびんきょくで　きってを　かいます。**4.** スミスさんは　スポーツクラブで　テニスを
します。

B. 1. A: スミスさんは どこで ほんを よみますか。B: としょかんで よみます。2. A: スミスさんは どこで しごとを しますか。B: かいしゃで します。3. A: スミスさんは どこで きってを かいますか。B: ゆうびんきょくで かいます。4. A: スミスさんは どこで テニスを しますか。B: スポーツクラブで します。

VI. 1. かとうさんは まいあさ やさいジュースを のみます。2. かとうさんは まいばん おくさんと ジョギングを します。3. かとうさんは まいしゅう スポーツクラブに いきます。

VIII. 1. おおきい おてら 2. (おてらの) にわで

Lesson 11

III. A. 1. 1) スミスさんは ともだちに てがみを かきます。2) スミスさんは のぞみデパートの しゃちょうに てがみを かきます。3) スミスさんは ぎんざの ホテルに てがみを かきます。4) スミスさんは にほんごの がっこうに てがみを かきます。2. 1) スミスさんは ともだちに でんわを します。2) スミスさんは のぞみデパートの しゃちょうに でんわを します。3) スミスさんは ぎんざの ホテルに でんわを します。4) スミスさんは にほんごの がっこうに でんわを します。3. 1) スミスさんは ともだちに メールを おくります。2) スミスさんは のぞみデパートの しゃちょうに メールを おくります。3) スミスさんは ぎんざの ホテルに メールを おくります。4) スミスさんは にほんごの がっこうに メールを おくります。

B. 1. 1) A: スミスさんは だれに てがみを かきますか。B: ともだちに かきます。2) A: スミスさんは だれに てがみを かきますか。B: のぞみデパートの しゃちょうに かきます。3) A: スミスさんは どこに てがみを かきますか。B: ぎんざの ホテルに かきます。4) A: スミスさんは どこに てがみを かきますか。B: にほんごの がっこうに かきます。2. 1) A: スミスさんは だれに でんわを しますか。B: ともだちにします。2) A: スミスさんは だれに でんわを しますか。B: のぞみデパートの しゃちょうに します。3) A: スミスさんは どこに でんわを しますか。B: ぎんざの ホテルに します。4) A: スミスさんは どこに でんわを しますか。B: にほんごの がっこうに します。3. 1) A: スミスさんは だれに メールを おくりますか。B: ともだちに おくります。2) A: スミスさんは だれに メールを おくりますか。B: のぞみデパートの しゃちょうに おくります。3) A: スミスさんは どこに メールを おくりますか。B: ぎんざの ホテルに おくります。4) A: スミスさんは どこに メールを おくりますか。B: にほんごの がっこうに おくります。

IV. 1. スミスさんは かようびの 10じに のぞみデパートで たかはしさんに あいます。2. スミスさんは すいようびの 7じに レストランローマで ささきさんの ごしゅじんに あいます。3. スミスさんは もくようびの 11じに さっぽろししゃで ししゃの ひとに あいます。4. スミスさんは きんようびの 6じはんに ホテルの ロビーで なかむらさんに あいます。

V. 1. はい、ときどき たべます。2. いいえ、あまり しません。3. いいえ、ぜんぜん みません。

VII. 1. スミス: ワインを 1ぽん おねがいします。みせの ひと: はい。2. スミス: サラダを ふたつ おねがいします。みせの ひと: はい。3. スミス: アイスクリームを よっつ おねがいします。みせの ひと: はい。

IX. メールを おくり(ます)

QUIZ 2 UNITS 3–5

I. 1. や 2. に、と 3. が、が 4. は、に、の 5. と、に 6. に 7. で、を 8. で、に 9. X、で、を 10. X、に 11. から

II. 1. だれ 2. どこ 3. なに 4. いくつ 5. なんにん 6. いつ 7. だれ 8. どこ 9. なんじ 10. いつ 11. なに、だれ

III. 1. あります 2. ありません 3. いきません 4. みます、みません 5. よく

UNIT 6

Lesson 12

IV. 1. これは あたらしい くるまです。2. これは ふるい ビルです。3. これは たかい セーターです。4. これは あまい ケーキです。5. これは おいしい りんごです。2. スミスさんは せんしゅう きれいな レストランで しょくじを しました。

VIII. 1. スミスさんは せんしゅう しずかな レストランで しょくじを しました。2. スミスさんは せんしゅう きれいな レストランで しょくじを しました。

X. 1. スミス: (a) えきから ちかいですね。(b) べんり ですね。2. スミス: おもしろい えですね。3. スミス: とても ふるい とけいですね。4. スミス: きれいな はなですね。

XII. きれいな

Lesson 13

III. A. 1. A: スミスさんは だれに とけいを あげましたか。B: すずきさんに あげました。2. A: スミスさんは だれに きょうとの おみやげを あげましたか。B: なかむらさんに あげました。

B. 1. A: すずきさんは だれに とけいを もらいましたか。B: スミスさんに もらいました。2. A: なかむら さんは だれに きょうとの おみやげを もらいましたか。B: スミスさんに もらいました。

C. 1. A: スミスさんは すずきさんに なにを あげましたか。B: とけいを あげました。2. A: スミスさんは なかむらさんに なにを あげましたか。B: きょうとの おみやげを あげました。

IV. A. 1. チャンさんは クリスマスに すずきさんに デジカメを あげました。すずきさんは クリスマスに チャンさんに デジカメを もらいました。2. すずきさんは バレンタインデーに チャンさんに きれい な スカーフを あげました。チャンさんは バレンタインデーに すずきさんに きれいな スカーフを もらいました。

B. 1. A: チャンさんは クリスマスに すずきさんに なにを あげましたか。B: デジカメを あげました。2. A: すずきさん は バレンタインデーに チャンさんに なにを あげましたか。B: きれいな スカーフを あげました。

C. 1. A: チャンさんは クリスマスに だれに デジカメを あげましたか。B: すずきさんに あげました。2. A: すずきさんは バレンタインデーに だれに きれいな スカーフを あげましたか。B: チャンさんに あげました。

D. 1. A: チャンさんは いつ すずきさんに デジカメを あげましたか。B: クリスマスに あげました。2. A: すずきさんは いつ チャンさんに きれいな スカーフを あげましたか。B: バレンタインデーに あげ ました。

E. 3. A: チャンさんは たんじょうびに すずきさんに なにを もらいましたか。B: はなたばを もらいま した。4. A: すずきさんは たんじょうびに チャンさんに なにを もらいましたか。B: セーターを も らいました。

F. 3. A: チャンさんは たんじょうびに だれに はなたばを もらいましたか。B: すずきさんに もらいま した。4. A: すずきさんは たんじょうびに だれに セーターを もらいましたか。B: チャンさんに も らいました。

G. 3. A: チャンさんは いつ すずきさんに はなたばを もらいましたか。B: たんじょうびに もらいまし た。4. A: すずきさんは いつ チャンさんに セーターを もらいましたか。B: たんじょうびに もらいま した。

VI. にほんごの ほんを もらいました。

Lesson 14

III. A. 1. なかむら: きのうの パーティーの りょうりは おいしかったですか。チャン: はい、おいしかったで す。スミス: いいえ、おいしくなかったです。2. なかむら: きのうの おまつりは にぎやかでしたか。 チャン: はい、にぎやかでした。スミス: いいえ、にぎやかではありませんでした。

B. 1. かとう: きのうの コンサートは どうでしたか。チャン: とても よかったです。スミス: あまり よく なかったです。2. かとう: きのうの バーゲンセールは どうでしたか。チャン: とても やすかったで す。スミス: あまり やすくなかったです。

V. にちようび、にぎやかでした。

UNIT 7

Lesson 15

I. 1. コーヒーを のみませんか。2. ゴルフを しませんか。

II. A. 1. A: しゅうまつに いっしょに ぎんざに いきませんか。B: ええ、いきましょう。2. A: しゅうまつに いっしょに しょくじを しませんか。B: ええ、しましょう。3. A: しゅうまつに いっしょに すもうを みませんか。B: ええ、みましょう。4. A: しゅうまつに いっしょに ひるごはんを たべませんか。B: ええ、たべましょう。

B. 1. A: しゅうまつに いっしょに ぎんざに いきませんか。B: ざんねんですが、つごうが わるいです。2. A: しゅうまつに いっしょに しょくじを しませんか。B: ざんねんですが、つごうが わるいです。3. A: しゅうまつに いっしょに すもうを みませんか。B: ざんねんですが、つごうが わるいです。4. A: しゅ うまつに いっしょに ひるごはんを たべませんか。B: ざんねんですが、つごうが わるいです。

IV. A. 1. らいげつ さっぽろで ゆきまつりが あります。2. あした たいしかんで パーティーが ありま す。3. かようびに よこはまで サッカーの しあいが あります。

B. 1. A: らいげつ さっぽろで ゆきまつりが あります。いっしょに いきませんか。B: いいですね。いきま しょう。2. A: あした たいしかんで パーティーが あります。いっしょに いきませんか。B: いいです ね。いきましょう。3. A: かようびに よこはまで サッカーの しあいが あります。いっしょに いき ません か。B: いいですね。いきましょう。

VI. 1. すずき: どようびに いっしょに しょくじを しませんか。2. チャン: ええ、しましょう。3. すずき: なにを たべましょうか。4. チャン: おすしは どうですか。5. すずき: いいですね。6. すずき: なんじ に あいましょうか。7. チャン: 6じに あいませんか。8. すずき: はい、そうしましょう。

VII. でんしゃ、にちようび

Lesson 16

I. 1. ちずを　かきましょうか。 2. この　ほんを　かしましょうか。

II. 1. スミス: ドアを　あけましょうか。なかむら: ええ、おねがいします。 2. スミス: しゃしんを　とりましょうか。すずき: いいえ、けっこうです。 3. スミス: まどを　しめましょうか。なかむら: ええ、おねがいします。 4. スミス: エアコンを　けしましょうか。すずき: いいえ、けっこうです。

III. 1. わたしは　かさが　あります。 2. わたしは　えいがの　きっぷが　あります。 3. わたしは　にほんごの　じゅぎょうが　あります。 4. わたしは　やすみが　あります。 5. わたしは　じかんが　あります。 6. わたしは　かいぎが　あります。

VI. 1. すずき: コピーを　しましょうか。 2. スミス: ええ、おねがいします。 3. すずき: なんまい　しましょうか。 4. スミス: 3まい　おねがいします。

VII. すずきさんが　かきます。

QUIZ 3 UNITS 6–7

I. 1. に　2. を　3. が　4. が　5. が、X

II. 1. どんな　2. だれ　3. どう　4. どこ

III. 1. きれいな　2. おいしい　3. しずかではありません　4. にぎやかでした　5. おもしろくなかったです

IV. 1. みませんか、あいましょうか　2. つけましょうか、あけましょうか

UNIT 8

Lesson 17

III. 1. でんきを　つけて、ドアを　しめます。 2. でんわばんごうを　きいて、でんわを　します。 3. うちで　ほんを　よんで、レポートを　かきます。

IV. 1. A: あした　なにを　しますか。B: ぎんざで　かいものを　して、えいがを　みます。 2. A: あした　なにを　しますか。B: レストランで　ひるごはんを　たべて、びじゅつかんに　いきます。

V. 1. スミスさんに　あって、いっしょに　テニスを　しました。 2. ドアを　あけて、でんきを　つけましょうか。

VI. 1. A: きのう　なにを　しましたか。B: ろっぽんぎに　いって、しょくじを　しました。 2. A: きのう　なにを　しましたか。B: ともだちに　あって、いっしょに　すもうを　みました。

VIII. 1. A: きのう　しごとの　あとで　なにを　しましたか。B: ともだちに　あって、いっしょに　えいがを　みました。 2. A: きのう　しごとの　あとで　なにを　しましたか。B: デパートに　いって、かいものを　しました。 3. A: きのう　しごとの　あとで　なにを　しましたか。B: バーで　ワインを　のんで、タクシーで　うちに　かえりました。

IX. 1. スミスさんは　きんようびに　こうべに　いって、ゴルフを　します。ゴルフの　あとで　ともだちの　うちに　いきます。 2. スミスさんは　どようびに　きょうとに　いって、やまもとさんと　しょくじを　します。しょくじの　あとで　ふるい　おてらや　にわを　みます。

XI. a) [テレビ]

Lesson 18

II. 1. ちょっと　まってください。 2. しゃしんを　とってください。 3. もう　いちど　いってください。 4. ペンを　かしてください。 5. ピザを　とどけてください。

III. A. 1. A: すみません。メールアドレスを　かいてください。B: はい。 2. A: すみません。メニューを　みせてください。B: はい。 3. A: すみません。かいぎの　しりょうを　もってきてください。B: はい。

V. 1. つぎの　しんごうを　ひだりに　まがってください。 2. ふたつめの　かどを　みぎに　まがってください。 3. まっすぐ　いってください。 4. デパートの　てまえで　とめてください。

VII. たかはしさん、ファックス

UNIT 9

Lesson 19

III. A. 1. たかはし: (チャンさんは)　どうやって　かいしゃに　いきますか。チャン: あざぶで　バスに　のって、とうきょうえきで　おります。とうきょうえきから　かいしゃまで　あるきます。 2. たかはし: (すずきさんは)　どうやって　かいしゃに　いきますか。すずき: よこはまえきで　でんしゃに　のって、とうきょうえきで　おります。とうきょうえきから　かいしゃまで　あるきます。

B. 1. チャン: 8じに　でます...8じ　20ぷんに　つきます。 2. すずき: 7じに　でます...8じに　つきます。

V.　1. スミス: とうきょうから　にっこうまで　どのぐらい　かかりますか。なかむら: でんしゃで　1じかんはん　かかります。2. なかむら: なりたくうこうから　ホンコンまで　どのぐらい　かかりますか。チャン: ひこうきで　5じかん　かかります。

VIII.　1. チャン: ひこうきは　なんじに　なりたを　でますか。2. りょこうがいしゃの　ひと: 11じに　でます。3. チャン: なりたから　ホノルルまで　どのぐらい　かかりますか。4. りょこうがいしゃの　ひと: 7じかんぐらい　かかります。5. チャン: ありがとうございます。

IX.　ちかてつ、30ぷん

Lesson 20

II.　1. まどを　あけても　いいですか。2. この　イヤーホーンガイドを　つかっても　いいですか。3. この　えの　しゃしんを　とっても　いいですか。4. ここで　たばこを　すっても　いいですか。5. あした　やすんでも　いいですか。

III.　1. すずき: おきゃくさんに　カタログを　みせても　いいですか。かとう: はい、どうぞ。2. すずき: おきゃくさんに　サンプルを　おくっても　いいですか。かとう: はい、どうぞ。3. すずき: あさって　やすんでも　いいですか。かとう: はい、どうぞ。

IV.　1. スミス: おてらの　しゃしんを　とっても　いいですか。おてらの　ひと: すみませんが、ちょっと...。2. スミス: にわに　はいっても　いいですか。おてらの　ひと: すみませんが、ちょっと...。3. スミス: ここで　おちゃを　のんでも　いいですか。おてらの　ひと: すみませんが、ちょっと...。

VI.　1. みせの　ひと: ここ／こちらに　おなまえと　ごじゅうしょを　おねがいします。2. スミス: すみません、ペンが　ありません。3. スミス: この　ペンを　つかっても　いいですか。4. みせの　ひと: はい、どうぞ。5. スミス: ありがとう。

VII.　3じはん、かいぎしつ

Lesson 21

III.　1. しゃしんを　とらないでください。2. ドアを　しめないでください。3. でんきを　けさないでください。4. くるまを　とめないでください。

IV.　1. ここは　でぐちですから、くるまを　とめないでください。2. ここは　みせの　まえですから、くるまを　とめないでください。3. ここは　ちゅうしゃきんしですから、くるまを　とめないでください。

VI.　かいぎしつ、かいぎ

QUIZ 4　UNITS 8–9

I.　1. に　2. を、に　3. で　4. で、を、に　5. から、まで、で　6. に、✕　7. に、を、に、に　8. は、から、を

II.　1. なに　2. いつ　3. どうやって　4. どのぐらい

III.　1. かかない　2. けします　3. のんで　4. とらない　5. しめて　6. あけます　7. みて　8. こない　9. します

IV.　1. みて　2. かって　3. おしえて　4. まがって、いって　5. もらって　6. とめないで

UNIT 10

Lesson 22

III.　A.　1. A: チャンさんは　いま　なにを　していますか。B: レポートを　かいています。2. A: なかむらさんは　いま　なにを　していますか。B: コピーを　しています。3. A: かとうさんは　いま　なにを　していますか。B: かいぎしつで　せつめいを　しています。4. A: ささきさんは　いま　なにを　していますか。B: おきゃくさんと　はなしを　しています。5. A: すずきさんは　いま　なにを　していますか。B: たばこを　すっています。6. A: たかはしさんは　いま　なにを　していますか。B: 1かいで　エレベーターを　まっています。

B.　7. B: いいえ、おきゃくさんと　はなしを　しています。8. B: いいえ、コピーを　しています。9. B: いいえ、レポートを　かいています。

VII.　c) [(スミスさんは)　おきゃくさんと　はなしを　しています。]

Lesson 23

VI.　1. グリーンさんは　しぶやに　すんでいます。そして、ＡＢＣフーズに　つとめています。2. なかむらさんの　いもうとさんは　さっぽろに　すんでいます。そして、ぎんこうに　つとめています。3. チャンさんの　おねえさんは　ホンコンに　すんでいます。そして、デパートに　つとめています。

VIII.　1. スミス: レストランとうきょうの　じゅうしょを　しっていますか。すずき: はい、しっています。2. スミス: さっぽろししゃの　ファックスばんごうを　しっていますか。すずき: いいえ、しりません。

XI.　03の　3944の　6493です。

Lesson 24

III. A. 1. スミスさんは　ビールが　すきです。スキーが　じょうずです。にほんごが　わかります。2. チャンさんは　コーヒーが　すきです。ダンスが　じょうずです。フランスごが　わかります。3. ささきさんはワインが　すきです。テニスが　じょうずです。ちゅうごくごが　わかります。

B. 1. スミスさんは　おさけが　すきではありません。ダンスが　じょうずではありません。ちゅうごくごが　わかりません。2. チャンさんは　ビールが　すきではありません。スキーが　じょうずではありません。かんこくごが　わかりません。3. ささきさんは　ウイスキーが　すきではありません。ゴルフがじょうずではありません。ドイツごが　わかりません。

C. 1. スミス: はい、すきです。スミス: はい、わかります。2. チャン: はい、すきです。チャン: いいえ、わかりません。3. ささき: いいえ、すきではありません。ささき: はい、わかります。

D. 1. なかむら: いいえ、じょうずではありません。2. なかむら: はい、じょうずです。3. なかむら: いいえ、じょうずではありません。

V. 1. たかはし: おちあいさんは　ピアノが　じょうずです。ジャズが　すきです。2. たかはし: こじまさんは　すいえいが　じょうずです。うみが　すきです。3. たかはし: あんどうさんは　えが　じょうずです。うきよえが　すきです。

VII. フランスご

Lesson 25

II. 1. わたしは　テレビを　みたいです。2. わたしは　たかはしさんに　あいたくないです。3. わたしはふるい　かぐを　かいたいです。4. わたしは　じゅうどうを　ならいたくないです。

V. 1. いしゃ: どうしましたか。チャン: ねつが　38ど　あります。2. いしゃ: どうしましたか。チャン: のどが　いたいです。3. いしゃ: どうしましたか。チャン: こしが　いたいです。

VI. 1. A: わたし　まいしゅう　ジョギングを　しています。B: いいですね。わたしも　したいです。2. A: わたし　まいしゅう　おちゃを　ならっています。B: いいですね。わたしも　ならいたいです。

VIII. c)

QUIZ 5 UNITS 10–11

I. 1. が　2. に　3. で　4. が　5. に
II. 1. しています　2. しっています、しりません　3. いきたかったです
III. 1. すきです　2. じょうずではありません　3. します　4. しません

CD SCRIPT FOR EXERCISES

Lesson 1, Exercise V
おんなの　ひと：スミスさんは　エンジニアですか。
たかはし：　　　いいえ、べんごしです。

Lesson 2, Exercise VIII
おんなの　ひと：すみません。スミスさんの　でんわばんごうは　なんばんですか。
たかはし：　　　ゼロ　さんの　さん　よん　ご　きゅうの　きゅう　ろく　ろく　ゼロです。
おんなの　ひと：ありがとうございます。

Lesson 3, Exercise VI
スミス：　　すみません。ジムは　なんじからですか。
フロント：7じはんからです。
スミス：　　どうも　ありがとう。

Lesson 4, Exercise IX
スミス：　　　あれは　ビデオカメラですか。
みせの　ひと：はい。
スミス：　　　いくらですか。
みせの　ひと：38,000えんです。

Lesson 5, Exercise VII
スミス：　　　すみません。あのビールは　どこのですか。
みせの　ひと：アメリカのです。
スミス：　　　あれは　いくらですか。
みせの　ひと：300えんです。
スミス：　　　じゃ、あれを　10ぽん　ください。

Lesson 6, Exercise X
なかむら：スミスさんは　あさって　どこに　いきますか。
スミス：　デパートに　いきます。
なかむら：だれと　いきますか。
スミス：　ともだちと　いきます。
なかむら：そうですか。

Lesson 7, Exercise X
すずき：チャンさんは　いつ　おおさかししゃに　いきますか。
チャン：もくようびに　いきます。
すずき：なんで　いきますか。
チャン：ひこうきで　いきます。
すずき：そうですか。

Questions:
1. チャンさんは　いつ　おおさかししゃに　いきますか。
2. チャンさんは　なんで　おおさかししゃに　いきますか。

Lesson 8, Exercise VIII
Ms. Nakamura is talking about her building.

1. 1 かいに　ぎんこうが　あります。
2. 2 かいに　ゆうびんきょくが　あります。
3. 3 がいに　レストランが　あります。

Lesson 9, Exercise VII
スミス:　　　　すみません。ちゅうしゃじょうは　どこですか。
おんなの　ひと: スーパーの　となりです。
スミス:　　　　ありがとうございます。

Lesson 10, Exercise VIII
チャンさんは　どようびに　ともだちと　でんしゃで　かまくらに　いきました。かまくらで　おおきい　おてらを
みました。おてらの　にわで　ひるごはんを　たべました。

Lesson 11, Exercise IX
なかむら: チャンさんは　よく　おかあさんに　でんわを　しますか。
チャン:　いいえ、あまり　しませんが、よく　メールを　おくります。(**NOTE:** が means "but." See Note 1, p. 205)

Lesson 12, Exercise XII
なかむら: あした　ともだちと　はこねに　いきます。
スミス:　はこねは　どんな　ところですか。
なかむら: きれいな　ところですよ。

Lesson 13, Exercise VI
きのうは　スミスさんの　たんじょうびでした。スミスさんは　ともだちに　にほんごの　ほんを　もらいました。

Question: スミスさんは　たんじょうびに　ともだちに　なにを　もらいましたか。

Lesson 14, Exercise V
すずき: チャンさん、にちようびに　なにを　しましたか。
チャン: あさくさで　おまつりを　みました。
すずき: どうでしたか。
チャン: とても　にぎやかでした。

Lesson 15, Exercise VII
すずき: スミスさん、にちようびに　いっしょに　にっこうに　いきませんか。
スミス: ええ、いきましょう。
すずき: なんで　いきましょうか。
スミス: でんしゃは　どうですか。
すずき: ええ、そうしましょう。じゃ、にちようびに。

Lesson 16, Exercise VII
スミス: すずきさん、フランスたいしかんは　どこに　ありますか。
すずき: ひろおです。ちずを　かきましょうか。
スミス: ええ、おねがいします。

Question: だれが　ちずを　かきますか。

Lesson 17, Exercise XI
なかむら: チャンさん、しゅうまつに　なにを　しますか。
チャン: どようびに　しんじゅくに　いって、テレビを　かいます。
なかむら: そうですか。

Question: チャンさんは　どようびに　なにを　かいますか。

Lesson 18, Exercise VII
かとう: チャンさん、たかはしさんに　かいぎの　しりょうを　ファックスで　おくってください。
チャン: はい、わかりました。

Lesson 19, Exercise IX
スミス: すみません。かいしゃから　のぞみデパートまで　どのぐらい　かかりますか。
なかむら: ちかてつで　30ぷんぐらい　かかります。
スミス: そうですか。ありがとうございます。

Lesson 20, Exercise VII
スミス: すみません、3じはんから　かいぎしつを　つかっても　いいですか。
なかむら: はい、どうぞ。
スミス: ありがとうございます。

Lesson 21, Exercise VI
かとう: ごごから　かいぎが　ありますから、かいぎしつの　エアコンを　けさないでください。
チャン: はい、わかりました。

Lesson 22, Exercise VII
ささき: スミスさんは　どこですか。
チャン: いま　3がいの　かいぎしつで　おきゃくさんと　はなしを　しています。
ささき: そうですか。

Question: スミスさんは　いま　なにを　していますか。

Lesson 23, Exercise XI
スミス: すみません。レストランローマの　でんわばんごうを　しっていますか。
なかむら: はい。03-3944-6493です。
スミス: ありがとうございます。

Question: レストランローマの　でんわばんごうは　なんばんですか。

Lesson 24, Exercise VII
かとう: らいしゅう　フランスの　ししゃに　いきます。
スミス: ひとりで　いきますか。
かとう: いいえ、チャンさんと　いきます。チャンさんは　フランスごが　じょうずですから。

Lesson 25, Exercise VIII
なかむら: スミスさん、しょうらい　どんな　ところに　すみたいですか。
スミス: そうですね。ちいさい　まちに　すみたいです。
なかむら: そうですか。

Japanese-English Glossary

おとこの ひと: man, 72
おなか: belly, stomach, 233
おなまえ: (another person's) name, 96
おにいさん: older brother, 215
おねえさん: older sister, 215
おねがいします: please (get me . . .), 8, 96
おのみもの: beverage, 105
おはいりください: please come in, 59
おはようございます: good morning, 49
おまつり: festival, 62, 132
おみこし: portable shrine, 150
おみやげ: gift, souvenir, 124
おもしろい (です): interesting, 113, 114, 133
おります: get off (a vehicle), 180, 181
おんがく: music, 92
おんせん: hot spring (resort), 67, 69
おんな: female, woman, 21
おんなの こ: girl, 80
おんなの ひと: woman, 21

か: (question-marking particle), 2, 6, 48, 222
～か (かん): day(s), 180
が: (as subject marker), 68; but (conjunctive usage), 169, 170, 205; (instead of は), 57, 58; (used with すきです, じょうずです, いたいです, etc.), 222
カート: cart, 83
カード: (business) card, 193; (credit) card, 36
カーネーション: carnation, 123
カーペンター: Carpenter (surname), 229
～かい/がい: floor, story, 70
かいぎ: meeting, conference, 22
かいぎしつ: conference room, 82
かいぎを します: hold a meeting, 167
かいさつぐち: ticket gate, 141
かいしゃ: company, the office, 9
かいだん: stairs, 206
ガイド: guide, 189
かいます: buy, 88, 91, 92, 160, 163, 178
かいものを します: shop, 91
かえります: return, go home, 48, 51, 52, 160, 162, 163, 178, 197
かかります: take (time), 179, 180, 181
かぎ: key, 11
かきます: write, 98, 100, 160, 162, 163, 178, 197
かぐ: furniture, 234
がくせい: student, 5
～かげつ: month(s), 181
かさ: umbrella, 11
かしましょうか: shall I lend you?, 150; かします: lend, 150, 151, 172
かぞく: family, 69
かた: shoulder, 233
カタログ: catalog, 169, 189
～がつ: month, 61
かつぎます: carry (on one's shoulders), 150

がっこう: school, 101
カップ: cup, 43
かど: corner, 171
かとう: Kato (surname), xiii
かない: (my) wife, 99
かばん: briefcase, tote bag, 71
かびん: vase, 122
かぶき: Kabuki, 89
かまくら: Kamakura (town), 75
かようび: Tuesday, 60
から: because, 98, 141, 142; from, 21, 22, 61
からい (です): hot, spicy, 113, 114
カレー: curry, 115
かんこく: South Korea, 41
かんこくご: Korean (language), 226
かんじ: kanji, Chinese character(s), 225

ききます: ask, 98, 162, 163; listen (to), 91, 92, 160, 162, 163
キス: whiting, 98
きたぐち: north exit, 143
きって: stamp, 38
きっぷ: ticket, 124
きてください: please come, 131; きます: come, 48, 49, 50, 51, 52, 160, 162, 163, 178, 196, 197
きに しないでください: don't worry about it, 200; きに します: worry (about), be bothered (by), 200
きねんび: anniversary, 129
きのう: yesterday, 51
きぶんが わるいんです: I don't feel well, 157
きゅう: nine, 10
きゅうじゅう: ninety, 23
きょう: today, 51
きょうと: Kyoto, 52
きょねん: last year, 51
きれいです or きれいな: pretty, clean, 110, 111, 113, 116, 133
キロ: kilogram, 42
きを つけて: take care, 161
きんえん: no smoking, nonsmoking, 197
ぎんこう: bank, 7, 22
ぎんざ: Ginza (district), 52
きんようび: Friday, 59, 60

く: nine, 10
くうこう: airport, 50
くがつ: September, 61
くすり: medicine, 78
くすりや: drugstore, 78
ください: please give me, 28, 29, 38
くだもの: fruit, 224
クッキングスクール: cooking school, 232
くに: (my) country, 105
ぐらい: about, approximately, 120
クラス: class, 235
クラブ: (exercise) club, 94; golf club, 155
グリーン: Green (surname), xiii

クリスマス: Christmas, 126
くるま: car, 41, 61
くろい (です): black, 38
くれます: give (to me), 110

けいたい: cell/mobile phone, 11
ケーキ: cake, 115
ゲーム: game, 115
けしゴム: eraser, 78
けします: turn off, 151, 160, 163, 178, 197
ケチャップ: ketchup, 199
けっこうです: be fine, be all right, 36; no thank you, 112 → いいえ
けっこん: marriage, 129
けっこんきねんび: wedding anniversary, 129
げつようび: Monday, 60
けんどう: kendo, 231

こ: child, 80
ご: five, 10
～ご: language, 35
こうえん: park, 50
こうくうびん: airmail, 171
こうさてん: intersection, 171
こうじょう: factory, 161
こうちゃ: tea, 90
こうばん: police box, 78
こうべ: Kobe (city), 167
コート: coat, 124
コーヒー: coffee, 43, 90
コーヒーカップ: coffee cup, 43
ごがつ: May, 61
ここ: here, 82
ごご: p.m., in the afternoon, 22
ここのか: the ninth (of the month), 61
ここのつ: nine, 39
こし: lower back, 233
こじま: Kojima (surname), 219
ごじゅう: fifty, 21, 23
ごじゅうしょ: (another person's) address, 174
ごしゅじん: (another person's) husband, 99
ごじゅっぷん: fifty minutes, 21
ごぜん: a.m., in the morning, 23
こちら: this one, 3
ことし: this year, 51
こども: child, 215
この: this (used before a noun), 20, 39
こばやし: Kobayashi (surname), 219
ごはん: meal, 26
コピーを します: make a photocopy, 156
ゴルフを します: play golf, 95
これ: this one, 9, 20; これは？: what about this?, 9, 10
ごろ: about, 85
こんげつ: this month, 51
コンサート: concert, 132
こんしゅう: this week, 51
こんど: this coming, 105

こんばん: this evening, 155
コンビニ: convenience store, 77

さあ: let me see, 220; さあ、わかりま
　せん: I don't know, 220
さいふ: wallet, 73
さかな: fish, 98
さかや: liquor store, 78
さき: ahead, 171
さくらびじゅつかん: Sakura Art
　Museum, 179
さけ: sake, 90
ささき: Sasaki (surname), xiii
サッカー: soccer, 142, 224
ざっし: magazine, 33
さっぽろ: Sapporo (city), 103
さっぽろししゃ: Sapporo (branch)
　office, 103
さとう: Sato (surname), 161
さとう: sugar, 199
～さま: Mr., Mrs., Ms., Miss, 97
さむい (です): cold, 113, 114, 133
サラダ: salad, 90
さん: three, 10
～さん: Mr., Mrs., Ms., Miss, 3
さんがつ: March, 61
さんじゅう: thirty, 23
サンドイッチ: sandwich, 90
さんにん: three people, 79
ざんねんですが、つごうが わるい
　です: I'm sorry, but it wouldn't be
　convenient (for me), 140, 144
サンフランシスコ: San Francisco, 184
サンプル: sample, 170
さんぽを します: go for a walk, 95

し: four, 10
～じ: o'clock, 21, 23
しあい: game, match, 142
しがつ: April, 61
じかん: time, 152
～じかん: hour(s), 180
しごと: work, job, 22
しごとを します: work, 91
ししゃ: branch office, 50
じしょ: dictionary, 35
しずかです or しずかな: quiet, 113,
　116, 133
した: bottom, below, under, 71
しち: seven, 10
しちがつ: July, 61
しっています: know, 204, 214, 215
しつれいします: good-bye, 49, 50
しながわ: Shinagawa (district), 217
しぶや: Shibuya (district), 57
しぶやえき: Shibuya Station, 175
します: do, 89, 92, 143, 160, 162, 163, 178,
　196, 197
ジム: gym, 26
しめます: close, shut, 151, 163, 196, 197
じゃ: well then, 28, 29
シャープペンシル: mechanical pencil, 35

じゃありません: is/are not, 2
じゃありませんでした: was/were
　not, 2
しゃしん: photograph, 151
ジャズ: jazz, 228
しゃちょう: president (of a company),
　101
じゅう: ten, 23
じゅういちがつ: November, 61
じゅういちじ: eleven o'clock, 23
じゅうおく: one billion (=1,000,000,000),
　29
じゅうがつ: October, 61
～しゅうかん: week(s), 181
シュークリーム: cream puff, 44
じゅうしょ: address, 10
ジュース: juice, 90
じゅうどう: judo, 233
じゅうにがつ: December, 61
しゅうまつ: weekend, 89
じゅうまん: one hundred thousand, 29
じゅうよっか: the fourteenth (of the
　month), 61
じゅぎょう: class, 152
しゅじん: (my) husband, 99
しゅっちょう: business trip, 57
しょうかいします: introduce, 230
じょうずです: be skilled; 222, 223, 224,
　225
しょうひん: product, merchandise, 169
しょうらい: the future, 235
ショー: show, 132
ジョギングを します: jog, 91
しょくじを します: have a meal, 114
ショコラショコラ: Chocolat-Chocolat
　(fictitious product name), 213
ジョンソン: Johnson (surname), 61
しりょう: data, information, material,
　documents, literature, 173
しろい (です): white, 175
～じん: -ese, -ian (person from), 4
しんかんせん: the Shinkansen, 61
しんごう: traffic signal, 171
じんじゃ: Shinto shrine, 69
しんじゅく: Shinjuku (district), 147
しんじゅくえき: Shinjuku Station, 147
しんせつです or しんせつな: kind,
　helpful, 113, 116
しんばし: Shimbashi (district), 147
しんばしえき: Shimbashi Station, 147
しんぶん: newspaper, 11

すいえい: swimming, 224
スイス: Switzerland, 39
(たばこを) すいます: smoke (a ciga-
　rette), 189, 190, 196
すいようび: Wednesday, 60
スーパー: supermarket, 22
スープ: soup, 90
スカーフ: scarf, 124
スキー: skiing, 224
すきです: like, 222, 224, 225

すきな: favorite, 122
すきやき: sukiyaki, 115
すぐ: soon, right away, 169
すし: sushi, 103
すしまさ: Sushimasa (fictitious sushi
　bar), 220
すしや: sushi restaurant, 103
すずき: Suzuki (surname), xiv
ステーキ: steak, 93
すてきな: fine, wonderful, lovely, 231
スパ: spa, 69
スポーツ: sport(s), 94
スポーツクラブ: gym, fitness/sports
　club, 94
スミス: Smith (surname), xiii
すみます: live, 204, 214, 215; すんでい
　ます: live, 204, 214, 215
すみません: I'm sorry, 17, 188; excuse me,
　21; すみませんでした: I'm sorry, 157
すもう: sumo wrestling, 144

セーター: sweater, 74
せつめいを しています: is/are
　explaining, 205, 207; せつめいを しま
　す: explain, 205, 206, 207
せなか: back, 233
ぜひ: by all means, certainly, 140, 149
ゼロ: zero, 10
セロテープ: Scotch tape, 78
せん: one thousand, 29, 30
～せん: (train) line, 187
せんおく: one hundred billion, 29
せんげつ: last month, 51
せんしゅう: last week, 51
ぜんぜん . . . ーません: not at all, 103,
　248–49
せんまん: ten million, 29

そうじを します: clean, 206, 207
そうです: that's right, 9, 10; そうです
　か: I see, 27
そして: and, 217
そちら: there, 49
その: that (used before a noun), 20, 37,
　232
そばや: buckwheat noodle shop, 76
ソファー: sofa, 71
それ: that (one), 20, 28
それから: also, in addition, 170
そろそろ: in just a short while, 129
そろそろ しつれいします: it's time
　to be going, I'd better get going, 129

タイ: Thailand, 4
～たい: want to, 222, 234
たいかい: large gathering, 142
だいがく: university, college, 7
たいしかん: embassy, 15
だいじょうぶですか: are you all
　right?, 157
タイじん: Thai (person), 4
たいへん: very much, extremely, 214

263

English-Japanese Glossary

Note: Idiomatic expressions have been omitted, as have counters, particles that do not translate into English, certain proper nouns, and some of the words listed in the Appendixes of this book.

The following abbreviations are used in this glossary:
adj. adjective
n. noun
v. verb

about: (of period, price, amount, etc.) ぐ
　らい, 120; (of time) ごろ, 85
above: うえ, 71
add: いれます, 197
address: ごじゅうしょ, 174; じゅう
　しょ, 10
after: 〜の あとで, 161
afternoon: ひる, 22
again: また, 131
ahead: さき, 171
air conditioner: エアコン, 153
airmail: こうくうびん, 171
airplane: ひこうき, 61
airport: くうこう, 50
all right: けっこうです, 36; よろしい（で
　す）, 161
alone: ひとりで, 49
already: もう, 207, 212
also: も (particle), 28, 29; それから, 170
a.m.: ごぜん, 23
and: そして, 217; や (particle), 69, 70
anniversary: きねんび, 129
apartment: マンション, 175
approximately: ぐらい, 120
April: しがつ, 61
arm: て, 233
arrive: つきます, 180, 181
art museum: びじゅつかん, 164
ask: ききます, 98, 162, 163
at: に (particle), 59, 60, 68
attorney: べんごし, 3, 5
August: はちがつ, 61

baby: あかちゃん, 199
back: (indicating position) うしろ, 71; (of
　body) せなか, 233
bad: わるい（です）, 132, 133
baggage: にもつ, 153
bakery: パンや, 79
ballpoint pen: ボールペン, 35
bank: ぎんこう, 7, 22
bar: バー, 93
baseball: やきゅう, 224
basement: ちか, 70
be: あります, 68, 69, 72, 77, 141, 142; いま
　す, 68, 72, 178; いらっしゃいます, 136;
　です, 2, 3, 77
because: から (particle), 98, 141, 142
bed: ベッド, 71
before: まえ, 71, 171; 〜の まえに, 162
behind: うしろ, 71
belly: おなか, 233
below: した, 71

bench: ベンチ, 157
beverage: おのみもの, 105
big: おおきい（です）, 38, 110, 112, 114
bill: おかんじょう, 106
billion: じゅうおく, 29
birthday: たんじょうび, 62
black: くろい（です）, 38
blanket: もうふ, 176
blouse: ブラウス, 124
blue: あおい（です）, 37, 38
book: ほん, 11
bookstore: ほんや, 78
boring: つまらない（です）, 132, 133
bottom: した, 71
bouquet: はなたば, 123
boy: おとこの こ, 80
branch office: ししゃ, 50
bread: パン, 78
break: やすみ, 22
breakfast: あさごはん, 26, 90
briefcase: かばん, 71
bring: もってきます, 170, 172
brochure: パンフレット, 188, 189
brother: あに, おとうと, おとうとさん,
　おにいさん, 215
buckwheat noodle shop: そばや, 76
bus: バス, 57
business card: カード, 193; めいし, 9, 10
business trip: しゅっちょう, 57
bus stop: バスてい, 84
bus terminal: バスのりば, 78
busy: いそがしい（です）, 113, 114
but: が (particle), 169, 170, 205; でも, 150
buy: かいます, 88, 91, 92, 160, 163, 178
by: で (particle), 59, 60, 170; by (the time):
　までに, 174
by all means: ぜひ, 140, 149
by what means: なんで, 60, 63

cake: ケーキ, 115
call: よびます, 168
cap: ぼうし, 124
car: くるま, 41, 61
carnation: カーネーション, 123
carry: (on one's shoulders) かつぎます,
　150; (in one's hands) もちます, 151
cart: カート, 83
catalog: カタログ, 169, 189
CD: CD（シーディー）, 30
CD player: CDプレーヤー, 30
cell phone: けいたい, 11
certainly: ぜひ, 140, 149
chair: いす, 71

check: おかんじょう, 106
check-in counter: チェックインカウン
　ター, 83
child: おこさん, こども, 215; こ, 80
chocolate: チョコレート, 126
class: クラス, 235; じゅぎょう, 152
clean: (adj.) きれいです or きれいな,
　110, 111, 113, 116, 133; (v.) そうじを し
　ます, 206, 207
clearance sale: バーゲンセール, 132
client: おきゃくさん, 191
clinic: びょういん, 78
clock: とけい, 11
close: しめます, 151, 163, 196, 197
coat: コート, 124
coffee: コーヒー, 43, 90
coffee cup: コーヒーカップ, 43
cold: さむい（です）, 113, 114, 133
college: だいがく, 7
color: いろ, 122
come: きます, 48, 49, 50, 51, 52, 160, 162,
　163, 178, 196, 197
company: かいしゃ, 9
computer: パソコン, 30
concert: コンサート, 132
concert hall: ホール, 147
condominium: マンション, 175
conference: かいぎ, 22
conference room: かいぎしつ, 82
convenience store: コンビニ, 77
convenient: べんりです or べんりな,
　113, 116
cooking: りょうり, 105
cooking school: クッキングスクール,
　232
corner: かど, 171
country, my: くに, 105
courier service: たくはいびん, 171
cream puff: シュークリーム, 44
credit card: カード, 36
cuisine: りょうり, 105
cup: カップ, 43
curry: カレー, 115
customer: おきゃくさん, 191

dancing: ダンス, 226
data: しりょう, 173
datebook: てちょう, 17
daughter: むすめ, むすめさん, 215
day: (period of) 〜か（かん）, 〜にち（か
　ん）, 180; (of the month) 〜にち, 61; (of
　the week) 〜ようび, 60
day after tomorrow, the: あさって, 52

267

270

Index

(改訂第3版) コミュニケーションのための日本語 第1巻 かな版テキスト
JAPANESE FOR BUSY PEOPLE I: Revised 3rd Edition, Kana Version

2006年 6月　第1刷発行
2009年 5月　第5刷発行

著　者　　社団法人 国際日本語普及協会
挿　画　　角 愼作
発行者　　富田 充
発行所　　講談社インターナショナル株式会社
　　　　　〒112-8652 東京都文京区音羽 1-17-14
　　　　　電話　03-3944-6493（編集部）
　　　　　　　　03-3944-6492（営業部・業務部）
　　　　　ホームページ　www.kodansha-intl.com
印刷・製本所　大日本印刷株式会社

落丁本・乱丁本は購入書店名を明記のうえ、講談社インターナショナル業務部宛にお送りください。送料小社負担にてお取替えします。なお、この本についてのお問い合わせは、編集部宛にお願いいたします。本書の無断複写（コピー）、転載は著作権法の例外を除き、禁じられています。

定価はカバーに表示してあります。

© 社団法人 国際日本語普及協会 2006
Printed in Japan
ISBN 978-4-7700-3009-2